ON
TREND

ON
TREND

THE BUSINESS OF FORECASTING THE FUTURE

DEVON POWERS

UNIVERSITY OF
ILLINOIS PRESS
Urbana, Chicago, and Springfield

A version of chapter 2, "Thinking in Trends," was previously
published as Devon Powers, "Thinking in Trends: The Rise
of Trend Forecasting in the United States," *Journal of Historical
Research in Marketing* 10, no. 1 (2018): 2–20.

Manufactured in the United States of America
1 2 3 4 5 C P 5 4 3 2 1
∞ This book is printed on acid-free paper.

Cataloging-in-Publication Data is available from
the Library of Congress
ISBN 978-0-252-04287-4 (cloth : alk.)
ISBN 978-0-252-08469-0 (paper : alk.)
ISBN 978-0-252-05173-9 (ebook)

Dedicated to Tonya Janell Powers, 1971–2017

Contents

Acknowledgments

Why write a book? All authors have at some point or another asked themselves this question. Books are arduous, impudent, ego-crushing. Books can never do all you wish them to do, and some sharp reader out there will pinpoint that and tell you. And there are just so many books in so many places—on library shelves and in bookstores, on ever-lengthening wish lists, in piles upon unread piles on nightstands. But write this book I did, and I am excited to share it with you. I wrote it because I want to live in a world where books matter, so I have written a book that matters to me and that I humbly hope comes to matter to you.

This book would not have come into being were it not for the wonderful people who populate my world, some of whom I knew long before this project and some of whom I came to know through it. I'm especially grateful to the seventy-two forecasters and futurists I interviewed: they invited me to their offices and conferences, talked to me on Skype, answered my emails at length, and otherwise allowed me to get a picture of the work that they do. In addition to these people, Susan Choi, Tessa Cramer, Ben Grinspan, and Maarten Leyts work in and around trends and provided invaluable knowledge, connections, insight, and support at various stages in the process. Thank you for answering my questions and teaching me the right ones to ask.

I visited several libraries for archival materials, including the New York Public Library; the Columbia Rare Books Collection; Harvard's Baker Library; the Hagley Library in Wilmington, Delaware; and the Hoover Institution at

Stanford. I am grateful to the librarians and archivists who helped me during those trips. Parts of this book were vetted at several scholarly gatherings, including the 2015 Culture45 conference at the University of Iowa, the Society for the History of Recent Social Science conference in 2016 and 2017, the 2016 US Intellectual Historians conference, and the International Communication Association conferences in 2017 and 2018. I also delivered chapters as lectures at the University of Michigan and the University of Wisconsin–Madison and gave a version of the conclusion at the PSFK CXI 2018 conference in New York City. Thank you to the audiences who listened to, read, and critiqued my work in those venues.

Danny Nasset at the University of Illinois Press brought enthusiasm and vision to this project from the very first moment I met him. He "got" what I wanted to do and gave me the time and freedom to pursue it. Since then, I have had the pleasure of working with many wonderful professionals at UIP, including Dustin Hubbart, Kevin Cunningham, Roberta Sparenberg, and Jennifer Argo. I would also like to mention Mary M. Hill, who improved this book through eagle-eyed copyediting; Jennifer Ferris, whose company, Kelsey Transcripts, transcribed the bulk of the interviews; and Kelly Burch, who deftly handled the index. To them and everyone else who worked toward making this book a reality, I send my sincerest gratitude.

Thank you to my colleagues, friends, and support system within Klein College at Temple University, including my deans, David Boardman and Deb Cai; Don Heller; Patrick Murphy; Brian Creech; Heather LaMarre; Edward Fink; Fabienne Darling-Wolf; Adrienne Shaw; Madga Konieczna; Tricia Jones; Soomin Seo; and all my colleagues in the Department of Advertising and Public Relations. Thank you also to Osei Appiah for hiring me, even though we never got the chance to work together.

At crucial moments during the writing process I had stimulating and encouraging conversations with a number of scholars whom I admire: William Baker, Derek Valiant, André Brock, André Carrington, Lonny J. Avi Brooks, Fred Turner, Tarleton Gillespie, and Craig Calhoun. The anonymous reviewers who read and critiqued this manuscript made it invaluably richer, and I am grateful for their generosity.

Three stupendous women read most or all of this manuscript as I was developing it. Melissa Aronczyk and I basically share a brain, and she was always on call to answer questions, quickly vet ideas, or slog through early chapter drafts. Stephanie Schulte has been my academic "twin" since 2009, and her wisdom, perspective, and friendship are evident throughout this book. Jessa Lingel, who was working on a book at the same time I was, agreed to exchange manuscripts and gave a thorough and very eye-opening read that helped me to crystallize several important arguments. Everyone, please go out and get her book too!

I am lucky to have a tremendous community of sharp, interesting, and supportive friends who have asked how my writing was going, sent me links they found about futurism, had dinner with me while I went on and on about some bizarre thing that I just learned, put me up when I came to their city, and generally made my life full as I wrote. Thanks to Belkys Garcia, Nadir Souirgi, Laurel Harris, Bridget McHenry, Christa Chatfield, Mika Johnson, Jamie Todd, Nina Hernandez, Adam Lewis, Marion Wrenn, Rory Arnold, Tony Nadler, Christina Morus, Gordon Coonfield, Chad White, Kelly Joyce, Shana Goldin-Persbacher, Nora Madison, Mathias Klang, Rebekah Modrak, Jon Shieber, Jessie Shimmin, Cindy Conti, Erin Christian, Sindhu Zagoren, Lauren Genovesi, Christopher Vyce, Nick Stropko, Ben Peters, Bilge Yesil, Susan Murray, Bethany Klein, Derek Johnson, Jonathan Gray, Jeff Pooley, Susan Luckman, David Parisi, Tom Perchard, Coline Milliard, Joseph Reagle, Brooke Duffy, David Hesmondhalgh, Jeremy Morris, Dave Park, Joel Oestrich, David Mindich, Asta Zelekauskaite, Brent Luvaas, Sue Stein, and all the professors of Philly Professor Beers.

Lee and Mandy Powers are my adorable parents. They are incredibly hardworking, funny, weird, and giving people who taught me to always finish what I start and mean what I say. I hope I have accomplished both here and have done them proud. To my husband, David Bennion, thank you for loving me and tolerating me always, even when I have crazy ideas and say absurd things and have to have my way. Thank you for making a home and a life with me, for being open and good and kind and patient, and for staying true to what you believe in. You are an inspiration.

In the middle of writing this book, my older sister, Tonya Powers, passed away. She was an extremely private person, and our personalities differed enormously. Nonetheless, I took for granted that she would be around during my future. I assumed that on some level we would figure out this growing older thing together. Though she'd never have expected it if she were alive, I dedicate this book to her. She taught me, in the most painful way, that you can never completely predict what tomorrow will bring.

ON
TREND

INTRODUCTION

On Trend

The New York offices of Sparks & Honey are open, embracing, and nonhierarchical. Perimeter walls burst with color—Sparks & Honey's hallmark hue of fuchsia dominates, but colors often background ideas, and the surfeit of ideas here has rendered the walls a rainbow. The wall nearest the entrance is bordered with headlines, all in caps, reading MICROTRENDS, MEGATRENDS, and MACROTRENDS. These are what Sparks & Honey call the "elements of culture," a "guiding framework" that serves to "translate the shifting global cultural landscape into leading edge insights" for their clients.[1] At the center of the room are several high tops and a conference table, all facing a wall covered with nine screens. There are two more screens nearby, one broadcasting news updates, another scrolling through headshots of the company's advisory board of "influencers." Merlin Ward and Ben Grinspan, bespectacled thirtysomethings, stand near the front of the room, readying notes. Merlin and Ben are the MCs for the Daily Cultural Briefing, which starts promptly at noon and which provides a glimpse into how this small but influential company turns culture into strategy.

The Daily Cultural Briefing is an hour-long presentation of around thirty curated "cultural signals" of the last twenty-four hours. A signal can be anything—a new product, a hip restaurant, a viral video—but it travels through media and, almost always, has some visually arresting component. The first third of the meeting is broadcast on Facebook Live. Merlin faces the camera and introduces himself and the event, and then he and Ben begin to cycle through stories. A smattering: Saliva swabs that provide fitness recommendations. "Un-Instagrammable" desserts made to look like ashtrays or kitchen sponges. Lemon-powered supercars. Medicinal mead. Professional fingerboarding. Robotic dogs.[2] The examples wash in and out, and as each one crests, the staffers chatter back and forth about its relevance. Some signals trigger long conversations (though long is relative—none is lengthier than a minute or two). Others float by with little more than a muttered "fascinating." Almost everything is "fascinating," but that's the point. Culture has been sifted, like sand, until only the most remarkable pebbles remain.

The Daily Cultural Briefing is only brief in duration. In ambit, it feels more akin to an all-night dinner conversation with your most tuned in friend, except there are thirty friends, and they started without you and are talking at top speed, and nobody eats anything except cultural soup. It's a sixty-minute barrage of video, insights, meaning. Each example is not simply what it appears to be initially; instead, it is a synecdoche, a tiny corner of a much larger whole. In reaction to a new episode of *The Glamorous Housewife*, a YouTube series that puts a modern spin on dated recipes, everyone jabbers about its "comedy meets DIY" aesthetic and the recent boom in "food renovation," which is revolutionizing how we approach cooking and dining. Later on, when the briefing lands on GetHuman, a start-up that makes customer service calls on behalf of its users, employees see a connection to the rampant "time poverty" that plagues harried professionals; GetHuman embodies the "lazy economy" that capitalizes on our desire to avoid the mundane.[3] There is something wild, even rattling, about how expeditiously miscellaneous events can scale up in terms of connotations, significance, and power. But to the Sparks & Honey staffers who, as CEO and founder Terry Young puts it, "eat culture for breakfast,"[4] signals such as these resonate with one or more of dozens of dynamics that are rippling through our culture; they represent subtle shifts in some bigger force. More importantly, signals are tethered to trends that are starting to reshape the world of today and that—they claim—will reshape tomorrow's even more so. And for the clients of this company—which is not quite an ad agency and not quite a marketing firm and not quite a management consultancy but which discovers the future in the here and now—the lesson of such foresight is clear: keep up with trends lest the world outpace you.

This is a book about companies like Sparks & Honey, their peers and their predecessors, and how their business in trends shapes consumer culture and the future.

Trends are expected in consumer culture. Developed economies always have some zeitgeist arresting the populace, some novelty or habit that sneaks into, then occupies, our collective awareness. That trends are so banal is what makes them so profound. We have come to accept that culture has a lifespan. *On Trend* will explore how a "trend" has become the commodity through which culture's lifespan is understood and circulated, bought and sold. Trends are, quite literally, the currency of cultural life. And because of their ability to normalize, codify, and anticipate change, trends are fundamental to understanding how consumer culture and capitalism operate today.

A small but powerful group of companies do critical work to circulate trends through consumer culture. In the pages that follow, I will introduce the professionals who do trend work: discovering trends, explaining them, predicting them, and even manufacturing them. I'll usually refer to these people as "trend forecasters" and to the business as the "trend industry," but their titles suggest a motley crew: cultural strategists, innovation directors, brand consultants, cool hunters. They work in marketing departments and advertising agencies, in think tanks and design firms; they are young and old, tragically hip and absolutely not so. But what they have in common is that their work is *futurist*. They get paid, some handsomely, to anticipate the future of culture. The trend industry that they constitute has been around only since the 1970s. And though they work somewhat in obscurity, they have achieved an influential role in churning consumer culture ahead.

If the future opens before us, paradoxically hopeful and ominous, trends are the vehicle we take there. In an aggressively capitalist, growth-hungry, and hyperconsumerist world—a world primed for disruption and steeped in the rhetoric of change—trends have become fundamental to how we live, work, play, shop, and learn. We may not always be aware of every tide that is washing over us. We may find the shifts petty or petulant. At times, we may actively resist them. But we accept, often without remark, that culture is in a constant state of unrest. We know that, via trends, culture will surely move on without us. This book seeks to defamiliarize, historicize, and rethink this state of affairs. It asks, How did we get here? Who had a hand in steering us down this path? How do they do what they do? And more—Why did we get here? How does the nature of cultural change shift when it is expected and forecasted? And if trends turn cultural change into a commodity, what price do all of us pay?

What Is a Trend?

"Trend" is an everyday sort of word with wide, even profligate, use. Magazines of every stripe burst with the season's latest trends; commentators read trends in job growth, public opinion, or stock prices the way fortune tellers read tea leaves, hunting for signs of prosperity or despair. On social media platforms, trends metamorphose into their gerund form, "trending," to provide twenty-four seven access to the hive mind. "It appears," writes Tarleton Gillespie in a recent commentary, "we are awash in these algorithmic glimpses of the popular, tiny barometers of public interest and preference."[5] In 2011 tech entrepreneur Jesse Kornbluth put it blunter still, remarking in the *New York Times* that "there's nothing trending faster in the whirl of sudden fame and fast fades than the thing itself—the phenomenon of trending."[6]

Such ubiquity might suggest that trending itself is a mere fad liable to outgrow its utility when the winds of technological fancy and lay vernacular blow in a different direction. Worse, it might seem as if the idea of a trend is so elastic as to be beyond theorization and, therefore, deep scrutiny. In this case, however, I'd suggest that the prevalence of trends makes it vital to understand them more deeply. Like sharing, algorithms, or memes, "trend" is a "keyword" that has achieved a noteworthy level of cultural penetration as a result of the growth of the internet, social media, and digital culture. Benjamin Peters in his book *Digital Keywords* explains that "keywords are the lexical operators of the current information age," presenting frames for thought and action.[7] Trends share much with other digital keywords insofar as, especially lately, they have become a way of structuring circulation and participation in a world where the internet has penetrated the lives of so many so thoroughly. Yet the importance of trends predates and transcends the online universe, even if the internet has heightened some of the key features of trends—a point I'll discuss more deeply below.

"Trend" has had multiple meanings over its history. The word first emerged in the 1600s to describe a physical bend, like the arc of a coastline or the curve in an anchor. Over time, "trend" came less to refer to the bent object itself and more to the "general direction" of how something moved—for instance, how a mountain range reached into the distance. By the late 1800s, the need for trend to refer to something physical slowly ceded to its meaning as a "general course, tendency, or drift"; trends could exist in ideas or behaviors. Around the same time, "trend" also became a way to refer to movement in data. For instance, the points on a graph could follow a "trend line."[8]

Once rendered abstract, trends served a wide range of functions. Within the social sciences, trends became a way to comprehend wide-scale and long-term social changes both qualitatively and quantitatively. A good example is the study *Recent Social Trends,* a massive sociological survey of contemporary life commissioned by President Herbert Hoover in 1929 and published in 1933. As Hoover noted in the report's foreword, "The task . . . was to inquire into changing trends," thus resulting in "emphasis on elements of instability rather than stability in the social structure."[9] The desire to manage instability also made trends useful to businesses as they learned to navigate the currents of mass consumption. The following appeared in the *New York Times* in the summer of 1924: "From the present indications about 90 per cent of the women's shoes that will be worn this fall will be black and about the same proportion of them will be pumps. . . . The style trend, it was said yesterday, is strongly toward the plainer effects, and the higher grade the shoes are the more pronounced is the tendency toward plainness."[10] Retail reports such as these had been appearing in the *Times*—along with other newspapers such as the *Boston Globe*, the *Los Angeles Times*, and the *Washington Post*—as early as 1910. Sales information about footwear, hat ribbons, waistcoats, and other fashionable goods mattered because it helped shape how businesses made marketing or purchasing decisions. As consumption became a greater part of the lives of everyday Americans, trends came to refer more specifically to consumer predilections, spreading beyond fashion to other products. Marketers were especially interested in trends, combining knowledge about social life and consumer behavior to devise better and more efficient ways of targeting shoppers.

As the above suggests, the concept of a trend has wide application. Momentary shifts in fashion and culture are thought of as trends; so too are tectonic transitions such as changing attitudes about race relations and global trade. Despite this variety, two important commonalities carry through. The first and most apparent is that trend is a label for *change*. The nature and extent of the change are variable, as is the way in which those changes are documented or seen. But a trend does not exist unless something has transformed, will transform, or is in the process of transforming. In one of the few scholarly treatments of trends, Jennifer Altehenger, Laila Abu-Er-Rub, and Sebastian Gehrig determined that they are "some of the most visible manifestations of changes within and between different popular cultures."[11] Following from this assertion, we can think about trends as a genre or category of social change comparable to other perceptible shifts such as revolutions, social movements, and economic cycles. To say that trends have generic qualities means that they possess similar features across numerous embodiments. Increasingly, trends define not only a familiar course of change but also specific industrial, social, or computational processes, especially those under capitalism.

Trends designate a particular relationship not just to change but also to time. Trends are *new*, but they are a certain style of new. When Ariel Levy, writing in the September 12, 2016, issue of the *New Yorker*, marveled at the trend of well-to-do urbanites partaking in ayahuasca, a psychedelic drug made from plants native to the Amazon, her report was both breathlessly presentist and zealously future-directed. One researcher quoted spoke of how rampant use of the drug had become, despite the fact that it remained under the radar of most people. "On any given night in Manhattan, there are a hundred ayahuasca 'circles' going on," she stated. The prevalence of the drug among San Francisco's tech sector caused another interviewee to express exasperation, remarking that "ayahuasca is like having a cup of coffee here." And Levy herself claimed that this drug, while fringe, held consequential implications. "If cocaine expressed and amplified the speedy, greedy ethos of the nineteen-eighties, ayahuasca reflects our present moment—what we might call the Age of Kale," she writes. "It is a time characterized by wellness cravings, when many Americans are eager for things like mindfulness, detoxification, and organic produce, and we are willing to suffer for our soulfulness."[12]

Never mind the oddity—so common among cultural reporting as to be almost invisible—that something taken by a subset of a privileged subculture in two sprawling, heterogeneous metropolises a continent apart somehow defines the "age" in which we all are supposed to be living. The rhetorical move is not unique to this reporter nor to the *New Yorker*, and it speaks to how epochal assumptions about trends are deeply etched into the conventions of cultural interpretation. Additionally, it highlights the capacity of trends to collapse the distance between the past, present, and future by showcasing how the world of tomorrow exists today—even if its existence is secret from the mainstream. As I researched this book, I had more than one trend forecaster paraphrase to me William Gibson, who has been apocryphally cited as claiming that "the future is already here—it's just unevenly distributed." Trends, then, are the vessels that carry and distribute the future. As they do so, they establish—and promise, albeit with qualification—that a select few determine the tastes, lifestyles, and ways of being for the rest.

It should be clear from the above that trends implicate people. The trends you will encounter in this book are social and cultural, and the forecasters you will meet are experts in human motivation and behaviors. For some, this means honing in on the needs that they believe underlie all human behavior with an eye toward how they flare up uniquely in different periods and contexts. Others prefer a high-level focus on the changing world; from there, trends shape the parameters and fault lines of what individuals do, desire, and think. Though trend professionals sometimes bicker about these distinctions, I see more similarities than differences in the approaches. At bottom, trends are interesting because of how they influence and are believed to influence social life—how they inform us about and encourage us to follow what other people are doing.

For businesses, staying atop trends can mean not just beating the competition but also having the ability to shape how culture unfolds in the first place.

In this book I'll define trends as impermanent cultural changes that indicate a trajectory of social influence. Impermanence is not a specific period of time, though—a trend can take years, months, or far less time to come into being. The definition is also purposely vague on where trends occur; I want to capture both changes in taste or preference and more sweeping social changes. What will be important to keep in mind throughout is that the concept of trends is necessarily elastic and contradictory. Trends summarize the imminent now and illustrate the distant future; they magnify tiny percolations and distill immense chaos. When trends become industrialized, marketed, and sold, they become instruments to make meaning, and money, off the prospect of constant change.

What Is Trend Forecasting?

Cultural change makes for good business, no matter what direction it goes.

Or so argued the Future Laboratory, a London-based trend agency that devoted an early 2016 report to what it called "Backlash Culture." "For too long, brands have pandered to popular sentiment and tried to be all things to all people," the agency noted, warning that "as we enter the second half of the Turbulent Teens, the rose-tinted and collaborative vision being peddled by Silicon Valley acolytes feels increasingly out of synch with the genuine consumer experience." Seen through the eyes of the Future Laboratory, Backlash Culture was everywhere: from global outrage at the Volkswagen emissions scandal to the vogue of protest; from "controversy courting" advertisements like those for the Squatty Potty to "dictatorial dining" at restaurants that abolished tipping in favor of living wages. The agency's advice was straightforward: by working with rather than against Backlash Culture, brands can position themselves as "uncompromising and directional, rather than just collaborative and conversational."[13]

Such a report provides a glimpse into the practice of trend forecasting, a multimillion-dollar industry that utilizes consumer research, marketing savvy, data, intuition, and social scientific methods to analyze, predict, manage, and manufacture trends in consumer culture. These consultants advise entities large and small across a wide range of product categories—from electronics to food, from fashion to government—and trade on their ability to help these organizations imagine, plan for, and navigate the future. Trend forecasters work in many types of environments. They can be found as independent freelancers; within trend-specific agencies; as a part of market and consumer research firms and innovation or brand consultancies; or in-house, either as subsidiaries of larger multimedia conglomerates or in future-focused departments of companies. They often work in conjunction with other kinds of advisors, such as management consultants, market researchers, brand strategists, advertising executives, or design professionals. Trend forecasting has clear overlaps with some of these activities, too, and in certain cases forecasters compete for contracts not with other trend forecasters but with other types of strategic advisement.

It is difficult to say how many people work in the trend industry. The profession does not have an official trade association or accreditation process. Only a handful of universities teach classes devoted to trend forecasting specifically, and far fewer have dedicated degree programs. The related subject of foresight, while more commonplace, is still rare when compared to most other academic fields. The lack of programs hardly matters, though, since most people who wind up in trend forecasting do not follow a prescribed educational or career path. On the contrary, many of the people I spoke to landed in forecasting entirely by chance. Scott Lachut, a New York–based forecaster, had followed a typical route. He graduated from Syracuse University with a BA in English and philosophy but with uncertain career goals. In 2008 a quest for writing and editing jobs landed him an internship at PSFK, an insights and trends company, where he now holds the title of partner and president of research and strategy. "There was a point when I was driving cross-country early on in my life where I recognized that I didn't have any marketable job skills seemingly," Lachut recalled. Yet because he excelled at writing, research, and critical thinking, winding up at PSFK "was quite a find for me and it finally set me off on a path" that played to his strengths.[14] Others I spoke with came to the trend industry through fashion, journalism, management consulting, or advertising, where exposure to the work of trend forecasters led them to want to make the leap themselves. Two immediate lessons arise from such circuitous career paths. First, because trend work is nebulous, even those who might be predisposed to do it may not land there right away. Second, most important to becoming a successful forecaster is a set of skills and a disposition toward the world rather than any particular training.

Adding to the confusion, trend work is an element of a wider futures industry, which scholars Luke Goode and Michael Godhe describe as the "institutions that enjoy the greatest powers of agenda-setting, horizon-setting and problem-defining in terms of the way society thinks and talks about the future."[15] To narrow down such a diffuse, heterogeneous field, I have zeroed in on *cultural trends*, meaning my subjects tended toward marketing, management consulting, branding, and consumer insights rather than tech forecasting, military planning, government, or transhumanism. In practical terms, that means that while forecasting trends is a major part of the work of all the professionals you will meet in this book, it's not the label that everyone would have chosen for themselves. For some, that's because trends occupy only a portion of what they or their companies do. Others, in true early adopter fashion, believe that the concept of trends has become passé through overuse. Still others gravitate toward another label, such as futurist, innovation officer, or strategist. The diversity of terms for this work further proves the obfuscated nature of trend practice. But there are other reasons for the lack of harmony around labels. For one, though trend forecasting has been around for close to five decades, the field has moved through phases of more and less prominence. The current excitement about it has elevated its power but also created an opportunity to contest its terms, scope, and players.

Semantic negotiations are fundamental to the growing power of trend labor as it seeks to guide a future marked by change and disruption. Put another way, what trend practitioners do is difficult to pin down by necessity because that is the best way to emulate and control a future filled with unknowns. As ironic as it may sound, for many businesses, such forms of reliable ambiguity are increasingly attractive. In May 2016 Vijay Govindarajan, a professor in Dartmouth's Business School, advocated in the *Harvard Business Review* a move toward "planned opportunism," which he argued was the best way to take advantage of the "nonlinear" changes besieging contemporary firms. "Planned opportunism requires sensitivity to weak signals—early evidence of emerging trends from which it is possible to deduce important changes in demography, technology, customer tastes and needs, and economic, environmental, regulatory, and political forces."[16] Think, then, of trend forecasting not only as expertise on trends but also as the professional embodiment of planned opportunism. It is future uncertainty made into a business.

Fluidity became fundamental to trend forecasting from its inception in the early 1970s as a commercial response to the era's challenging business and social circumstances. While the legion of crises then facing American capitalism and culture are well-known, it is particularly salient to remember that they did not occur in isolation. The compound effects of social, political, and economic changes such as feminism, environmentalism, civil rights, war, and economic instability provoked a widespread fear of change itself and the existential threat that the future presented. These changes were felt across many spheres and institutions, but they were particularly entrenched in business, which ardently embraced discontinuity and discovered the future as an exciting terrain for capitalist value creation.

Of course, worries about the pace of change and the nature of the future were certainly not new then. Such apprehensions date back hundreds of years and were felt with noteworthy intensity around the turn of the twentieth century. Yet we should keep in mind the wisdom of German historian Reinhart Koselleck, who has noted that "the more a particular time is experienced as a new temporality, as 'modernity,' the more that demands made of the future increase."[17] Before World War II, the anxieties of modernity drove a range of responses from religious, artistic, and political corners about how to address, respond to, and control the new. In the wake of the war and in light of the growth of cybernetics and computing, similar desires have stimulated distinctive strategies. One of these that took particular hold in the United States was "futurology," or the study of the future and the "science of forecasting."[18] First systematized by military strategists, futurology developed variously within the business, government, academic, and nonprofit sectors with the aim of better accounting for long-term developments and warding off apocalyptic possibilities such as nuclear war, economic collapse, and mass extinction. In the late 1960s and into the 1970s, the popularity of futurology gave birth to government initiatives, think tanks, policy groups, conferences, private firms, and a robust literature that occasionally included breakout best sellers like *Future Shock* by Alvin Toffler and *Limits to Growth,* coauthored by Donella Meadows, Dennis Meadows, Jorgen Randers, and Williams Behrens.

Trend forecasting is thus one of myriad examples of the ways in which the future began to structure contemporary action of the 1970s in profound and systematic ways. For sure, the future signified a period of time that was invoked to signal caution or cavalierism, to spark or stymie imagination. But it also became a concrete object of study that attracted its own specialized expertise, tailored methods of intervention, and—as trend forecasting attests—commercial imperatives. As psychology had done for the mind and economics for the market, futurology "disciplined" the future, making it intelligible as an intellectual field. But the course toward disciplinary status was uniquely complicated for futurology and arguably remains incomplete. Despite the prominent role of speculation and planning in many areas of life, outright claims to understand or to be able to manage the future are often received skeptically. That futurology has experienced criticism of this kind since its beginnings is in part an aspect of the struggles for legitimacy that plague all new areas of inquiry. Where futurology continues to differ from other fields is the degree to which so much of its disciplining took place outside of universities. While this is perhaps the sort of observation that surprises no one but an academic, I offer it to highlight the degree to which trend forecasters are not only self-proclaimed shepherds of the future but key producers of futuristic knowledge and methods that are often isolated from and even shunned within more conventional intellectual spheres.

Trend forecasting is far from the only profession that engages with the future or weighs in on the direction in which culture is heading. Cultural journalism, punditry, various kinds of social science, brand management, and advertising also track cultural developments, hedge bets, and issue proclamations in a range of media about their prospects, power, and implications. Additionally, trend forecasters share commonalities with other sorts of professional predictors who labor in various capacities both in and outside the firm to manage the inherent risk of future action; we can count advertising, marketing, and opinion research, as well as economists, accountants, and research and development teams, as playing these sorts of roles. In this sense, trend forecasters may be thought about as cultural intermediaries, a professional grouping originally identified by Pierre Bourdieu (1984) and more substantively theorized by Michael Featherstone (1987). According to Featherstone, intermediaries are generally understood as "an expanding class fraction centrally concerned with the production and dissemination of consumer culture imagery and information" who "act as cultural entrepreneurs in their own right in seeking to legitimate the intellectualization of new areas of expertise."[19] For trend forecasters, that "new area of expertise" has two parts. Most obviously, trend forecasters have expertise in trends, as much of their work involves identifying and labeling cultural dynamics. More broadly, trend forecasters have expertise in how the future will impact culture and, by extension, consumption. What they know is how to translate cultural developments—the flow of change itself—into market opportunities.

To explain what I mean, consider Edith "Edie" Weiner, a futurist and trend forecaster who has been working in trends since the late 1960s. Edie, her son Jared, and her daughter-in-law Erica run the Future Hunters, a company dedicated to identifying "emerging trends that will be important to you before they become part of the cultural and business vernacular."[20] Among the many services they provide is the quarterly, day-long trend summit, where Edie, Jared, and Erica present white papers on trends to executives and leaders among their current client base. After reading the white papers together, summit participants discuss their implications across the various sectors they represent. I attended two such summits, the most recent in June 2018, where one report proposed a rubric to evaluate the types of work most vulnerable to automation. Rather than conceive of high-skill versus low-skill professions, Future Hunters proposes valuing work that is LTOG (low throughput, off the grid) over HTUG (high throughput, on the grid). The company's idea is that jobs that require problem-solving skills, humanity, and the ability to adapt to unique situations should be more valuable than jobs that require workers to process information and perform routine tasks, however intricate or specialized they may be:

> Skilled tradespeople will be in high demand, home nursing services will be in high demand, trusted babysitters and dog walkers will be in high demand . . . just as radiologists will find their work taken over by smart systems that read images far faster and with greater accuracy based on larger data sets. Thinking in terms of LTOG and HTUG as the spectra along which jobs will fall, it becomes easier to know going forward which workers really need to be kept happy . . . and which will easily or before too long become high-priced redundant talent.[21]

A society that is recalibrated to reward LTOG skills—and that, in turn, relegates HTUG work to machines—obviously would have tremendous ramifications. Imagine how a retailer that pays its clerks minimum wage might prepare for a future in which kind, attentive, and enterprising salespeople are so in demand that their salaries, benefits, and work environments must correspond. Imagine how a university might refashion curricula to prepare students when "practical" job skills aren't writing code, mastering software, or learning to evaluate contracts but critical thinking, expression, and creativity. How might a federal job retraining program begin to emphasize traits like emotional literacy, humor, and interpersonal communication? What would our society be if we exalted nurses the way we now elevate Wall Street traders? While conversations about such shifts are not new, staying atop of these developments and critically assessing their implications doesn't necessarily fit into everyday work routines. During the trend summit, executives across sectors brainstormed about how they might begin to account for these dynamics within their companies through either creating new initiatives or establishing protocols. This, in a nutshell, is what the Future Hunters aims to do: to raise the urgency of impending changes and offer possible pathways forward.

The Future Hunters is a small family company, just three futurists and one support staff. Most trend forecasters employ fewer than fifty, and many companies are still run by their original founders. Piers Fawkes, who began PSFK in the early 2000s, remarked to me that "this industry is in many ways like a cottage industry," an observation I found to be very true.[22] The small size of trend firms and the industry in general makes their outsize impact even more striking. People I have interviewed have clients among some of the world's best-known companies, including CitiBank, Google, Apple, Samsung, Heineken, Allergan, H&R Block, Disney, Uber, Pepsi, Home Depot, Marriott, and many more. They also partner with smaller start-ups that are themselves carriers of the future.

In May 2016 I attended a seminar for PSFK that featured Jibo, a social robotics company, and Casper, a company seeking to upend the mattress industry. In the years since, Casper has grown in prominence; Jibo, less successful, nonetheless has been heralded as a necessary step toward domesticating robots. Trend forecasters therefore tackle the consumer future along several different fronts, by influencing its leaders, promoting its change agents, and dragging along Johnny-come-latelies. In this and many other ways, anticipation of change incites present activity and thereby sets in motion the futures that have been forecast.

While trend forecasting companies can be found in many parts of the world, they are most heavily concentrated in the industrialized metropolises of the Global North, including New York, Berlin, Amsterdam, and London. The assumptions about the future that arise from this positioning are many, but one of the most dominant is that meaningful change is actualized in these centers of media, technology, fashion, commerce, and the arts, either originating there or migrating gravitationally toward those locales from elsewhere. Stephan Paschalides, founder and CEO of Brooklyn-based insights agency Now Plus One, explained to me how he understands this process. "I'm of the opinion that New York has sort of stopped producing trends. I feel like it's too expensive for the super creative people to be here," he noted. "There's of course new ideas all the time. . . . I don't want to say we steal them, but we borrow them from other cities, from other countries, and sometimes we make them better."[23] Other forecasters admitted that living and working in major cities shaped their perspectives on the future in ways that were both illuminating and limiting. Clearly, what counts as a trend is geographically determined and rooted in the inequities of the global order.

Tracing Trends

Trends forecasters channel a long line of scholarly and popular writers who, since the mid-nineteenth century, have sought to systematically understand collective behavior, social influence, and the spread of ideas. The earliest incarnation of these commentaries marveled at "the crowd" and its recklessness—as did Charles Mackay, a Scottish journalist whose 1841 *Extraordinary Popular Delusions and the Madness of Crowds* peered into the long history of panics, bubbles, and crazes. "Men, it has been well said, think in herds," Mackay wrote. "It will be seen that they go mad in herds, while they only recover their senses slowly, one by one."[24] The irrationality and unpredictability of the crowd also invited study from Gustav Le Bon, a Frenchman who penned *The Crowd: A Study of the*

Popular Mind, a landmark in social psychology, in 1895. "Crowds, doubtless, are always unconscious, but this very unconsciousness is perhaps one of the secrets of their strength," he explained. He continued his decree: "The most striking peculiarity presented by a psychological crowd is the following: Whoever be the individuals that compose it, however like or unlike be their mode of life, their occupations, their character, or their intelligence, the fact that they have been transformed into a crowd puts them in possession of a sort of collective mind which makes them feel, think, and act in a manner quite different from that in which each individual of them would feel, think, and act were he in a state of isolation."[25] Le Bon's work thus began a long intellectual march toward making "the crowd" more comprehensible. Near the turn of the century, crowds of people were likened to a living body in which cells acting together could perform functions impossible in isolation. The functionalist biological view—that society should be conceived of as a social organism—became the "science" of the human world, one that could rival the natural sciences. For Gabriel Tarde, also writing in France near the turn of the twentieth century, society's biological underpinnings helped to explain how ideas and behaviors replicated throughout its systems. "The social being, in the degree that he is social, is essentially imitative," he wrote. "Imitation plays a role in societies analogous to that of heredity in organic life." Tarde thus proposed various concepts for thinking about how ideas travel and change as they move throughout a social body, including "universal repetition," "vibration," and "diffusion."[26] Diffusion has been most resilient, especially lately, among those who study how information flows within online networks.

In developing ideas about the forces behind social shifts among large, unstable, yet linked groups of people, Tarde and others also anticipated one common feature of trends: that as human as they may be, their suprahuman characteristics require concepts that amount to more than just a collection of individualized decisions, attitudes, or understandings. These early thinkers accurately recognized the degree to which social currents often feel like a force beyond anyone's direct control. Why, you might ask yourself, are ASMR, edible insects, or electric bikes suddenly in vogue? When did open marriage, microdosing on psychedelics, or minimalism move from marginal to comprehensible, familiar, even common? If these developments erupt as forces, establishing terms and laws to explain them not only makes sense of society's mysteries. It also is a necessary step toward being able to anticipate them, since one characteristic of laws is that they are applicable to new circumstances. One of the most basic and enduring laws that Tarde and others helped to introduce is the assumption that novelties spread through societies, passing from one person to another until they expire—in other words, that there is a natural life cycle to social change.

By World War II, biological metaphors for crowd behavior had largely fallen out of favor. The crowd itself was also supplanted by "the masses," which after decades of usage signaled not hordes of strangers teeming in the streets but atomized individuals who nonetheless could exhibit similarities and relative coordination. Trying to understand what affected the masses and with what result is one of the central questions of this era of social science, and it is far beyond me to review all of that here. But in the interest of thinking about trends, a few developments deserve mention—particularly those that examine the power of social relations.

David Riesman's now-classic *Lonely Crowd: A Study of the Changing American Character,* first published in 1950, provides a window into how relationships shifted sociological understandings of social dynamism. In his view, postwar America had given birth to a new social type: the other-directed person. Unlike those whose decisions were driven by an overriding sense of tradition or a firm internal core, for the other-directed, "their contemporaries are the source of direction"; they were driven by social desires such as popularity and sociability. Other-directed people are also rampantly consumerist, reflecting and reinforcing the gravitational pull of mass consumption: "The other-directed person's tremendous outpouring of energy is channeled into the ever-expanding frontiers of consumption" in much the same way the previous generation had focused on production.[27]

Riesman's work joined that of sociologists whose explorations into a wide range of sites—popular culture, voting behavior, taste and preference, mass communications—contended that interpersonal exchanges were at the root of overarching transformations in opinions and ways of being. In developing their famed theory of "personal influence" in the mid-1950s, for instance, communication researchers Elihu Katz and Paul Lazarsfeld wanted to comprehend how "the influence[s] of mass media are not only paralleled by the influence[s] of people; in addition, influences from the mass media, are, so to say, refracted by the personal environment of the ultimate consumer." Their research led them to conclude that "the beauty parlor, the disc jockey, the department store, while intended as means of selling commodities become, derivatively, agencies which affect the styles of life and ways of thinking of those whom they influence."[28] In other words, they were centers of influence that organized consumers' lives, framed their encounters with one another, and projected their ways of being to others—and as such magnified their power. Advertisers and marketers eagerly strategized around how these ideas could be used to better understand, predict, and control consumer behavior.

Perspectives such as these do much to enrich earlier sociological explanations by providing a way to talk about major cultural transitions in terms of singularized interactions. Think about it: as much as it might baffle us to understand why e-sports or pop-up restaurants have taken off, many of us also look to others for ideas on what to wear, how to speak, and what to do. We may know people who serve this purpose for us; we may talk with friends about things we read or watch, which reinforces their power upon us. Mid-twentieth-century sociologists understood that whether overt or subtle, the longing (and pressure) to follow others played a prominent role within the social order. For understanding trends, this insight was crucial: it indicated that the social influence had a normative direction, from the most influential to the most impressionable, from the leaders to the followers.

The last two decades have seen a roster of popular books broaching the topics of social influence and crowd behavior anew, paralleling the rekindled fascination about social connections that has accompanied the rise of the internet and social media. The most famous—perhaps infamous—of these is Malcolm Gladwell's *The Tipping Point: How Little Things Can Make a Big Difference*. Published as social media was on the brink of a popular breakthrough, the central claim of Gladwell's book is that "the best way to understand the emergence of fashion trends, the ebb and flow of crime waves, or, for that matter, the transformation of unknown books into bestsellers, or the rise of teenage smoking or the phenomena [*sic*] of word of mouth, or any number of other mysterious changes that marks everyday life is to think of them as epidemics. Ideas and product and messages and behaviors spread just like viruses do."[29] In an inspired and ultimately potent coinage, Gladwell identified the "tipping point" as the critical juncture after which the ubiquity of an idea, a catchphrase, a practice, or a product is all but assured. The idea of a tipping point also perfectly captured the era's newfound obsession with "virality," which resurrected biotic analogies and fastened them to the mapping of human systems. Other titles, from academics and popular writers alike, contributed additional nuance to an emerging conceptualization of networked influence and idea exchange. For Duncan Watts, whose 2004 book *Six Degrees: The Science of a Connected Age* helped to popularize the "science of networks," the complex connectivity underlying human and nonhuman systems called for transdisciplinary tools—from mathematics to sociology, from physics to business—that could generate new ideas and more powerful explanations. Wharton School professor Jonah Berger, whose work includes *Contagious* and *Invisible Influence*, has taken a different approach, reveling in the surprising correlations and power of others to impact how we make decisions.

These books continue to have great influence and, considered together, provide a third important insight about trends. As we continue to interpret why people do what they do, explanations based on biology or conformity come in conversation with technological analogies and, specifically, the language of networks. Networks are, in the words of theorist Wendy Chun, "a defining concept of our epoch," not only describing social worlds but also manifesting them.[30] Gladwell, Watson, Berger, and numerous others find networks all around them, and they use networks both literally and figuratively to discover patterns, trace cultural movement, and link otherwise unlike and unlinked happenings. Put another way, for them, one purpose of networks is to comprehend trends. Through networks, they see trends: randomness that reveals hidden order and collectivity that emerges only at scale.

We should remain mindful, then, of what the close connection between trends and networks indicates about the assumptions of our contemporary theories. It is not simply that the dominance of technology shapes how we see the social, though that is certainly the case. To return to Chun, "Networks both embody neoliberalism's vision of individuals as collectively dissolving society and foster analyses that integrate individual actions/tics into shareable trends/habits."[31] As the infrastructure for trends, networks have biases. Seen within networks, trends become a way to collect us individually and assume that we gravitate toward those who are like us. Even more, like networks, trends tend to presume that novelty is best understood not as uniqueness but as likeness. Finally, and perhaps most importantly, both networks and trends prove to be deeply recursive. They are always shaping that which they attempt to describe.

. . .

I began this project in earnest in 2016, and over the ensuing years I interviewed seventy-two trend and future professionals. In addition, I attended eight trend meetings, from hour-long briefings to multiday conferences, and conducted in-person research with multiple subjects in four countries: the United States, the United Kingdom, the United Arab Emirates, and the Netherlands. Other interviewees hail from or have done work in an additional eight countries: Brazil, Canada, Denmark, Kenya, Germany, Singapore, South Africa, and Turkey. I visited archival collections at Columbia, Harvard, the University of Southern California, and the Hagley Library, and several companies allowed me access to artifacts and materials that are not otherwise publicly accessible. (For more information about my materials, please see the acknowledgments.) This book is the culmination of this research, as well as the result of deep reading of primary and secondary sources.

Part 1 is historical, conceptual, and largely focused on the United States. It consists of three chapters. Chapter 1, "Trending," carries that omnipresent contemporary concept backward into a prehistory of trends and trend forecasting. I argue that "trends" became useful in the early twentieth century for reasons that will feel familiar to today's readers: they supplied an impetus to consume change, spoke to a pernicious anxiety about the future, and fueled a desire for strategies for managing uncertainty. Over the first half of the twentieth century, the trend increasingly offered a mechanism through which to comprehend and track rapid social transformation and then use that understanding to make informed decisions about future action. Social scientists, entrepreneurs, and cultural observers began to utilize the trend as a way to recognize social patterns, and they eventually solidified the rampant use of trends as metrics of consumer culture.

"Thinking in Trends," the second chapter, begins in the late 1960s. By then, trends had become commonplace for talking about flights of fashion and fancy. Also by this moment, the future had become an overwhelming worry as massive change ricocheted through American society and destabilized the most basic assumptions about the good life. Against this backdrop, trend forecasting emerged as an industry. I tell this story primarily via the career of Faith Popcorn, the world's most famous forecaster, who started a company called BrainReserve in 1974 and by the 1990s was known as the "Nostradamus of Marketing." Popcorn and her peers exhibit how the insights of a budding futurology came to be applied and marketized in the business realm.

Chapter 3, "Cool Hunting," deals with the market research fad of the same name, which came into popular consciousness in North America and Europe after a 1997 *New Yorker* article by Malcolm Gladwell (the article that prefigured the aforementioned book, *The Tipping Point*). Cool hunters of the 1990s and early 2000s scoured youth and subcultures for "cool"; documented those artifacts with photographs, video, and websites; and then sold their insights to companies interested in getting ahead of the curve. In other words, cool hunters operated as trend forecasters, embodying the next generation of the business. In exploring how this evolved, I show how cool hunters utilized visual anthropology and early digital tools to engineer new ways of tracking, documenting, and drawing meaning from social activity. Cool hunters thus show how important the hip underground would become to consumer culture and how trend forecasting became the ringleader of this conquest of the future of youth.

Part 2 takes a more multinational perspective to deliver a critical assessment of the contemporary trend industry. That story begins in the fourth chapter, "Trends, Inc." In it I detail how forecasters produce trends, revealing their styles of cognition, baseline assumptions, core methodologies, and strategic justifications. I likewise explore trend forecasting as a culture industry that paradoxically promises to be a steadying force for its clients while simultaneously thriving off uncertainty and risk.

These critical themes continue in the following chapter, "Global Futurity." Here, I look specifically at the global practice of trends. Not only is the trend industry situated in many parts of the world, but built into trend practice is the fevered drive to mine the world for profitable developments. I argue that in its quest for the new and the edgy, trend forecasting is both an idyllic partner in global union and an apparatus of further cultural colonization. The chapter focuses on Dubai and the Netherlands but spans several other locales.

Chapter 6, "Eventful Futures," digs into the politics of trend forecasting. Though trend forecasting is in many ways a progressive industry, it struggles with inclusion, especially racial inclusion; futurism has a long history of being overwhelmingly white and male. With this in mind, I think through what happens when trends aspire toward political change and, in turn, how other modes of future imagining can bring about more visionary, radical, and diverse futures. My primary example in this chapter is Afrofuturism, but I also consider other issues of political relevance such as gender relations, automation and class politics, and environmentalism.

In the book's conclusion, I take stock of trends in the context of a world that has been thoroughly trended. Against the backdrop of the current cultural assessment of "trending"—in the wake of Cambridge Analytica, fake news, and the like—I wonder whether we can extend that conversation to address our cultural approach and acceptance of the trend in general. As scholars, critics, consumers, and practitioners, how can we channel the awesome power of trends in ways that enable us to better imagine collective futures? How can the trend forecasting industry become more ethically minded, more inclusive, and more sensitive to how it uses its social perch? And if we consider the trend to be not a natural outcome of life but instead a manufactured commodity created in the service of a mostly undemocratic future, what should we do, if anything, to change how we live?

As comprehensive as I've attempted to make *On Trend,* there are a few obvious shortcomings. The most apparent lapse is the lack of diversity in my interview subjects. The majority lived in the United States and the Netherlands, a bias that colors my own perspective in ways both overt and subtle. I have done my best to make those biases known when I was aware of them. Most subjects were also white and economically privileged, a reflection of industry demographics, as well as a product of my own research process. Subjects also tended to be between the ages of thirty and fifty-five, with few who were younger or older; about half were women, and though several identified themselves to me as gay, lesbian, or queer, far more did not express this aspect of their identity openly. I think through the issues of identity, with a focus on race and socioeconomic class, in chapters 5 and 6, but the topic infuses my thinking throughout. Disclaimers aside, I do think the book reflects both the trend industry as it currently stands and what a researcher of my background and means was able to learn.

Readers may be surprised that there is not more here about tech. Surely, technology plays a central and growing role in our society and culture, and it's a big part of the various discussions that take place over the following pages. But this book is not about "tech forecasting," meaning I don't go into detail about what technologies will be coming down the pike, and I haven't spent time with tech forecasters who focus entirely on those questions in all their technical specificity. Data science is also mostly absent, and not just because that suits my scholarly leanings. The use of data was rapidly changing within trend forecasting during the time of my research and not yet something widely adopted or standardized. I hope scholars who succeed me can make sense of the topic more astutely than I have.

On Trend has a blended scholarly genealogy, drawing from business history, cultural studies, future studies, media studies, and branding and promotional culture, with a hardy journalistic sensibility. The mélange reflects my intellectual persona and values, but it is one that may strike certain readers as nontraditional. Likewise, while I have written as a critical scholar, I have done so with a deep fascination and heartfelt admiration for the people and practices I have studied. I am sure this will strike some readers as misplaced, perhaps even compromised. To me, a critique that cannot humanize its object of study or offer practical insights is not useful. I appreciate that my subjects are smart and introspective, that this is their life's work, and that most of them are simply trying to do their best. At the same time, I maintain a healthy skepticism and a genuine worry about the power of trends to habituate change, to extend inequality, and to flatten cultural difference. I have observed forecasters' problematic assumptions and deficiencies, and I have had the privilege to think broadly and historically about the industry's implications. My concerns and ideas, and my belief that they must be understood historically, may appear to other, different readers of this book to be pedantic, impractical, or unnecessary. However, one thing I learned well from hanging out with business types is how much they appreciate an outsider perspective. I am hopeful that my views will help them to see themselves differently and that it will create the potential for useful collaborations and thoughtful revisions.

And to those readers who might have picked up this book simply because it seemed interesting, I say this: thank you. *On Trend* will reveal things you may not know about how consumer culture operates. The people and practices that comprise the following pages may at times seem strange, unbelievable, even absurd. Quite likely, the work that they do may be off your radar. But be certain that what *you* do is on theirs. And be certain, too, that the future they see holds power to shape the future you will live. This is what makes trend forecasting as exciting as it is disquieting. And this is what raises the urgency to understand what it means—historically, practically, and critically—to be on trend. That is the aim of this book.

PART ONE

CHAPTER 1

Trending

Remember eating Tide PODs? Remember President Dotard? Remember #The-Dress? (It was *definitely* gold and white.) Remember the ice bucket challenge and the mannequin challenge, the Harlem Shake and Gangnam Style, plane bae and distracted boyfriend and all the things you should have done by thirty-five? It's entirely plausible that you remember none of these things. They are pop culture ephemera, memes and trivia, social media folderol that bred newspaper headlines, bits on radio morning shows, and segments on the nightly news. It's also plausible that you never noticed some of these moments. Maybe you're not American, not middle-aged, not coastal, or not on Twitter. Maybe you gave up trying to follow *right now* a long time ago. Either way, each captured enough attention to warrant even more attention. Each drove—if only for a fleeting, utterly forgettable instant—a wave of cultural conversation.

In contemporary parlance, each trended.

The unique contemporary connotation of trends began in 2006, when Google Trends first launched.[1] Google Trends tracked the frequency of search terms, which could be compared to other terms or analyzed by geography. Two elements of this new feature made it immediately compelling. The first was its emphasis on time-dependent data; Google Trends changed each day, providing a window into behaviors that were tantalizingly of-the-moment. Second, and relatedly, was the nature of the observations these search data provided. Seen in aggregate, search terms allowed us to draw conclusions that previously had been difficult or impossible to ascertain, giving meaning to what the mass of us were searching at any given time.

Twitter followed two years later with its own trending feature, and that feature has been even more consequential. Twitter Trends consists of an algorithmically updated list of popular hashtags, which Twitter sorts geographically. Something can trend in Topeka but not Tallahassee, in Croatia but not Chile. In an enthusiastic blog post from that inaugural season, one writer proclaimed that "at a glance I'm able to see what the world considers important in this moment, which lights a path to explore what matters to me."[2] Claiming that the summation of tweets amounted to something "important" was perhaps a bit of a stretch; pundits, then as now, debated Twitter's purpose and viability.[3] Even so, the effect of Twitter Trends has been unmistakable. It provides a handy proxy for popularity, quickly asserting its utility as a synonym for cultural relevance.

Many other companies use trending algorithms to organize their content and draw conclusions about user behavior. "Trending" therefore feels like an innovative response to a contemporary dilemma. In some ways, it is. As we search, click, tweet, snap, and hashtag our way through our media ecosystems, trending evaluates our behaviors en masse, reminding us that we participate in a greater whole. Tarleton Gillespie, a media and information scholar, identifies this as how trending algorithms "call together publics rather than fracturing them."[4] In revealing what's nascent, ascendant, or burbling in our midst, trends provide a window into who we are and where we've been. Trending is not just a passive mirror of culture, though. It actively creates it. Trending algorithms not only select what to reveal and focus on but also set up further decisions to be made on account of those actions—gathering more attention or serving as a barometer of public sentiment, for instance. (For this reason, some critics have argued that trending algorithms should be abandoned, noting that their opacity and gameability make them a "worthless metric"; Facebook, in response, eliminated trending in 2018.)[5]

Thinking about trends in terms of futurism clarifies what Gillespie calls the "self-affirming" nature of trending.[6] Trends may gather the recent past to make claims about the present, but they always aspire to guide the future. Their goal is to shape perception and compel action. In this sense, the problems trending addresses, as well as those it creates, are of distinctly older vintage. Since the turn of the twentieth century, stewards and observers of culture have attempted to gather information to detect cultural patterns and with those make best guesses about the future. Then, as now, they were driven by the anxieties that arose from what felt like rapid, uncontrollable change. Then, as now, they put the latest technologies to work to assist them in making these determinations. And then, as now, professionals emerged to wield and sharpen these tools and to make them consumable.

This chapter focuses on how trends became a solution to the problems of modernity—a way to apprehend cultural information and make decisions about the future. Trends became an important technology in the late nineteenth and early twentieth centuries because they addressed two urgent problems within a swiftly modernizing society. The first problem, driven by the growth of the social sciences, concerned how to distill generalizable social patterns from the rising amounts of data being collected about the world. The second problem stemmed from the attempt to find applications for this new knowledge: Could patterns, once discerned, aid the work of prediction? A range of professions imagined trends as the key to understanding the future and gaining control and advantage in a world of unyielding change. From there, trends became firmly attached to consumer culture and began their passage into the commodity they are today.

What I offer below is a prehistory of cultural trend forecasting, whose story I begin formally in the next chapter. Though historical, the tale I tell here in many ways reflects our own time. Our obsession with knowing where culture might go and monetizing that knowing is long-standing. Our belief that some people are ahead of others and thereby lead cultural change is deeply rooted. And our confidence that with the right tools we can control the future is an unshakeable aspect of our humanity, our resolve, and our folly.

Trends in Data

The modern career of trends began amid the rise of university-based social sciences disciplines and their varied methods of systematic social observation. Ethnography grew in popularity in the late nineteenth century, originally popularized as part of a positivistic, imperial project of collecting empirical data about non-Western cultures.[7] In the early 1900s the Chicago school of sociology pioneered a similar procedure via the notion of fieldwork, gathering qualitative evidence from the surrounding world to make inductive generalizations about social ills.[8] Collected observations of these varieties could be used to indicate normal or common tendencies among or between examples, which the word "trend" was sometimes used to describe. In 1898 an American anthropologist named Alice C. Fletcher wrote in a study of the Omaha tribe of an unusual song she heard during a hair-cutting ritual; it "rises and dwells upon the tonic, which is rare in Indian music, the general trend of the songs being from high to lower tones."[9] Sociologists around the turn of the twentieth century found their own trends, in legislation, philosophy, in habits, and in sensibilities, as they took stock of the world and its diverse manifestations of social order.[10]

Quantitative methods and statistical analyses had also made inroads into the social sciences by the late nineteenth century.[11] As the idea that social life could be subjected to the scientific method came into vogue, evolving methods, complex mathematical formulae, and growing data sets served to unveil patterns in the social as never before, based, as Ian Hacking has argued, on the idea of "normalcy and deviation from the norm." In particular, even as determinism was losing its grip over the hard sciences, the emergence and growing power of statistical probabilities revived the quest to discover laws of social behavior.[12] Turning toward averages, likelihoods, patterns, and change over time, the social sciences became newly empowered, obsessed with the idea that scientific acuity would display the hidden intricacies of social operation.

The development of social sciences grounded in the precepts of scientific method was both a cause and a symptom of a diminishing focus on individual agency within complex societies. Instead, there was a growing acceptance that "human events were caused not by personal intentions and actions close at hand, but by impersonal, distant, and less apparent causes."[13] In the emerging subfield of "social forces," these ideas compelled researchers to identify, grasp, and measure the business cycle, social progress, public opinion, or reforms like prohibition or feminism—social dynamics that were not always visible in the strict sense but that widely impacted day-to-day life. "Social forces there are; obvious in manifestation or detected by accident, subtle in working or terrific in explosion . . . but they are not yet brought within scientific description," noted Franklin H. Giddings, chair of sociology at Columbia and a foundational figure in the field.[14] The view of society Giddings promoted at Columbia centered on expanding its measurement. "Social forces," once identified, could shed new light upon society's operations. "A man is said to be doing well if he succeeds in a business venture, whereas the particular success is due in part to the prosperous conditions, a social force," explained William F. Ogburn, at the time also affiliated with Columbia sociology. "When a man fails in business, his failure is interpreted in terms of personal inability, whereas the business crisis and depression—a social force—may be the cause."[15] The implications were obvious: better understanding of the forces themselves not only provided more sympathetic readings of social phenomena but also could better coordinate action and might even protect against fiasco.

What later came to be known as "social indicators" research presents another iteration of the growing power of macrolevel forms of knowing. Beginning in the mid-1800s, American reformists began using statistics to argue for the necessity for social interventions. Statistical information gathered about problems such as crime, poverty, and alcohol use was then employed to develop "a condition of society involving collective responsibility rather than an unfortunate or reprehensible condition of individual persons."[16] Early social indicators research helped to identify the general trajectory of society, as well as its less desirable aberrations, in order to shape both activist and policy action. It was governmental in all senses of the word: it became the tactics of the state and its reformers, but it was also used to instill a sense of norms and aspirations within the people themselves.[17]

A scientific, statistically grounded understanding of society focused on the measurement of social action, and a distillation of large-scale processes epitomized trend-oriented ways of thinking, as strongly underscored by a major study of American society published in 1933 and fittingly named *Recent Social Trends*. Commissioned by President Herbert Hoover in 1929, the fifteen-hundred-page study, funded by a $560,000 Rockefeller grant, was the result of years of work by a team of social scientists, including Charles E. Merriam, founder of the Social Science Research Commission; Alice Hamilton, the first female faculty member at Harvard; and Wesley C. Mitchell, one of the founders of the National Bureau of Economic Research. Nearly thirty chapters across two volumes surveyed society from an exhausting range of different angles—population, technological invention, occupational patterns, education, racial and ethnic groups, the family, leisure, religion, the arts, consumption, and more. "The Committee's procedure . . . has been to look at recent social trends in the United States as interrelated," read the report's introduction, "to scrutinize the functioning of the social organization as a joint activity."[18]

While the report was criticized for its expense, tardiness, and lapses (most egregiously, its failure to anticipate the Great Depression), it was also praised for providing a never-before-seen panorama of social life. As John Dewey wrote in a 1933 review, "We are undergoing a great disturbance of social equilibrium, and that the present great social problem, affecting all lines of social activity, is the problem of coordination and integration. There is nothing startlingly new in this conclusion. . . . But none the less to have assembled the material from every facet of our many-sided social life which supports in detail the generalization, to have given the only comprehensive picture of the resulting confusion, and clear-cut depiction of the whole problem is a great service."[19] In Dewey's view, to gather a surfeit of social information was not only to ascertain more meaningful and representative truths about society's currents and dilemmas but also to present sharper tools for chipping away at modern problems.[20] "The social sciences were imbued at their inception with a new understanding of history and with high expectations of modernity," explained Dorothy Ross in her now-classic history of the genesis of American social sciences. The guiding edict of the social sciences was the "future of modern society," and properly used, they could bring about social advances.[21] *Recent Social Trends* not only supplied a total picture of a rapidly shifting society but also created a means of making inferences about the days ahead. Ogburn, who served as director of research for the President's Research Committee on Social Trends, said of the report, "The very term trend suggests the future. . . . [W]hen a study of trends of the immediate past is made for purposes of planning and policies, the attention is focused at once on the future."[22] Understanding the future as a terrain susceptible to careful intervention, the report's trends became ways to talk about, represent, and exert technocratic control over the future.

Despite its shortcomings, *Recent Social Trends* made clear how trends could be used in the service of modernity. I invoke the term "modernity" here specifically to speak to the enormous suite of rapid social changes that overtook industrialized countries especially around the early twentieth century—multifaceted shifts such as urbanization, industrialization, mass consumption, mass communication, and secularization. In the mire of these, the signature characteristic of modernity was "the rise of novelty as an essential category of experience."[23] Novelty signifies more than the quickening pace of new things, ideas, and developments—it also suggests the privileging of the new over the traditional. Philosopher Marshall Berman asserts that modernization "nourished an amazing variety of visions and ideas that aim to make men and women the subjects as well as the objects of modernization, to give them the power to change the world that is changing them."[24] For Frederic Jameson, a literary theorist, modernity means that "a new age is beginning, that everything is possible and nothing can ever be the same again; nor do we want anything to be the same again; we *want* to 'make it new,' get rid of all those old objects, values, mentalities, and ways of doing things, and somehow be transfigured."[25] Both thinkers contended that massive change accompanied hyperawareness of change and the desire on the part of many to be the agents of that change. The result was a society forward gazing in triplicate: because the mire of transformations felt like nothing that had happened before; because the unyielding discourses about change echoed from every corner; and because of the collective yearning not to be left behind and, even, to get ahead.

Trends should be considered not just a word whose meaning modified amid the surges of modernity but an evolving, modern representational technology functioning both to stand in for and to capture the dynamism of a world unstable. Trends became part of the discourse of high-level change and a strategy for projecting that change forward to a time otherwise unknown. *The Trend*, a short-lived magazine founded in 1911, explained it this way: "Insight into the past and interpretation of the present gives a foresight of the future."[26] Such temporal slippage—that past revealed present, that present predicted future—would become commonplace whenever trends were invoked. What is important to point out here is that this strategy is deeply rooted in modernization, which, for all the discussion of its eclipse by other cultural epochs in the years since, bequeathed a powerful predisposition toward novelty that remains with us.

As trends performed transactional work between the past, present, and future, they became firmly nested within the forecasting professions. Forecasting—"to anticipate or predict a future condition or event through the analysis of data or through rational study"—arose in a variety of arenas in the late nineteenth and early twentieth centuries, vanquishing colloquial ways of knowing through numbers, data, and calculation.[27] It was during that time that "prediction became a ubiquitous scientific, economic, and cultural practice," writes historian Jamie Pietruska in her book *Looking Forward: Prediction and Uncertainty in Modern America*, "and forecasts, accurate or not, offered illusions of control over one's future."[28] Two cases, those of weather forecasting and economic forecasting, illustrate how the emergence of forecasting relied upon trends.

In the case of the weather, scientific meteorology began to displace almanacs, prophecy, and other popular ways of understanding the climate in the late 1800s.[29] In other scholarship, Pietruska writes that the establishment of the US Weather Bureau in 1891 was part of "turn-of-the-century efforts to redefine weather forecasting as a modern scientific practice and to relegate weather prophecy to the realm of pre-modern quackery."[30] Weather forecasting still involved a great amount of uncertainty, however, but when that uncertainty was recast as probability rather than guesswork, rational calculation displaced hunch, tradition, and spiritual knowledge. Emerging forms of weather forecasting also relied upon systematic study of the past as a method for establishing the likelihood of future weather situations. The niche practice of "weather typing" in the early twentieth century is just one example: assuming that the atmosphere "repeats its own past," weather typers built registers of weather activity drawn from an enormous number of locations, then would try to find conditions that were similar to what the area in question was currently experiencing.[31] More common, meteorologists and climatologists took into account a location's climate or "average" weather as they developed expectations, determined cycles, and studied seasonal variability. Mathematical concepts such as time series (how data change over time) and trend lines (plotting a course among a data set to better observe its general direction) were helpful toward this process.

For example, a 1921 article on the "secular variation" of climate looked at the relationship over time between sunspots and temperature, noting that the best way to grasp the bigger picture was not to look at the relatively short intervals of years or even decades but to trace the "secular trend" over many decades.[32] Henry Helm Clayton, a popular meteorologist in the late nineteenth and early twentieth centuries, was likewise a believer in sunspots and weather periodicity; his weather bulletin explained that "the purpose of the forecast is to indicate the *trends* in weather over a given period of time in the future."[33] Trend knowledge also helped to connect weather to other phenomena it affected—for instance, how weather might relate to crop yields and thus prices.[34]

The latter point directly correlates with the growth of economic forecasting. The financial panics of the late nineteenth century drove researchers both in and beyond business to search out ways to better manage economic uncertainty (and some, curiously enough, were inspired by developments in the weather sphere).[35] I have already mentioned efforts from within economics, sociology, and statistics to identify and understand the business cycle. Such work depended upon improved information about business operations such as commodity prices and volumes of imports and exports. In turn, armed with this knowledge, entrepreneurs—among them, now-legendary figures such as Roger Babson, John Moody, and Warren Persons—"were the first to envision the possibility that economic forecasting could be a field, or even a profession; that the systematic study of a vast range of statistical data could yield insight into future business conditions." While forecasting took many different forms in its early days—from quasi clairvoyance to meticulous data gathering to protomodeling and extrapolation—the field made liberal use of trends. In some cases, forecasting adhered so strictly to monitoring trends that there was little appreciable difference. While he was secretary of commerce, Herbert Hoover promoted the use of "trend analysis" to execute government forecasting, which included the development and circulation of economic figures and statistics. He believed that awareness of economic conditions would provide disinterested accounts that, unlike private forecasts, had no incentive to either overstate or misrepresent reality.[36] Econometrics, which became established during the Great Depression, was another instance of trends being used to model the economy and forecast its behavior.[37]

So far I've focused primarily on how trends became valuable implements for the scientific management of social life, making visible quantitatively derived and temporally dependent social facts. As historian Theodore Porter aptly notes, "The quantitative technologies used to investigate social and economic life work best if the world they aim to describe can be remade in their image."[38] Trends did precisely that: by providing a method for measuring social phenomena and extrapolating their state, those facets of the world were reconstructed, intelligible not as independent episodes but as located along a dynamic continuum that stretched from the past into the future. The power of trends went beyond their capacity to be measured, however. Through anthropology, journalism, marketing, and consumer arenas such as fashion, trends would also become a catchall for describing patterns within culture and the spread of happenings across a differentiated social spectrum. By the middle of the twentieth century, trends would develop a different relationship to the notion of forecasting and would become deeply embedded within the idea of culture.

Trends in Culture

Trends were modern, flexible, representational. They would become cultural, marketable, and advisory. Thanks to early twentieth-century social sciences, "trend" became synonymous with the movement of ideas and data, especially that which could be graphically represented, statistically calculated, or scientifically examined. Yet as quantitative researchers continued to elucidate trends' features over the middle decades of the twentieth century, trends gained a more common colloquial meaning that referred to shifts in contemporary taste, style, or "consumption patterns and behaviors."[39] The new understanding could be ascribed, in part, to the ascendance of consumer culture and the stratification of social groups that accompanied it. But it also had to do with the widespread acceptance of anthropological ideas about culture, which lent credence to new styles of qualitative cultural observation. By the 1960s "culturalized" trends and their machinations would fully saturate the fibers of American life.

Deciphering how trends became intrinsic to consumable culture begins with the word "culture" and its varied conceptions. Raymond Williams famously noted in his 1976 book, *Keywords: A Vocabulary of Culture and Society,* that culture is one of the most complex terms in the English language, a snarl of overlaps, faulty assumptions, and antagonisms. Culture refers to the idea of being civilized, tasteful, or virtuous in comportment and demeanor. Another meaning pertains to intellectual and creative labor ("the arts"), while the third meaning of culture refers to the entirety of customs, mores, and norms that are shared by a society.[40] All these definitions are significant to understanding trends, but it is the last connotation—culture as a way of life—that lends itself most directly to techniques of observation that facilitated "seeing" trends. Forging the connection between culture and the whole of social life is generally credited to Ruth Benedict's popular *Patterns of Culture,* first published in 1934. A study of "living culture" of the Pueblos of New Mexico, the Kwakiutl of North America, and the Dobu of Papua New Guinea, Benedict's book conceptualized culture as "the systematic body of learned behavior which is transmitted from parents to children"—customs, habits, and ways of being that were geographically and historically specific.[41] The implication of such ideas was far-reaching for Westerners in general and Americans in particular. Benedict contended that "advanced" Western lifestyles were accidents of culture rather than some absolute pinnacle of progress. Likewise, the individualism so central to American selfhood was now itself a product of cultural learning. Being "culture-conscious" was Benedict's antidote to bigotry, and it could be turned inward just as well as it could be turned outward.[42]

The 1930s was the era when Americans fostered "the sense of awareness of what it means to *be* a culture, or the search to *become* a kind of culture." In one sense, this "domestication of culture" meant that American culture turned into an object: something identifiable, intelligible, and subjectable to trained observation and earnest reflection.[43] But the domestication of culture also democratized it. Once the province of trained professionals to discern about foreign peoples, culture was now by, for, and apparent to everyone. Moreover, in Benedict's view, culture exuded its influences in ways large and small: "Taken up by a well-integrated culture, the most ill-assorted acts become characteristic of its peculiar goals. . . . The form these acts take we can understand only by understanding first the emotional and intellectual mainsprings of that society."[44] Or, if culture is "personality writ large," as Margaret Mead once proposed, then it flowered not only in the similarities across a community but also in how individuals' behavior could emblematize something larger.

All of this alludes to how the idea of "patterning" aids the perception of cultural trends as we understand them today. Benedict argued that "a culture, like an individual, is a more or less consistent pattern of thought and action."[45] If culture overarches these patterns, linking them into some kind of knowable whole, then beliefs, behaviors, and ways of life may indicate one's culture, just as much as culture may shape one's beliefs, behaviors, and ways of life. Observed patterns become ways of connecting the individual to the sociocultural and from there tracing larger developments, forces, and shifts. Certainly, the quantitative study of individual attitudes and motivations also revealed patterns, as I noted earlier; patterns were also central to the growth of opinion research during the 1930s and beyond.[46] Yet the growing awareness and acceptance of anthropological patterning during the interwar period served two distinct purposes. First, it sanctioned the use of ethnography as a means of knowing culture through forms of observation not easily conformed to quantitative metrics. Second, it reified culture, allowing singular actions to become representative and supraindividual dynamics to take on their own agency.[47] Trends operated through both, born of the assumption that the micro and the macro related to and could be read within, through, and into one another.

Documenting the adoption of trends as a means of speaking about cultural patterns is less straightforward than tracing their penetration into quantitative observation. Here, I have relied on the somewhat imperfect proxy of etymological shifts—how the changing use of language tells us something about changing ideas and evolving concepts. As I noted earlier, "trend" had long connoted general tendencies. In the first decades of the twentieth century, the word was also used to describe shifts in commodity supply, including fashion items and dry goods. But, over time, intangible trends in culture became more easily graspable and more contingent upon consumer demand or social vogue. For instance, consider a 1935 *New York Times* article covering an exhibit at the National Academy on the "American Trend." The piece explores how the works, all relatively recent, expose "the unfolding American sequence," where, "in general, the palette is seen to have freshened."[48] Another *Times* article from the same year declared that "the trend in education is toward 'individuation'"; the superintendent of New York City schools was advocating for a curriculum that valued individual students' needs as a way to promote equality.[49] Joining trends in commodity output, stock prices, and birth rates—that is, trends that could be counted or determined statistically—there were trends in shortwave broadcasting programming, trends in American-style fashion in Chinatown, trends toward decadent fiction and overly long motion pictures.[50] These trends, reflective of cultural happenings, could also be used to make suggestions about the future. In an article on the "office building outlook," Phillip C. Hodill, president of the National Association of Building Owners and Managers, remarked on the "trend toward special purposes," sharing his opinion that "office buildings in the future will consist of new buildings for special purposes or, where the situation justifies, the addition of new space." He based his ideas on "progress" in building regulation, such as the creation of new regulatory bodies and the updating of building codes.[51]

What these and myriad other cultural trends of this period have in common is that they emerged not just from patterns but within the change in patterns over time. Trends arise not just through similarity but also through difference: how practices stand out against what is expected, usual, or normal, or how the present differs from the past and suggests what might be in the future. Of course, observations about change in society did not begin with the modernity or with trends, and I have already detailed how one of the effects of modernity was to make change a built-in assumption of social life.[52] What I want to highlight here is how qualitative observation of patterns could be employed to deduce and influence changing tastes, sensibilities, attitudes, or practices, even in the absence of numbers, or what we might today call "hard data."

Cultural trends have much to do with the rise of consumer culture. Consider, for example, historian Michael Kammen's point that by the 1920s "commerce and culture could no longer be tidily compartmentalized"; though then as now many cultural activities are not market-based a priori, he argues that cultural touchstones were increasingly purchasable goods.[53] Moreover, just as culture became thoroughly consumerist, consumerism became cultural, which joined anthropological understandings of culture and those that indexed expression, taste, and refinement. Cultural values in all their various permutations came to be expressed through mass market behavior, giving new power to those who manufactured and adjudicated culture and new meaning to consumer decisions.

Though mass consumption had been growing in the United States since the nineteenth century, the "consumer culture" that became engrained between the late 1920s and the end of World War II had several notable features. Advertising—especially the imagistic, persuasive ads created by newly established advertising professionals—was a cornerstone of this new cultural condition, as it both encouraged the consumption of culture and broadcast cultural norms. Through their symbolism and sloganeering, advertisers functioned "to identify as 'decisively American' precisely those habits or traits most conducive to avid spending: an open mind, fierce individuality, a boundless appetite and curiosity for new things, a readiness to accept the modern, and a determination to find quality and satisfaction."[54] Moreover, American advertising professionals fancied themselves as great civilizers, using advertising's scientific credentials to bring about social and moral progress.[55]

The explosion of mass communication was likewise central to the construction of American consumer culture.[56] Radio, the cinema, popular fiction, phonographic records, and magazines were the products of industries as intent to manufacture and sell products as the makers of automobiles, foodstuffs, and perfume. More significantly, their content interpolated audiences whose association with these programs, songs, and stories gave them alternative options for communities that were not as beholden to geography. In discussing this effect in radio, media historian Susan Douglas has noted that the medium "hastened the shift away from identifying oneself—and one's social solidarity with others—on the basis of location and family ties, to identifying oneself on the basis of consumer and taste preferences."[57] In radio, divisions like the Red and Blue networks split radio listeners along likes and dislikes, with Red airing "popular entertainment," while Blue broadcast "refined and sophisticated programs," creating common ground among those who listened to the same stations.[58] In turn, scholars, market researchers, and radio programmers made and infixed a range of assumptions about audiences based upon their listening habits. "Evidence appears to be rather large that listener tastes and preferences are definitely improving with regard to certain types of radio offerings," noted one 1941 study. "There seems to be no question, however, that the vast majority of American radio listeners are still largely uncritical, and that a minority of people consciously use radio as a cultural agency."[59]

Somewhat paradoxically, despite the fact that consumerism democratized culture by attaching a price tag, consumer differentiation persisted in the cultural landscape, acutely so into the 1930s.[60] And as is clear in radio—where the "price" was not dollars per se but instead time spent listening to advertising—ability to pay was not the only determinant of one's consumer decisions. Instead, consumer choice became a core element of one's lifestyle and a prism through which to see other kinds of differences manifesting. In turn, consumer differentiation along cultural lines thus formed one of the building blocks of consumption, reflected and reinforced in the market's composition.

The "brows" of culture have come to be one of the signatures of how taste distinctions mobilized the market around a belief in tiers of unified cultural sensibilities. Originally drawn from late Victorian era phrenology, a racist system that believed that the height of one's brow indicated one's intellectual capacity, the terms "highbrow" and "lowbrow" later came to identify cultural products, as well as to what extent one could appreciate those objects.[61] Highbrow culture included that which was elite, genteel, and superior, that which was aimed at (and often reserved for) the well-to-do. Lowbrow, or "mass," culture, on the other hand, was base and crude. Between those two was middlebrow culture, an aspirational cultural position that advocated neither the elitism of the highbrow nor the supposed crudeness of the low but instead provided an option that was as accessible as it was beneficial and was almost compulsively "middle."[62]

Highbrow, middlebrow, and lowbrow were hardly exact classifications, and they were invoked as much to disparage the imagined preferences of others as to associate oneself with peers. Especially in the 1940s and 1950s, cultural distinctions became critical battlegrounds, with cultural critics such as Dwight Macdonald leading the charge against "midcult," highbrow increasingly disparaged for its elitism, and intense handwringing over the effects of low culture like rock music and comics on youthful consumers. Further, brows maintained the racist, sexist, and classist biases that first produced them even as they moved away from naming such differences in an explicit sense; jazz music, pulp fiction, and "vulgar" entertainments were disparaged in vain hopes of preserving the purity of white, upper-class, masculine intellectualism (and its philistine corollaries). Cultural choice was never as clear-cut as the discourse of brows allowed. Yet the equivalence being drawn between consumption and culture would not be quickly discounted, nor would its ability to reproduce the market in its own image.

The ABCD categorization system, pioneered by Paul Cherington of the advertising agency J. Walter Thompson in 1924, was even clearer in the linkages it forged between taste, class, and a host of other variables and lifestyle manifestations.[63] Recognizing that "the United States is not a single market" but rather "a collection of markets which have certain factors in common," the ABCD system was meant to provide an "arbitrary classifications of families" that would be useful in conducting door-to-door consumer research.[64] The groups were determined as follows:

- Class A. Homes of substantial wealth above the average in culture that have at least one servant. The essential point, however, in this class is that the persons interviewed shall be people of intelligence and discrimination.
- Class B. Comfortable middle class homes, personally directed by intelligent women.
- Class C. Industrial homes of skilled mechanics, mill operators, or petty trades people (no servants).
- Class D. Homes of unskilled laborers or in foreign districts where it is difficult for American ways to penetrate.[65]

ABCD's criteria generalize between how much money one made and how one behaved in life, which could in turn be used to explain how one would behave in the marketplace. Though "culture" as used here still connotes refinement, identities brought under the helm of anthropological culture are present, including intelligence, taste, profession, ethnicity, and gender. Consumer categorization provided a shortcut that would both represent and produce difference in consumer culture.

The evolution of a differentiated consumer culture has two main takeaways relevant in a historical treatment of cultural trends. First, the marriage of consumption and culture suggests that the market could be considered a proxy for cultural changes. This follows historian Lizabeth Cohen's argument that the market, long thought of as primarily economic, became a space of political action for consumers and a place where they could exercise their rights and perform their identities.[66] My point is that marketplace activity was not just politicized. It was "culturalized" too because of the ways that consumer choices displayed, and were seen to display, cultural identities. Changes to consumption habits could therefore reflect wider cultural changes that themselves were no longer conceivable apart from consumerism. A second relevant point is that a stratified marketplace established a directionality to this change, as changes often transferred between groups with distinct and hierarchized preferences. Aspiration and imitation had been considered aspects of social life since the 1900s, but in the wake of consumer culture they became features of the market.

Thorstein Veblen's 1899 *The Theory of the Leisure Class* established the modern understanding of the relationship between status and consumption.[67] Noting that "the possession of goods . . . becomes a conventional basis of reputability," Veblen challenged neoclassical economics by suggesting that sociality rather than mere supply and demand foregrounded economic drives. Importantly, he argued that "pecuniary emulation," or the desire to imitate those of greater wealth, inspired accumulation: "In any community where goods are held in severalty it is necessary, in order to his own peace of mind, that an individual should possess as large a portion of goods as others with whom he is accustomed to class himself; and it is extremely gratifying to possess something more than others."[68] Such a theory of social imitation corresponds to developments in social psychology by Gabriel Tarde and others who considered how social systems mimicked biological systems of heredity.

Veblen's impact amplified in the ensuing decades, especially after 1935, as economists, sociologists, and early market researchers investigated how status consumption and social influence affected market behavior.[69] For instance, institutional economics, which attracted prominent adherents such as Wesley Mitchell and John R. Commons in the early decades of the twentieth century, focused its critical analyses on consumption, social dynamism, and group behavior and favored "collective action" over the neoclassical concept of rational self-interest.[70] Likewise, in his landmark 1936 book, *The General Theory of Employment, Interest and Money*, John Maynard Keynes embraces some Veblenian ideas, arguing for the positive effects of status consumption on the economy.[71] For sociologist and market research pioneer Paul Lazarsfeld, social and psychological influence underpinned consumer motivation. When interviewing a consumer, market researchers had to be mindful of the "outside influences which affected his choice," such as advertising, advice from friends, and word of mouth.[72]

Growing acceptance of the social side of consumption, whether it was understood as imitation, emulation, distinction, or influence, affirmed dynamism and change as inherent features. Consumer culture meant not only a continual influx of new goods and not only that advertisers aggressively tried to shape the meaning of these goods but that consumers' decisions to adopt or abandon products and to copy or reject what the people around them were doing were key drivers of demand. Historian Susan Matt, writing about the early twentieth century, explains that the abundances of mass consumption, combined with the rise of secularism, the celebration of individualism, and the popularity of Darwinian theory, resulted in a society that "seemed to endorse movement, change and competition" and where envy, once a frowned-upon emotion, was accepted and even celebrated as an incentive to buy.[73] The desire to "keep up with the Joneses" meant that Americans consumed under the cultural expectation to both constantly change and do so covetously, with an eye trained on those just ahead of them.

Fashion was where these dynamics played out most vividly, and, not coincidentally, fashion is also where "trends" have governed changes and patterns most thoroughly and conspicuously. The following passage is from *Recent Social Trends*, commenting on the growing phenomenon of "knock-offs" in fashion retail:

> Formerly there were definite seasonal changes in the style of women's apparel. Now many New York stores report that there are no seasons, but a change in merchandise from month to month. Fifteen years ago a manufacturer was safe in preparing for volume sale models that were fashionable in Fifth Avenue shops the year before. Today it is frequently less than a week after a model has been shown in the window of one of the exclusive couturiers of 57th Street or 5th Avenue that it appears at $6.95 or $3.95 in the 14th Street serve-yourself stores.[74]

Here we have evidence of two types of trends: the quickly changing shifts in color, cut, or design and the longer-perioded pattern of accelerating imitation. The passage also points to emulation in the Veblenian sense: trends that follow from high to low, elite to everyday. Such movements had been common in fashion for centuries, but during the modern period fashion designers codified them and industrialized constant change, mimicry, and obsolescence in apparel. Similarly, through changes in color and design, fashion became a way to promote and hasten the consumption of other kinds of goods. Regina Blaszczyk acknowledges this in *The Color Revolution*, a history of color in fashion: "Color came to be seen as a solution to the problems of under-consumption that afflicted the mass-production economy."[75] Automobiles, home furnishings and décor, and other goods could also follow trends and, in so doing, become more deeply enmeshed in the process of consumer acculturation, differentiation, and competition.

Forecasting was a central element of fashion industrialization. One of the earliest interventions was the creation and widespread adoption of shade cards, which French dye houses first created in the late nineteenth century. Shade cards aided textile mills and fabric sellers in deciding what colors to manufacture for the upcoming season, with the hope that a consumer could find matching goods across a range of shops. By the early twentieth century, dye houses distributed their shade cards worldwide.[76] From there, color forecasting began to standardize and streamline color adoption across the fashion industry.[77] The Textile Color Card Association (TCCA) of the United States, started in 1915, can be counted among the first true forecasting bodies. As it systematized color choice, TCCA also brought scientific management into fashion production, following other businesses in an increasing focus on efficiency, productivity, and waste reduction.[78]

The spread of color forecasting was closely related to the rise of style and fashion trend forecasting. By the late nineteenth century, Paris had firmly established itself as the world's fashion capital and the originator of styles that would later be taken up in other localities. For this reason, fashion information from Paris became highly coveted, and agencies and professionals cropped up to sell fashion knowledge and expertise.[79] The forecasting businesses existed in addition to extensive journalistic coverage of fashion, which did its own work to foster trend circulation. But fashion trend forecasting has several beginnings, depending on what one chooses to focus on. In the next chapter, I will explore processes of trend hunting and trend setting that destabilized the rigid top-down transference of trends, especially the dominance of Paris.

Not every industry was as malleable as fashion, and as the next chapter will detail, the full flowering of forecasting within cultural industries would not take place until after World War II. Nevertheless, the early twentieth century has much to teach us about how trends became an instrument of prediction across a wide range of fields—a way to foresee but also control future decision making. Trends made data more manageable and predictable; they also provoked newness even as they endeavored to contain it. Trends helped track the movement of consumer culture; they also helped institutionalize its avarice and disparities. A concept that emerged to contend with modernity became instead its consummate symbol. Trends brought the future ever closer to the present and in doing so pushed it even farther out of reach.

CHAPTER 2

Thinking in Trends

In a 1986 *New York Times* profile, columnist William Geist marveled at the predictive acumen of Faith Popcorn, CEO of a New York trend forecasting agency called BrainReserve. "Ms. Popcorn *knows* that white wine and light beer are history, things the rest of us won't come to realize for about two years," Geist reported. "She thinks the Duchess of York, Sarah Ferguson, may make 'gritty honesty' popular. And she somehow sees the Reagans' new cavalier King Charles spaniel leading to designer brand dog food." Observing that Americans, generally speaking, were a "trendy lot," Geist explained how Fortune 500 companies, blindsided by the pace of social change, kept Popcorn's telephone ringing "off the hook" as they sought BrainReserve's advice for navigating shoppers' whims. This presented a dilemma for Popcorn, who complained of trend fatigue. "She becomes so tired of trends," noted Geist, "that sometimes she secretly loves to go to the supermarket and see people buying cholesterol and Red Dye No. 2."[1]

BrainReserve had begun twelve years earlier, when Popcorn and her then business partner, Stuart Pittman, left their jobs as creative directors of Smith/Greenland advertising agency to start a new company. In the mid-1970s BrainReserve's mission was simple if cryptic: to "gather all the smartest people I could find to solve whatever problem was at hand."[2] Early on, the company's method was just as open-ended as its mission. A typical project began this way: "The two partners visit the client . . . analyze the marketing and the media and together with the client work out the 'problem statement.'" They then recruited "at least four outside brains," who partook in a freewheeling problem-solving session. "They either tell me how to improve an idea or come up with a better one," Popcorn noted at the time.[3] As imaginative as these techniques may have been, though, most companies were uninterested. "I had this company, and it made nothing," Popcorn later relayed. "I pitched cold. People were like, 'What are you talking about?'"[4]

How a company with an ambiguous purpose and struggling sales pitch ended up a hotly desired consultancy with its finger on the pulse of the zeitgeist provides a lesson in how the concept of "trend" had evolved. By the late 1960s, trend was more than just a widespread social pattern. More and more, it signified popular fancies—a usage that coincided, I argue, with a paradigmatic shift. Trends transformed from simply au courant into currency: shorthand to identify and extract value from both micro and macro cultural changes. The shift was reflected in and reinforced by new forms of expertise that emerged to identify and distribute trend knowledge. And trend forecasters like Popcorn embodied this expertise par excellence, launching an entire field dedicated to advising executives on where culture was heading.

This chapter focuses on the growth of American trend forecasting between the early 1970s, when the industry established itself as distinct from advertising and market and opinion research, through the mid-1990s, when the language of trends crested in popular discourse. Several important figures factor into this story, though none loom quite as large as Faith Popcorn, whose career maps neatly onto this time frame; BrainReserve was one of the first dedicated trend forecasting agencies in the United States, and Popcorn's best-selling 1991 book, *The Popcorn Report*, exemplified and in many ways galvanized the trend frenzy of the latter period. The emergence of trend forecasting highlights the ascendancy of trends as the lingua franca of cultural change, functioning metaculturally to package the movement of culture as inherently sellable. Trend forecasters participated in and were precipitates of the broad reimagining of the cultural landscape in the terms of the market and of all actors within it as somehow on its timeline—early adopter or laggard, on trend or out of fashion.

The progression of "trend" and trend forecasting continues a story about cultural research. Forecasters had to figure out how to "read" the culture, and many of their techniques echoed, paralleled, borrowed from, and led methodologies of the social sciences. The previous chapter outlined how some social scientific techniques adapted to the corporate sphere, but there are plenty of other examples. Psychology was quickly adopted for the purposes of advertising early in the twentieth century; the commercial utility of communication research came with its inception; and research into social groups, frequently spearheaded by university-trained sociologists, instigated forms of market segmentation that evolved after the 1950s. Yet the role of trend forecasters is noteworthy for at least a few reasons. It shows how a roster of qualitative research techniques—including ethnography, content analysis, environmental scanning, diffusion studies, and scenarios—became choice business strategies at the very moment that computer-driven quantitative techniques were growing in prominence and power. Trend forecasting is, therefore, not just a sterling example of how business represents a prolific site for the development, consumption, and—some might say—co-optation of social science. Even more noteworthy is the reason why forecasters turned toward these methods: because they offered a means to detect, describe, and shape the future, which was an increasingly important and profitable frontier of corporate activity.

The desire to know, understand, and control the future has a solid place in human history, and predictive impulses have been systematized, codified, and thoroughly marketized since the late nineteenth century. The futurological turn of the early 1970s grew out of both social scientific developments and popular tracts that enraptured a populace obsessed with and unnerved by the hastening speed of change. Trend forecasters rode this wave of fascination, turning to "applied futurism" in their quest of forecasts that might calm anxious executives or, in some cases, stoke those anxieties to produce profitable results.[5] The work forecasters did for corporations concretized the future of culture: it was not something messy, amorphous, and mysterious; instead, it was more intelligible, navigable, and marketable.

The Future of the Corporation

The late 1960s and early 1970s form a period of significant change in the United States. The era is a complex tapestry of shifts both impermanent and enduring: widespread political activism, growing environmentalism, rising postindustrialism, slowing economic growth, and diminishing confidence in social, economic, and political institutions of all kinds. Like other institutions, American businesses struggled to grasp the profundity of the transformations, but what heightened their consternation was the degree to which many companies previously had ignored social and cultural issues without harm. Amid such intense changes, perhaps the most transformative of all was the recognition of change itself: years of tradition, security, and understanding rapidly ceding to the unmanageable, the uncontrollable, and the unknown.

One person who sought to explain the new environment was Alvin Toffler, a former labor journalist for *Fortune* magazine. Toffler was not the first to call attention to the vast social transformations afoot, but his 1965 *Horizon* magazine article, "The Future as a Way of Life," crystallized their far-reaching implications. He named it "future shock," a feeling similar to the "culture shock" of "bewilderment, frustration, and disorientation" that Peace Corps volunteers and other Americans traveling abroad experienced. Yet future shock afflicted inhabitants of their own country and was even more disorienting. At least travelers "have the comforting knowledge that the culture they left behind will be there to return to," while "the victim of future shock does not."[6] Toffler spent nearly five years expanding these ideas into *Future Shock*, the comprehensive book that became a global best seller. In it, Toffler vividly describes a society in the midst of an "abrupt collision with the future" in which "millions of ordinary, psychologically normal people . . . will find it increasingly painful to keep up with the incessant demand for change that characterizes our time." Breakneck change was rattling every social foundation to its core—from the family to work, from medicine to politics. To cope, "the individual must become infinitely more adaptable and capable than ever before," and social institutions needed to start immediately to support and funnel this transformation. "A challenge of such proportions demands of us a dramatically new, more deeply rational response toward change," Toffler wrote near the book's conclusion. "By making imaginative use of change to channel change, we can not only spare ourselves the trauma of future shock, we can reach out and humanize distant tomorrows."[7]

Future Shock triggered deep reflection among its business readership. In the pages of *Advertising Age*, Theodore J. Van de Kamp, a marketing director, identified a "nightmare of unpredictability" that future shock had wreaked, openly wondering, "Is the corporation as we know it today able to exist in the Age of Future Shock?"[8] Carl Spielvogel of McCann Agency moaned that he was "constantly amazed at the number of persons in the agency business who have yet to read as basic a book on change as Alvin Toffler's *Future Shock*," even though the foundations of their businesses were suddenly shaky.[9] The chairman of the board of Hanes Dye and Finishing ordered copies for all the company's top brass; at McKinsey, the consulting firm, *Future Shock* was excerpted for the company's internal newsletter; Lloyd Singer, vice president of Motorola, ranked it among "the most important works of our time."[10] *Future Shock*, if not required reading for the executive class, at the very least turned into a lodestar, a reference point, and a provocation. "Planning will no longer be considered another management function. . . . [I]t will be recognized as the *way* to manage," wrote Edward Green, a corporate planner, in a piece on the book in *Management Review*. "We can't predict the future with accuracy, but we can't plan for the future until we create an estimate of what we believe will happen."[11]

Green's response, typical of his contemporaries, also highlights one of the most striking aspects of reading *Future Shock* nearly fifty years on: how closely Toffler's pronouncements align with the way that business has come to talk about itself. Whatever challenge the book offered or fears it might have incited have been thoroughly absorbed into the rhetoric, if not the logic, of American business. This is perhaps not surprising. Toffler, though plainly critical of many institutions and driven to effect meaningful transformation, was neither particularly anticapitalist nor progressive. Moreover, he was well versed in the literature of influential business thinkers of his time, such as John Diebold, author of 1952's *Automation* and champion of technological transformation, and Peter Drucker, whose 1969 book *Age of Discontinuity* articulated the nascent mandate for perennial innovation. Likewise, as Walter Friedman writes in his history of economic forecasting, capitalism "is a uniquely future-oriented economic system in which people make innovations, apply for patents, watch interest rates, and in other ways 'bet on the future.'"[12] Capitalism without some eye toward what lies ahead would be difficult if not impossible to fathom. But the embrace of *Future Shock* within corporate culture cannot be fully explained by these reasons. What helped propel Toffler's work toward wholehearted acceptance among executives, managers, marketers, advertisers, and planners was its resonance with an intellectual movement striving not only to bring the future into view but to anticipate it fully and shape it methodically. The future's movement, fluctuation, and risk were first revelations and then assets to be capitalized upon by companies newly infatuated with flexibility, as well as by those that positioned themselves as uniquely able to grasp complexity and ambiguity.

Methods for managing the future broke decisively, imaginatively, and mystically with their scientifically rational predecessors in the wake of World War II. The postwar period birthed within strategic planning an "ostensibly secular prophecy in which the primary objective was not to foresee *the* future but rather to schematize, in narrative form, a *plurality* of possible futures" through a complex marriage between cybernetics and Eastern mysticism.[13] As early as 1959, a management theorist like Stafford Beer could assert that the "exceeding complexity of management systems ... required acknowledging the irreducible multiplicity of possible outcomes."[14] Likewise, in his *Horizon* piece, Toffler noted that "the willingness to speculate freely, combined with a knowledge of scientific method and predictive techniques, is coming to be valued in precisely the place where, in the past, the greatest emphasis has been placed on conservatism and feet-on-the-ground 'realism.'"[15] As companies in the 1960s and 1970s began to focus more on competition and strategy—spurred in part by the mounting power of management consultants—the status quo of earlier eras disintegrated, and managers increasingly saw the future as an unclear but necessary question.[16]

Two methods, both developed by military strategists at think tank the RAND Corporation, assisted corporate managers in exploring the future more easily. The first is scenario planning. In its earliest incarnation, scenario planning involved the systematic imagination of an array of possibilities for a given situation. Planners would then produce narratives as a way to envision the ramifications of these options in detail.[17] The most legendary early corporate usage of scenario planning was by Royal Dutch Shell; scenario planning was fully integrated into company practice in the early 1970s.[18] Prior to adopting scenario planning, Shell's forecasting techniques foresaw price stability, incrementally growing demand, and little reason to suspect that any volatile changes would reshape the oil markets.[19] However, thanks to the efforts of Shell executives Pierre Wack and Ted Newland, both deeply interested in the work of Herman Kahn, renowned RAND strategist and author, Shell began to utilize scenario planning methods to conceive of potential changes to come, such as higher prices, political volatility, and decreasing demand.[20] Instead of simply attending to issues that immediately pertained to their bottom line, "companies like Shell would have to pay attention to many things that had never concerned them before."[21] When ill-defined social and cultural risks became a part of the mix, profitability hinged upon assuming uncertainty rather than certainty.

In 1964 another group of RAND associates developed a second systematic method of qualitative future prediction. Known as the Delphi method, it was a long-range forecasting technique that "used a sequence of questionnaires to elicit predictions from individual experts"; those predictions were summarized and then "fed back" to the respondents in an iterative, bias-proofing process.[22] Theodore Gordon, who along with Olaf Helmer-Hirschberg authored a seminal report at RAND on science and technology forecasting, later explained, "We set about inviting people who were likely to have something to say," including "science fiction writers and policymakers and luminaries in their field."[23] Delphis grew to be wildly popular, with major corporations such as General Electric, Kaiser Aluminum, and TRW, Inc., commissioning their own Delphis during the mid- to late 1960s.[24] Delphis were crucial in standardizing the practice of corporations seeking advice from experts far beyond their specific trade.

Corporate usage of Delphi and scenario planning showed the tremendous advantages that could come from assiduous future speculation. "The future is our only field of power, for we can only act on the future," wrote Bertrand de Jouvenel, noted French futurist and author of *The Art of Conjecture*, which appeared in English in 1967.[25] If the future was *not* predetermined and *not* just like yesterday but instead up for grabs, it was a field of competition, negotiation, and opportunity that companies neglected at their peril. It was a space in which companies had to expect the unknown and plan deliberately for it. As one book on long-range forecasting noted, "Understanding of the problems arising from uncertainty helps the planner see which uncertainties or which effects of uncertainties might be reducible and which are irreducible."[26] The future increasingly became a way to manage the present—not only to set desired futures in motion but also to render readying for the future a constant business posture. Savvy managers could use ambiguity to their advantage, seizing upon controllable elements, better preparing for multiple contingencies, and acting to turn the future in their favor.

Management's approach to the future focused much of its attention on macrolevel drivers of social, cultural, political, and economic change: population data, political conflicts, economic indicators, technological progress, and social movements. These were the same factors that some social scientists, influenced by the developments in futurology, had started to again think about as "trends."[27] But the rise of trends also depended on change occurring at the microlevel: how individual consumers made decisions, formed allegiances, and accepted or rejected newness. Marketers took the lead in making sense of these issues, drawing less from military planners and more from communication research, sociology, and social psychology. Much like their colleagues in management, they would come to find insecurity, mobility, and rebellion acceptable rather than regrettable and animating rather than worrying.

America's Tastemakers, the influential two-part study issued by Opinion Research Corporation in 1959, exemplified how marketers began to make such realizations. The first report warned that market research had gotten it backward: "Habitually, our observations focus on convenient categories—sex, income, education, etc.—that may obscure rather than illuminate the process of change." Because "consumer behavior determines sales trends, industry performance, national indices—and not vice versa," what was needed was a theory of consumer change, which the report called the "Mobility Theory of Market Prediction."[28] Based on the idea that there is "a group of people whose behavior patterns will be followed later on by the mass," the report identified "high mobiles" as those inclined toward change across a range of choices, behaviors, and identities.[29] These consumers, who were "early adopters," as well as "leaders," could "act as a sensitive barometer of upcoming change in American values" and "consolidate old trends and start new ones in our values, in styles and tastes, and ultimately in product preference."[30] The advice was clear: marketing should concentrate the most effort not on particular demographics per se but on these trendsetting change agents.

As marketing was becoming more focused on consumer dynamism, the school of "marketing management" prioritized marketing as central to all levels of business decision making.[31] In an interview in *Nation's Business* in 1963, Malcolm McNair, Harvard Business School professor and marketing pioneer, explained that "there is the older point of view on marketing, which is that it is essentially a job of selling, the job of the sales manager and all the activities that relate to it. That is a somewhat limited point of view. Today most of us in marketing think of it as a concept that envelops all of management. All business has to be market-oriented. Essentially, marketing comes before production. That might sound paradoxical but unless you can sell merchandise there is no point in producing it."[32] With marketing dictating production, research about consumers took on new dimensions. Market segmentation and motivation research were already well established; to augment them, marketers of the mid- to late 1960s began to look more intently at buyer behavior and to reenvision how segments might be comprised.[33] For example, in 1966 Professor McNair pressed retailers to assume that their buyers were "youthful in mind and spirit, increasingly affluent, increasingly au courant of the culture in which they live, increasingly sophisticated, increasingly concerned with self-expression, and increasingly concerned with the development of individual good taste."[34] The movement toward a more refined understanding of consumers was further buoyed by the rise of psychographics, the "development of psychological profiles of consumers and psychologically-based measures of life styles," which *Advertising Age* named one of the most important advances of 1968.[35] Around the same time, marketers, who as a group were predominantly white and male, began to think seriously about marginalized groups such as African Americans, senior citizens, and women, especially as these groups began to seek out empowerment within the marketplace and a "credibility gap" increasingly separated corporations from their customers.[36] All of this was a sea change from earlier practices of "consumer engineering" and planned obsolescence, in which top-down, superfluous updates to a product's shape or color duped consumers to buy.[37] Instead, new fashions could emerge from anywhere. As one observer put it, "New social concepts no longer percolate down—they percolate *up*."[38]

Diffusion research readily supplied a way to comprehend the organic origins and granular transfer of tastes. While diffusion can be traced back to the early 1900s, as both social psychologists and anthropologists sought to understand how ideas spread across social systems, a noteworthy revival in diffusion studies took place in the 1950s within communication and sociology, both bleeding into and drawing from the overlapping territories of opinion research and marketing.[39] Newer studies corresponded with sociological interest in popular culture, fads, and fashions, which were becoming more legitimate areas of study during the same period.[40] Diffusion was also closely related to prominent scholarship about opinion leadership, such as Elihu Katz and Paul Lazarsfeld's 1955 *Personal Influence*, which underscored "the importance of social pressures in motivating people to expose themselves and be receptive to the influence of communications."[41]

But it was Everett Rogers's *Diffusion of Innovations*, published in 1962, that deserves credit for amplifying these new ways of thinking about consumer behavior and proclivities. Though the book was not intended as a work of marketing per se, to this day the taxonomy it presented remains a dominant way for classifying consumers. Borrowing from the schema put forward in *Personal Influence*, as well as *America's Tastemakers* and rural sociology, Rogers hypothesized that different groups of people would be primed to ideas at different times; these groups were "innovators," "early adopters," "early majority," "late majority," and "laggards."[42] While this system somewhat coincided with standard demographic categories such as age and social status, its advantage was the degree to which it allowed for conceiving of consumers in an ordinal fashion, as leaders and followers who could take to different novelties at different times. A temporal, aspirational classification of consumers thus made it possible to "forecast" their behavior. In theory, this meant that product consumption could be mapped like weather as it moved across a population.[43] Chester Wasson, marketing professor and consultant, noted as much in the *Journal of Marketing* in 1968: "Not only with fashion, but with product acceptance in general far more is predictable than is generally thought."[44] In effect, theorizing consumption as waves of adoption would give rise to a new, much more powerful form of consumer engineering that exploited social behavior. And with certain consumers as bellwethers of others' imminent behavior, the future existed not intangibly "out there" but in the flesh.

The act of differentiating consumers spatially and temporally took hold strongly in the world of fashion, where forecasting snowballed in the 1960s. Of course, fashion was the ultimate erratic commodity; as Herbert Blumer noted in 1969, "Its touch is not light. . . . It sets sanctions of what is to be done, it is conspicuously indifferent to criticism, it demands adherence, and it bypasses as oddities and misfits those who fail to abide by it."[45] Over the course of the twentieth century, seasonal variations in color, cut, and fabric were the norm, especially in women's apparel, and textile manufacturers had worked together since the 1910s to determine, for instance, what hues would come to market when.[46] But it wasn't until the 1960s that fashion became a globally competitive business where designers tried both to get ahead of other designers and to mine youth and the street for looks. Pioneers in the fashion forecasting industry, such as Ohio-born, London-based David Wolfe, designated themselves as hunters for these looks and consumers, whether on the streets of Chelsea or the runways of Paris, which they then ferried back to American retailers.[47]

The forecasting of bodies, values, and styles, whether in fashion or food, automobiles or appliances, would put "the innovator" at center stage. Innovators, as initiators of new ideas, looks, and values, very quickly became cherished consumers—not only valuable targets for a sales pitch but also a resource to be discovered, studied, and followed by everyone, including corporations. Early adopters were likewise sought after. Though they didn't create change, their leading-edge acceptance made them central to understanding how the mass market might behave. But finding these subgroups and deciphering their wisdom was no easy task. The period's climate of social rebellion, married to a long-standing fascination with the hip cool of the Other, meant that many changes that would come to affect the mainstream—long defined as white, middle class, suburban, straitlaced, and heterosexual—got their start among places and people that companies had long ignored or avoided, such as urban ghettos, gay nightclubs, and punk enclaves. In this way and others, the marking of certain people as "ahead" or "behind" the curve proved both deeply political and often predatory, aligning with tactics of market segmentation that amplified social differences and gave businesses new levers of control.[48] Likewise, this turn in strategy depended on a level of cultural understanding beyond one's business that many simply did not have time for. Management consulting, for all its know-how, was hardly up to this task. What was needed instead were professionals willing to identify pockets of trailblazing culture, no matter how off the beaten path they were, and report back from the trenches. What was needed were translators, who would explain microlevel action in terms of collective behavior and use it to bear both good and bad news. And such wisdom would be irresistible if it could be cast as the solution to a future that everyone agreed was a distressing problem.

Popcorn Reports

Before she was Faith Popcorn she was Faith Plotkin, the Manhattan-born daughter of Jewish attorneys. Born in 1947, Popcorn attended New York University, though she "didn't like school" and "barely" managed to complete her degree. ("I spent most of my college years . . . in bars with my professors," she later recalled.)[49] After graduating in the late 1960s, she began her career in advertising; by the early 1970s, she was vice president and creative director at Smith/Greenland, a small yet lucrative New York advertising agency known for its gutsy and off-kilter campaigns.[50] Popcorn—who, legend has it, assumed the alias after a boss had repeated difficulties recalling her given name—recalls a "romantic and adventurous" workplace where hardworking creative women could escape, at least moderately, from the industry's rampant sexism. "We worked until eleven o'clock every night, and we worked every single weekend," she has said. "And we came up with really brilliant stuff."[51]

Nonetheless, Popcorn became "disillusioned" with advertising and the cookie-cutter approach to selling that even renegade agencies like hers could produce.[52] Her entrance into the advertising profession coincides with the creative revolution, when many agencies shed their conformist image and embarked on a radical reenvisioning of what advertising was and how it was done. As William Tyler, director of creative services at Benton and Bowles, explained in *Advertising Age*, "Some call it creative freedom. Others, creative permissiveness. Still others, creative anarchy. Whichever, it is the closest thing to a revolution the ad business has experienced."[53] Following the lead of Bill Bernbach, whose agency, Doyle Dane Bernbach, generated some of the era's most memorable ads, agencies began to play down advertising's scientific credentials and unleash the imaginations of their creative departments. Those employees, in turn, delivered a different kind of advertising: more knowing, more visually daring, and more in line with countercultural and socially critical themes. When they didn't find their ideas sufficiently appreciated by their bosses, they often left to start their own firms.[54]

When Popcorn and Stuart Pittman struck out on their own in 1974, then, they were part of the exodus of creatives whose new companies "expanded the boundaries of advertising, pioneered a thousand new techniques and formulas, and opened paths that their larger competitors would soon follow."[55] The change surging through the advertising profession transcended improved or hipper tactics for selling; it birthed entirely new methods that reimagined the tenor and purpose of advertising. As they had among their marketing colleagues, these practices involved absorbing, apprehending, and getting out ahead of culture, as well as finding ways to understand and exploit uncertainty.

In a letter dated May 8, 1975, Popcorn and Pittman pitched their new company as an antidote to market malaise. "These are unusual times for many companies," they wrote in a letter to R. A. Pittman, vice president of marketing at Brown and Williamson Corporation. "The conventional methods of motivating the consumer most often don't work." They continued: "To meet this unprecedented problem we have come up with an unprecedented solution. The formation of BrainReserve: a task force of seven of the most innovative and respected creative talents in America. For the first time these people have been brought together, to work together, on a single problem: a combination unavailable at any advertising agency, boutique or on a freelance basis. . . . Having no preconceptions to start with, our solutions are wide-ranging and nonconformist."[56]

As the name BrainReserve suggests, Popcorn and Pittman's team solved problems with brain power, harnessing the ideas of people who weren't constrained by the norms or functions of a traditional agency. The original team of reservists included a number of "advertising stars," including Shirley Polykoff, the mind behind Clairol's famous "Does She or Doesn't She?" advertising campaign of the 1950s, and Ornofrio "Patch" Paccione, a top ad executive and photographer who had learned the business from Paul Rand, the legendary commercial artist.[57] At BrainReserve meetings, participants used the "applied art" of creative brainstorming that had become popular after the 1953 publication of Alex Osborn's *Applied Imagination*. These group problem-solving sessions were an early hallmark of a particular brand of creativity, in which the market provides the framework for perceiving the creative act as such.[58]

In addition to their creative "brain trust," members of BrainReserve combed through magazines, newspapers, and other venues to familiarize themselves with the client, the industry, and the pertinent cultural developments. They also surveyed stakeholders, such as customers and salespeople, so they could present a complete picture of the company and its issues.[59] It was a process that blended advertising, marketing, and management consulting, and it resulted not just in ideas for advertising campaigns but also in marketing opportunities and product extensions. An example: for Consolidated Cigar, one of the company's first clients, BrainReserve proposed a cigar for women and a fruity cigar aimed at marijuana smokers.[60]

BrainReserve's techniques evolved as the company matured. Initially in the business of generating "super ideas to make consumers part with their dollars in the poor economy," Popcorn and Pittman soon realized that BrainReserve was "in a position to help companies which, because of long-range marketing plans, are caught by rapid social changes."[61] Their style of forecasting scrutinized cultural life and explained it to clients in ways they could understand and hopefully profit from. With Campbell's Soup, another early client, BrainReserve called attention to the rise of fresh foods, pressing the canned soup king to prepare for revised consumer expectations.[62] In efforts such as this, BrainReserve was selling more than its awareness of change. Central to the company's success was that cultural change itself could be a commodity extracted to benefit not only corporations but also BrainReserve.

Other companies were also beginning to marketize cultural change. Independent futurist groups date back to the early 1960s, when a few RAND strategists splintered off to start organizations with broader scopes than military planning. In 1961 Herman Kahn, for instance, founded the Hudson Institute, where he and his research staff worked with companies including Xerox, Boeing, Coca-Cola, Union Carbide, and Time Inc.[63] Olaf Helmer-Hirschberg and Theodore Gordon were among those who joined Frank P. Davidson to create the Institute of the Future in 1968; among their objectives was to "adapt engineering and operations research techniques to the social sciences," as well as to produce an annual "Future State of the Union" report.[64] Such groups were not merely the offspring of RAND alumni. Two years earlier, the World Future Society, helmed by Edward Cornish, set up shop in Washington, DC. Within a year, the society had published the first issue of *The Futurist* magazine, which became an important public sphere for self-identified futurists. Universities also became centers for futures research. An example is the long-standing Stanford Research Institute, which by the early 1970s was consulting industries far beyond its original clientele of the military and oil mining, including government, scientific bodies, and corporations of many varieties.[65]

While a number of these groups profited from their forecasts, it wasn't until the 1970s that the forecasting sector boomed, making "futurist" a bona fide job category. Theodore Gordon, who departed the Institute of the Future in 1971 to form the Futures Group, a management consulting firm, quipped: "It's not exactly a household word, but for all I know there may already be an SIC [Standard Industrial Classification]." He continued:

> How would it read? "Futurist: one professionally concerned with the future, describing, usually through systematic methods, what might be, not singly but in consistent and probabilistic sets." As a breed, futurists are thus non-determinists, anti-nihilists, rationalists. They are scattered in government and industry planning groups; in universities which are teaching about change, how to understand it and bring it about; in research institutions, devising methods and applying them to tough problems of social policy; or in private consulting groups, trying to bridge the gap between theory and reality, trying to make the tools work in pragmatic, real-time applications involving immediate decisions.[66]

One "real-time application" for futurist work took place within the life insurance industry, where Edie Weiner began her career. A twenty-year-old college graduate in 1969, Weiner was hired at the Institute of Life Insurance under

Harold Edrich, a sociologist who ran the institute's social research team. At the time, Edrich's group was working on an instrument to monitor changing values and attitudes that they called the monitoring attitudes program (MAP). Elsewhere in the company, Arnold Brown proposed the creation of a "mechanism" for tracking social change that resulted in what came to be known as the trend analysis program (TAP). TAP produced periodic reports that encapsulated the overhaul of contemporary society. As noted in the institute's first report, from June 1971, TAP "is based on the concept that at least some of the changes in society result from changes in ideas and that publications are the means whereby ideas circulate through society. Regularly and systematically monitoring publications can serve to identify ideas with potential impact on our business and to track their progress or diffusion through society."[67] Weiner soon came to the attention of Brown, and she began contributing to the TAP reports. When Brown was promoted to vice president in 1972, Weiner took over running the program. For the next five years, she coordinated dozens of volunteer readers, who collectively studied more than seventy publications for indications of social, economic, technological, and political change. Weiner, Edrich, and Brown left the institute in 1977 and founded their own eponymous consultancy. There they began to produce trend reports for clients beyond insurers, including J. Walter Thompson (advertising), Hoffmann–La Roche (pharmaceuticals), SRI International (a nonprofit scientific research institute), and *Esquire* magazine, using a technique they called environmental or "strategic" scanning. As Weiner and Brown later explained in their book, *Supermanaging,* environmental scanning was "a new kind of radar to systematically scan the world and signal the new, the unexpected, the major, and the minor."[68] "A lot of what was changing was pattern recognition, and that had to be intuitive," Weiner later explained. For Weiner, no amount of quantitative data or computer modeling could substitute for a highly developed "curatorial" sense groomed to pick up on signals of change.[69]

Weiner's work exemplifies the centrality of trends to the work of professional futurism. A somewhat mocking *Saturday Review* piece on "the rise of the predicting profession" did sympathize with futurists with regard to the sheer impossibility of their object of study: "All they can do . . . is to study the way trends progress and interact, and speculate about events that may change the course of those trends."[70] Trends, as it turned out, were even more useful than that. They were the ideal conceptual tool for integrating high-level societal understanding with low-level bursts of cultural populism; they bundled the future and made good business. As one business school guide stated, during the 1970s there were a "growing number of research and consulting firms offering a variety of services that monitor the environment—identifying changing trends and opportunities as well as potential problems of importance to companies." The guide advised that despite their cost, these trend services "are still of great value to those corporations that must anticipate these changes and developing trends."[71]

Most futurist agencies promoted themselves as trend specialists. The Futures Group, Gordon's firm, developed several trend products, including PROSPECT, a service that monitored a hundred consumer and pharmaceutical trends; FU-TURSCAN, a self-service system that allowed companies to customize their scans; and Trend Impact Analysis, a method that combined historical data and trend extrapolation with expert judgment to account for the possibility of "unprecedented future events."[72] Future Option Room, run by Jerry Glen, Scott Dankman, and Roy Mason, began in the early 1970s to "synthesize information from a variety of fields into condensed formats to give you the best future options," focusing on "how changing social values and trends could affect your growth."[73] High-profile pollsters who were aware of the techniques being developed by futurists also got into the sale of trends. Yankelovich, Skelly and White, helmed by renowned pollsters Daniel Yankelovich and Florence Skelly, worked on a number of trend products, including Corporate Priorities, Monitor, and YouthMonitor.[74] Even the *New York Times* made a foray into this field. Subscribers to its Information Bank would have access to an "online service that permits daily tracking of information," accessing more than a thousand articles that could be "a dependable source of facts, trends, ideas."[75]

The *New York Times* example shows the increasing entanglement of futurism and information filtering and management. Information services made sense as futurological devices in light of information surplus, where news of threats or opportunities might flare up from anywhere. As the average businessperson could not keep tabs on every relevant news source, especially when print news could be difficult to access, futurists emerged to fill a much-needed void: they found and curated information; they subscribed and read for you. While the *New York Times* Information Bank was more than futurological, several similar services with an emphatically futurist bent cropped up in the 1970s, including *Changes*, a daily news digest distributed by a Canadian company called ORBA, and *Future Abstracts*, published by Futuremics, an information service. For $110 per year, a *Future Abstracts* subscriber in 1975 would receive every month "the latest information about the future literally at your fingertips" on forty-eight five-by-eight-inch index cards, filled with reports on "films, tapes, games, and journals; abstracts of university theses and unpublished papers; graphs, statistical data, trend projections, and bibliographies."[76]

Information was thus a critical aspect of trend forecasting. Acting much like Pierre Bourdieu's "cultural businessman," who "is at one and the same time the person who exploits the labor of the 'creator' by trading in the 'sacred' and the person who, by putting it on the market, by exhibiting, publishing, or staging it, consecrates a product which he has 'discovered' and which would otherwise remain a mere natural resource," forecasters' keen understanding of cultural happenings allowed them to define what was truly remarkable and what was mere noise, defining patterns and themes that, though visible, might otherwise go unnoticed.[77] Their consecrative power oversaw not just cultural production or practice but also, crucially, reporting and criticism. In effect, the forecaster, who worked metaculturally, "focuses attention on the cultural thing, helps to make it an object of interest, and, hence, facilitates its circulation."[78]

Of all the trend forecasters, perhaps none epitomized this metacultural role as well as John Naisbitt. Born in 1929, Naisbitt was the president of the Naisbitt Group, a service that spotted trends for corporations. A 1982 *Wall Street Journal* profile called him a "professional trend-watcher" who made big money forecasting cultural shifts. "Just as economists have crafted a profitable industry forecasting interest rates and the gross national product, Mr. Naisbitt and others have made businesses of predicting broad social, economic and political developments," the reporter noted. "Their clients seem to see in the trend-watcher's service an orderly way of keeping abreast of events that they don't control but with which they must come to grips if they are to stay in business."[79] That same year, Naisbitt collected his observations in *Megatrends*, a book that by 1985 had sold more than six million copies and that continues to shape the language of forecasting.[80] Defining megatrends as "broad outlines that will define the new society," Naisbitt identified ten transformations that his group had excavated over their years of newspaper "content analysis."[81] Megatrends were not fly-by-night fads but consequential, unavoidable shifts that would set society on a new course. The concept of megatrends has since become a standard trope within the trend forecaster's arsenal. While many companies also discuss smaller, faster-moving trends, most identify parent trends in which microtrends are nested.

At BrainReserve, the metacultural work came in three guises. The first was its development of consumer research reports, first produced in 1980. "Americans are not really the connoisseurs of wine they appear to be," began a splashy *New York Times* feature on the report entitled "Inside Consumers' Minds." "Warned of the perils of salt, Americans miss it badly and crave well-spiced food. People are not wildly enthusiastic about the new small cars. They are not so interested in open marriage or divorce as they used to be. And youth, as an American cult, is out." The findings alone already stood out in a context where communal marriage was still a buzzword and Betty Crocker ruled American kitchens with her wholesome, unassuming cookbooks. BrainReserve's proc- lamations not only defied convention but also recommended that "sweeping changes in marketing and product innovation" answer them.[82] "Nobody ever believed me, ever, and still to this day they don't believe it," Popcorn has since remarked.[83] But as BrainReserve became a source for pithy, bold, and prescient cultural prediction, Popcorn's star continued to rise, especially after Pittman exited the company in 1984. "Along with the wind, time and tide, the tectonic plates, the Judeo-Christian tradition, and the Byzantine tax code, Faith Pop- corn had been irresistibly shaping our life," noted William McKibben in the *New Yorker*'s Talk of the Town in 1986. "Is Faith Popcorn the ur of our era? Is she the oversoul incarnate? And, if so, is she nice? We can report that she is as nice as she is omniscient, and that is almost totally."[84]

"Oversoul incarnate" was exaggerating things, but McKibben's joke spoke to the second role that BrainReserve, specifically Popcorn, occupied: a guru of trends who doled out burnished nuggets of cultural interpretation. Variably called the "Nostradamus of Marketing," the "Trend Oracle," and other hyperbolic titles through much of the 1980s and early 1990s, Popcorn was a favorite in pub- lications like the *New York Times*, *Newsweek*, the *Wall Street Journal*, and *Fortune*; in 1987 one reporter went so far as to call her "one of the most interviewed women on the planet."[85] "I was always interesting to the press, maybe it was my name or something," Popcorn later reflected. When journalists telephoned, "the only thing . . . that I could ever talk about was what was going to happen"—and the more outlandish the quote, the better.[86]

Once identified as an omniscient source for information (and fandangle), Popcorn and BrainReserve could work metaculturally in another way by ped- dling BrainReserve's unique take on trends. A 1985 client report exploring the market for premium dog food explained that such a product could harness two significant social currents: the country's drift toward more traditional products (in line with growing social conservatism) and consumers' newfound penchant for premium goods. Another report, for a fast food client in 1987, explained how urgent it was to cater to buyers inclined toward convenience, small indulgences, and variety.[87] BrainReserve's work was thus doubly trend-oriented. It labeled trends but also marketed the trends it identified to its clients, whose obedience became an affirmation of BrainReserve's work. Over the years, Popcorn and her team refined their own list of "megatrends," which continued to serve as a prism to adjudicate their clients' products and services. BrainReserve's trends were a particular take on the world that did not vary from client to client; instead, clients conformed to the trends as Popcorn saw them.

In 1991 Popcorn published *The Popcorn Report: Faith Popcorn on the Future of Your Company, Your World, Your Life*. Collecting her observations over the years, the book presents scenarios for the future, an outline of ten key trends, and advice on how to keep one's business looking ahead. "Trends are predictive because they start small, then gather momentum," Popcorn wrote. "To make your product or business on-trend, you'll need to understand how the trends work together to define the future." Each of the ten trends occupies its own chapter and is festooned with a crackerjack name such as "Cashing Out," "Down-Aging," or "99 Lives." The chapters include examples of real brands that responded (or didn't) to the trends, as well as make-believe products that illustrate a trend's applicability. For instance, regarding the "Fantasy Adventure" trend ("vicarious escape through consumption"), Popcorn rattles off ways that companies might adapt: "What about the return of Scent-a-Rama movies, with scents pumped into the theater? Or Escapist Rooms, where scenes and sounds are projected on the wall; for instance, a trip to Kenya or Paris. A California company is actually proposing that in the future tourists should come to theaters built at the entry-ways of America's great national parks and view a film on a giant wraparound screen—without ever stepping foot in the parks themselves. Benefits: No more tiring walks, no more tour buses infringing on nature."[88]

In addition to its list of trends, *The Popcorn Report* explained BrainReserve's other cleverly named forecasting tools and products. TrendView, for instance, was a seminar for "20 to 1500 people" that would educate attendees on what the future portended. TalentBank consisted of on-call experts from different professions ("more than two thousand") whom BrainReserve reached out to for insight or brought together for ideation sessions. What the company called "brailling the culture" was a hybrid of nonstop ethnography and environmental scanning—reading, listening to, and watching media but also surveying anyone and everyone regarding their views about culture. TrendTrek, another quasi-ethnographic tool, involved "a field trip to a cutting-edge location that stimulates fresh thinking about new products and services." Additional "proprietary" methodologies included particular approaches to critical thinking, market research, and expert consultation.[89]

The book was a hit, for a time catapulting Popcorn from niche celebrity to household name. Popcorn's book also inspired a number of people to try their own hands at trend forecasting, making her responsible in key ways for the industry's expansion both domestically and internationally. Recognition came at a cost. To this day, Popcorn's name frequently provokes either qualification or defense among her peers and competitors, signaling the level of controversy that continues to surround her and her work. Even during the height of her fame—and likely because of it—Popcorn received frequent ridicule. "Is Faith Popcorn for real?" wondered one story from *The Futurist* magazine, noting that her "unforgettable" name detracted from her credibility.[90] Others were even less kind. In a scathing exposé in the *New Republic*, Ruth Shalit criticized Popcorn, questioned her methods, and shamed the companies that shelled out millions for her advisement. "The familiar rap on Faith Popcorn is that she is an old-fashioned scam artist, hoodwinking corporations and journalists with elegant spin on the glaringly obvious," wrote Shalit. "The scarier truth may be that she fills a genuine spiritual gap in corporate America"—a sense of worth for executives akin to "'the economics of meaning.'"[91]

Conclusion

Though intended as a stinging rebuke, Shalit's words imparted a truth. We no longer question that the soul of corporate America needs perpetual saving. Popcorn's gospel was part of a far-reaching development to orient businesses to the hollowness of their cultural understanding and the necessity of facing the momentums that threatened their demise. Trend forecasters, whether situated as market consultants or freelance futurists, were determined not so much to foretell the future as to make sense of the torrent of cultural life as it unfolded. Theirs was an economics of meaning drawn from a medley of homegrown and borrowed strategies for comprehending the world and sold to people convinced that the future had become far too important to be left to chance.

In the end, asking whether Popcorn is some kind of prophet or simply a profiteer is not the most interesting question. Far more interesting is what her and her peers' successes say about the role and influence of cultural prediction. During the 1970s, trend forecasting helped turn a menacing future into an opportunistic one first by breaking down the barriers between corporations and the cultures in which they existed and second by offering the trend as a window through which to see the future of that culture prematurely. Two decades later, *Newsweek* would count trend forecasting among the decade's hottest vocations, even suggesting that it had become *too* popular and was thus due for a retrenchment.[92] In the intervening period, relentless volatility had become not only normalized in American life but also a basic element of business operations. Forecasting the future purported to quell this instability, but it actually accentuated it, in part by bracketing it, naming it, and recursively pumping it back into the culture.

It's a state of affairs that should sound familiar to us today as trends course at warp speed through our social media platforms and ever more sophisticated analytics aim to interpret their signals. Early trend forecasters presaged this development as they digested and deciphered information flows, conjured significance out of signs, and made confident recommendations about what companies should do tomorrow. Accuracy and inaccuracy are thus the wrong gauges to use when considering trend forecasters' futurism. In parsing culture into trends assumed to carry the world forward, trend forecasters neither predicted the future nor concocted it. Instead, they brought the future into being.

CHAPTER 3

Cool Hunting

The 2001 PBS *Frontline* documentary *Merchants of Cool* opens on a scene of teenage boys of varying racial backgrounds sitting in a semicircle. A white man—business casual, thirty-twoish—joins them and begins peppering them with questions. "Has anybody ever done a focus group before?" The boys look around a bit; one sheepishly raises his hand. They're apathetic, but the man forges ahead. "You know, it's all going to be sort of, like, what you guys think. You guys are sort of the experts today, and it's going to really be just you guys telling me your opinions," he effuses. "Tell me some of the things that are really hot right now, some of the things that are really big right now, popular trends, things that you sort of see everywhere. What's, like, going on? What's hot right now? Just shout them out."

Silence.

Next we hear the voice of media scholar Douglas Rushkoff, the host of this episode: "OK, so they're no more responsive than most teenagers, but that's not going to stop this market researcher, because the information he's looking for is worth an awful lot of money. At thirty-two million strong, this is the largest generation of teenagers ever, even larger than their baby boomer parents. Last year teens spent more than one hundred billion dollars themselves and pushed their parents to spend another fifty billion dollars on top of that. They have more money and more say over how they'll spend it than ever before."

Merchants of Cool delves into youth-focused marketing, whose increasingly cunning tactics have produced a world where, Rushkoff laments, "a walk in the street may as well be a stroll through the mall." The documentary was part of a growing chorus of criticism condemning the spread of commercialism into previously pristine arenas of cultural life: books such as *No Logo* and *One Market under God*; periodicals like *Adbusters* and *The Baffler*; and high-profile movements against sweatshops, global trade, and runaway conglomeration. In *Merchants of Cool* Rushkoff investigates how, over the 1990s, corporations had developed new strategies for monitoring and appealing to young consumers and in the process had tried to turn youthful cool entirely toward their purposes. "To win teens' loyalty, marketers believe, they have to speak their language the best," he notes. "So they study them carefully, as an anthropologist would an exotic native culture."

Keeping up with youth's ever-changing whims had even given rise to a novel breed of market researcher: the "cool hunter." To explain this development, Rushkoff interviews Malcolm Gladwell, who had written a *New Yorker* article about cool hunting a few years earlier. "Cool hunting is structured around, really, a search for a certain kind of personality and a certain kind of player in a given social network," Gladwell says, a sober look on his face as he speaks to the camera. "For years and years on Madison Avenue, if you knew where the money was and where the power was and where the big houses were, then you knew what was going to happen next. And cool hunting was all about a kind of revolution that sets that earlier paradigm aside and says, in fact, it has to do with the influence held by those who have the respect and admiration and trust of their friends." We next meet DeeDee Gordon, one of the cool hunters Gladwell profiled in both his *New Yorker* article and his 2000 book, *The Tipping Point*. As a shot pans across a picture of a wide-eyed Gordon, Rushkoff marvels at her capacity to command top dollar for her skills. Gladwell offers some additional commentary. "How good is she? I think she's as good as anyone is at this game," he states. "And it's something—it's a difficult thing to quantify, of course. It's not a science. It's really a question, ultimately, of how much do you trust the person who's doing the interpretation and how good are their instincts."

Between the mid-1990s and the mid-2000s, "cool hunting" came of age. At first blush, cool hunting appears as little more than market research under millennium tension, one example in a long line of corporate attempts to understand, anticipate, and ultimately shape consumer desire. Fast-paced, youthful, and nonlinear, cool hunting pantomimed the trends it followed. To the dismay of Rushkoff and other critics, it took advantage of that isomorphism, blatantly exploited it, and inevitably ruined the very thing it sought to unearth. "That's the paradox of cool hunting: It kills what it finds," Rushkoff explains in *Merchants*. "As soon as marketers discover cool, it stops being cool."

Seen from other angles, cool hunting told more complicated tales. Following in the footsteps of trend forecasters who had successfully marketized cultural prediction in the 1970s, a new fleet of services emerged during the 1990s and promised to tame the future by showing companies where youth culture was going. They prided themselves on understanding "cool"—a word that described not only the edgiest trends but also a trajectory of influence predicated upon quick change, flattening social hierarchies, and the ongoing transfer of subcultural capital into economic capital. Taking advantage of emerging mobile and digital technologies and low-tech solutions, cool hunters made the terrain of cool more visible and trackable. In addition, as practice-oriented disciplines such as marketing began to make novel usage of ethnography, semiotics, and cultural studies, a new sphere for applied social science arose, presenting both professional opportunities and existential challenges for sociology, anthropology, and other fields.

The evanescent popularity of cool hunting likewise exposed how trends dictate the circulation of knowledge. On the one hand, cool hunting capitalized on a growing belief that subcultures were the new tastemakers and that opinion leaders could be found on the margins—a fact that justified its existence as much as its methods. On the other hand, cool hunting became a flashpoint that instigated debate about these forms and flows of expertise among those who had the most to gain (and lose) by their ascendance, including journalists, public intellectuals, academics, and cool hunters themselves. It is in this way that cool hunting, despite its brief tenure, provides an instructive case for rethinking how the shape of the future is contingent upon who is asked and empowered to foretell it.

The Subcultural Market Doctrine

In 2001 the BBC premiered a three-part series about the cool hunting phenomenon, appropriately entitled *The Coolhunters.* Early on in the second episode, we meet Robert Hanson, European president of Levi's, as he sits outside company headquarters in Brussels. "We have a really rigorous process of development, where four times a year our designers are sent out of Brussels and out of Europe, really, for six weeks to do intensive research on all the major capitals around the world," Hanson says. "Simultaneously we've built a network of what we call trend scouts, who are based in all the major urban capitals in Europe, and

we'll expand that to include other cities in the world over time. These are generally people who live in and among the opinion-leading target that we look at,
who tend to be the ones that originate trend. And those people bring us more
organic ideas—they're things that are out there in the kind of energy of what's
happening with opinion-leading young people. And from there, ideas emanate."

For a capsule description of cool hunting, it would be hard to do better than
Hanson's. Throughout *The Coolhunters*, marketers, designers, and scouts, most
under the age of thirty-five, traipse around the globe collecting novelty: they
comb Beijing shops for denim textiles, sample cuisine in Morocco, and scru-
tinize footwear in Camden Town in London. At times, it seems that the job of
cool hunters is to be professional young people in all their hip, curious, and
discerning glory. "The scouts are selected on the basis of their lifestyle and
cultural interest," notes the narrator later on in the episode as the scene shows
trend scouts poring over items in an open-air market. A pixie-like woman holds
up a furry cropped jacket, seeking approval from a lanky young man dressed
head to toe in black. "Cool!" she exclaims. They laugh.

Cool had come a long way from its postwar origins. Then, Beat writers, makers of film noir, and European existentialists embodied a postwar cool that had
sprung from the marrow of African American jazz—a stance that signaled "authenticity, independence, integrity, and nonconformity."[1] By the time of Levi's
cool hunters, some fifty years on, cool had proliferated but also commercialized,
and it belonged as much to brand-conscious insiders as artsy outsiders.[2] Cool
remained a mark of distinction, but commodification insured that cool would
also be a form of knowledge that could be decoded, extracted, and imitated. Cool
became valuable—less to those who authored it than to those who learned how
to sell it.

Cool hunting was not the first or only attempt to harness this value. In its
use of cool as prognostic, however, cool hunting evidenced a powerful new consensus—among advertisers and marketers but also journalists, academics, and
public intellectuals—that the rules of cultural influence had inverted. Money
and power still mattered; nobody disputed that. However, when it came to matters of taste, cultural influence followed a different path, from the periphery to
the center and from marginalized, oppositional groups to dominant, compli-
ant ones. Cool hunters were worker bees naturally attuned to buzz; what made
them invaluable resources was their location "in and among the opinion-leading
target," as Hanson phrased it. Cool hunting is better seen, then, as an effect of
what I call the "subcultural market doctrine," an increasingly widespread set
of assumptions that viewed subcultural groups as trendsetters and thus market leaders. The subcultural market doctrine, upheld not just by commercial

enterprises but also by its staunchest critics, caricatured oppositional groups and diluted what subculture meant. Additionally, by making claims about the predictive nature of subcultures, it also erected an increasingly rigid framework regarding how culture changed, and it ultimately suggested the helplessness of subcultures in the face of consumer capitalism.

The subcultural market doctrine derived in large part from the rise of "subculture" as a dominant principle within the social sciences. Anthropologists had long been interested in subcultures as social groups within societies. Amid the proliferating market segmentation of the 1960s and 1970s, marketers began to embrace anthropology's version of subculture not just to talk about racial minorities, youth, and the working class but also to imagine subgroups organized around taste, lifestyle, and other consumer choices.[3] So conceived, subcultures were potential markets deserving of targeted address. They were also incubators of habits, lifestyles, and products that might eventually reach the mainstream, which meant white, middle-class, and middle-of-the-road buyers. Subculture established a conceptual shorthand for monitoring crossover between markets, presuming that entrance into the white mainstream was the peak achievement. The idea that subcultures could dictate mainstream trends was novel enough that scholar George Field coined a term for it in 1970. What he called "status float" was a theory of why "some fashions, as well as some analogous non-fashion phenomena, climb up the status pyramid from below."[4]

Subculture as used within marketing and business bore an uncanny resemblance to sociological understanding of the term. Since the early twentieth century, sociologists had used subculture to think about deviance and nonconformity, especially among youth.[5] However, during the latter half of the twentieth century, critical sociology—especially the faction influenced by cultural studies—began to consider subcultures as resistant groups that displayed their rebellion less in antisocial behavior than in rituals, taste, and expressive practices, especially among the working class. As British sociologist Dick Hebdige's 1979 book *Subculture: The Meaning of Style* argued, the existence of groups such as punks, mods, and teddy boys "has signaled in a spectacular fashion the breakdown of consensus in the post-war period." Using semiotics and ethnography to decode subcultural lifestyle, Hebdige found subcultures that were rich in insubordinate and political gestures. He also found a situation ripe for capitalist exploitation. "Each new subculture establishes new trends, generates new looks and sounds which feed back into the appropriate industries," he noted. Cycles of rebellion and "recuperation" ensured that "the fractured order is repaired and the subculture incorporated as a diverting spectacle within the dominant mythology from which it in part emanates."[6]

Though Hebdige's focus was on youthful rebellion, his ideas gained widespread purchase among academics in the 1980s thanks to theories of "active" audiences that were popular in sociology and anthropology, as well as in English, communication, and other fields. In a latter-day reflection on that period, anthropologist David Graeber observed that "what was taken to be true of rebellious youth came to be seen as true, if perhaps in a less flamboyant fashion, of all consumers."[7] If all consumers were capable of defying the dominant order, the reasoning went, then those who studied culture should unearth and celebrate those rebellions and argue for their significance. Scholars in the 1980s and 1990s wrote about the agency and resistance of affinity groups, whether romance readers or TV connoisseurs, music fans or mall shoppers. In effect, they tacitly endorsed the position that the best way to think about these subgroups was as subcultures who made meaning and protested norms through their consumer behavior.

The belief that consumers were subcultures and subcultures were consumers—and that subversion was inherent to their mode of being—found its natural habitat during the mid-1990s within consumer culture theory (CCT), "a family of theoretical perspectives that addresses the dynamic relationships between consumer actions, the marketplace, and cultural meanings."[8] CCT's interest in "subcultures of consumption" stemmed from the idea that brand choice and allegiance were often more revelatory than race, gender, or age in understanding consumer behavior. In a foundational piece that established the "subculture of consumption" as a conceptual tool for both researchers and marketers, John Schouten and James McAlexander engaged in fieldwork among Harley-Davidson motorcycle riders to learn their habits and core assumptions. What they found were groups of riders, primarily white and male, who took to their "hogs" as a form of defiant escapism. "For bikers the Harley is the antithesis of all the sources of confinement (including cars, offices, schedules, authority and relationships) that may characterize their various work and family situations," they wrote. "The myth of the Harley and its supporting symbolism is one of total freedom." This libertarian spirit, strongly infused with hypermasculine Americanism, proved strongly magnetic; hardcore Harley enthusiasts regularly defended their turf from dabbling "weekend warriors."[9]

As the Harley scholarship exhibits, a subculture need not be youthful or bohemian to attract parasitic emulators; it need not be progressive or avant-garde to be "resisting" some sort of "mainstream." The subcultural market doctrine could be applied fluidly and even illogically, making for slippery mainstreams and generic resistance. Marketers also caught subcultural fever, resulting in bizarre reversals where subcultures born of structural inequalities turned into grist for lifestyle choices. In the mid-1990s, hip hop turned into precisely this kind of target. Writing in *American Demographics* in 1996, Marc Spiegler attempted to explain the recent affiliation between an upscale brand like Tommy Hilfiger and a rap artist like Biggie Smalls. "On the surface, it seems Hilfiger and others are courting a market too small and poor to matter," he writes, referencing the black urban youth who originally performed and listened to rap. On the contrary, "scoring a hit with inner-city youth can make a product hot with the much larger and affluent white suburban market." He then cautions: "To take advantage of this phenomenon, you have to dig into how hip-hop culture spreads from housing projects to rural environs, understand why hip-hop is so attractive to suburban whites, and discern the process by which hip-hoppers embrace products. . . . What draws white teens to a culture with origins so strongly linked to the inner city, and so distant from their suburbia's sylvan lawns? Clearly, rebellion is a big factor."[10]

With these examples, my aim is not to dismiss the possibility of counterhegemonic subcultural forms or to refuse the existence of something we might call "co-optation." Clearly, Harley-Davidson riders and black rap fans have different histories, ambitions, and concerns—as do any number of other subcultures we could discuss. My point is more fundamental. I contend that the subcultural market doctrine has proven a widespread, remarkably uniform, and endlessly malleable framework into which a variety of groups could be inserted to serve similar ends. Its central tenet was that, properly understood, subcultures supplied profitable target markets and ongoing icons of inspirational resistance. In other words, they were cool.

Cool hunting depended on these ideas, and so it is not surprising that the subcultural market doctrine proved especially powerful when applied to youth. Since the early twentieth century, marketers have prioritized young people as impressionable consumers who could influence older consumers both as family members and as symbols to aspire to, no matter a person's age. The rise of the baby boom helped codify and universalize youth marketing practices, which remained in place long after boomers were no longer young.[11] Ever since then, the idea of "generation" often structures and overdetermines youth behavior, and during the 1990s, this played out in reference to Generation X. In North America, Generation X (sometimes also known as the "baby bust") typically consists of those born after the baby boom who were in their late teens and twenties during the 1990s. Mythologized in Douglas Coupland's 1991 novel *Generation X: Tales for an Accelerated Culture*, which follows three friends in Southern California as they struggle for self-definition and against an older generation's expectations, Generation X became a pop culture phenomenon and a demographic preoccupation across numerous fields. Imagining GenX as a class subjugated by baby boomers also proved an irresistible frame for theorizing 1990s youth culture. For instance, in *Microphone Fiends: Youth Music and Youth Culture* (2014), Andrew Ross celebrates the "resistance" inherent in rave culture, hip hop, and alternative rock: "It may be that a new kind of social domination, with the fantasy of lost youth at its center, has come into being. The cultural and political forms of that domination are rooted in a middle-aged, regressive nostalgia that youths have no alternative but to recognize and resist under conditions not of their own choosing. Their resistance . . . is often lodged against a generation who claim to have invented the 'politics of youth.'"[12]

Corporations of the 1990s were just as enamored as academics with youthful resistance. Thomas Frank's *Conquest of Cool: Business Culture, Counterculture and the Rise of Hip Consumerism*, published in 1998, mostly gained recognition as an eye-opening study of how and why this infatuation erupted during the 1960s. Be that as it may, Frank is clear that his own time, the 1990s, replicated the earlier era's tendencies:

> Beginning in 1991–92 . . ., American popular culture and corporate culture veered off together on a spree of radical-sounding bluster that mirrored events of the 1960s so closely as to make them seem almost remarkable in retrospect. Caught up in what appeared to be an unprecedented prosperity driven by the "revolutionary" forces of globalization and cyber-culture, the nation again became obsessed with (of all things) youth culture and the march of generations. It was as though we were following the cultural stage directions of a script written thirty years before.[13]

Taking Frank's observation on its face, the idea that corporations touted youth and its subcultures as emblems of revolution is the epitome of the subcultural market doctrine. Frank is also a product of this history, complicit in cementing the portrayal of this era. The roles of truth teller and Jeremiah are ones that Frank spent years relishing as the longtime editor of the anticonsumerist magazine *The Baffler*, which chronicled the commercial co-optation of youth culture in general and of alternative subcultures in particular. What he perhaps failed to realize was the degree to which he depended upon and furthered the very conditions he detested. This happened not only by accident, insofar as businesspeople might read and learn from his ideas, a fact that he admitted.[14] It also happened intentionally, as his mission was to reduce complicated social processes into something easily graspable: youth culture as authentic and ahead, the mainstream as chronically behind, and the corporation as the locomotive chugging the process of co-optation along.

Whether seen through the eyes of eager marketers or nettled critics, the marriage of subcultural theory and market forces came about due to a shared belief that subcultures were no longer the outcasts from the mainstream but its true leaders. Subcultures may have always had distinctive cultures, but in assuming that they birthed the "cool" that everyone else would one day be enamored of, subcultures became carriers of the cultural future. Though usually understood as the natural, if new, order of things, the rule of cool was constructed via both deliberate marketing practices and sympathetic critics who began to conflate difference and rebellious leadership. In this context, trends were like diamonds, waiting to be unearthed by whoever arrived first, and cool hunting became one solution to the problem of excavation. And it is for this reason that cool hunting also became a character in a late twentieth-century morality play that pitted good against evil, authenticity against fakery, and capitalism against community.

"The Ascendancy, in the Marketplace, of High School"

"I'm the first one to say I am not trendy," asserts Jane Buckingham, founder and president of Trendera, a Los Angeles–based brand consultancy and trend forecasting firm. "I am not someone who innately finds the coolest fashion item or the best product. But what I am good at is understanding why people do what they do and saying, 'Oh, I think that's going to be a trend, because I think that person represents what people are into.'"[15]

Early on, Buckingham (née Rinzler) demonstrated a talent for being able to sense what might become fashionable, especially among people her age. In 1985, while a student at Horace Mann High School in New York, she stumbled across a book about teenagers written by a man in his forties. Annoyed by how out of touch the book was, Buckingham complained to her mother, a writer. "My mother said, 'Well, could you do any better?' And I thought, 'Well, at least I could do it from a teenager perspective.'" She resolved to write her own book. Buckingham sent surveys to hundreds of teenagers around the country on their thoughts and published the results in *Teens Speak Out*, a study in teenagers' "most intimate thoughts, feelings, and hopes for the future."[16]

Buckingham graduated from Duke University with a bachelor's degree in English in 1990. She went to work in advertising; *Teens Speak Out* made her a go-to expert on youth. Soon, she landed a position directing youth marketing at Boston's Houston Effler, at the time a hot upstart with a reputation for dynamism.[17] Still, Houston Effler was not a high-powered New York shop; it didn't have the biggest brands or the fattest budgets. "We couldn't spend the kind of money that they [big-name advertising firms] could spend on research," Buckingham recalls. "So we would have to do more grassroots things, like talking to people on the street or creating a network of young people to tell us what was going on," she recalled. The close-knit culture of Boston aided the firm's efforts. Converse, a client, was a local company; a stroll down Newbury Street or around Cambridge provided telltale clues as to how the shoes were doing. This boots-on-the-ground approach "just started to reveal trends," Buckingham explains. "And trends were both the big—what are people thinking—and the small—what are they buying, what are they wearing."[18]

In 1996 Buckingham left Houston Effler to start her own company, Youth Intelligence. Among her inspirations was Irma Zandl, a marketing doyenne who had published a widely read youth market report called the *Hot Sheet* since 1986.[19] Following Zandl's lead, Youth Intelligence began publishing the *Cassandra Report*, which Buckingham named in a cheeky aside to the ill-fated Greek prophetess. Where *Hot Sheet* relied on breaking out groups into traditional demographics like sex and age, the *Cassandra Report* aimed to "take it one step beyond, and really feel what the influencers are doing by finding these really cool people," she recalled. Demand for the service exploded quickly, and Buckingham gained a solid reputation as a soothsayer for Generation X.[20]

Gregory Skinner—whose former company, Mina, was the most prominent cool hunting firm in Canada in the 1990s—followed much the same course in his career. A lifetime aficionado of "cool things," Skinner graduated from McMaster University in 1989 with a degree in finance. After a brief stint working for an oil and gas company, he opted to try his hand at self-employment and gravitated toward youth marketing. "I'd see all these billboards and all this advertising, and oftentimes the catch, the slogans, or the positioning of it—I'd go, 'That is just so completely wrong,'" he explained. Deeply connected to the art and music scenes of 1990s Toronto, Skinner surmised that he could "leverage my own knowledge to help them, so I started my company."[21] At first, he wrote columns about youth for *Strategy*, a Canadian business magazine, and took short-term consulting gigs when opportunities arose. But after a major beer manufacturer sought him out, and he impressed the company with his insightfulness, projects started rolling in. The onslaught of new work required him to scale up his business:

> At the beginning, it's just me, and it's a hustle. . . . You have to be in the know, and you got to take in all this information, then you got to go talk to people and find out what's going on. And then you got to go report, and then you have to do all the admin, and so it was really a lot of work. . . . I started to make contact

with these people who knew stuff, like psychologists and people who threw parties, and fashion designers and DJs, and I'd say, "Hey, you know, we're doing this thing, do you mind working with me—like help me understand what's going on in your realm?" And so eventually I'm like, "You know what? If I get enough people with enough diversity coming together to work on solving a problem or getting the answers, then we can be way smarter than any one of us could be individually." So I started to build this network of people, and we called them moles. You know, like a spy.[22]

At its peak, Mina used eighty-five moles globally, a distributed network peopled with cool nodes. "There was no other way to get this information," Skinner noted. "You couldn't just Google 'what's going on in EDM?' You couldn't just Google, 'what's going on in technical fabrics for athletes?' You had to know someone who knew this stuff."[23] And because information was qualitative, it was often ad hoc, intuitive, and labor-intensive. As Skinner told a reporter in 1999, "If you have someone who's partying every night in the rave scene, they're going to be able to tell you the minute there are differences in the music and the clothes or the atmosphere. . . . You can't just go to a rave and watch kids dancing around for two hours and then think you know this segment."[24]

As recently as ten years prior, embedment with consumers—otherwise known as "consumer ethnography"—was a derided endeavor, especially among academics who saw applied anthropology as contamination of the real thing. And while industrial anthropologists first appeared in corporations in the 1930s to study workers, the notion that late twentieth-century businesses might take the same approach to their consumers was farfetched.[25] "The skills of anthropology were traditionally of no use to anyone except the British Empire," noted Steve Barnett in a 1986 *New York Times* story on his work with the Cultural Analysis Group at Planmetrics, a Chicago-based consultancy. Yet by that time, Barnett, who held a PhD in anthropology from the University of Chicago, commanded $2,000 per day analyzing human behavior on behalf of corporate clients.[26] As the 1980s progressed, what came to be known as "observational research" (or, more scornfully, "eavesdropping on consumers") gained acceptance among forward-thinking companies.[27] "A rather daring technique five years ago, the hiring of cultural anthropologists to observe and often videotape consumers in stores, malls and their own homes has become a standard practice for many large corporations and some leading advertising agencies," commented a reporter in the *New York Times* in 1989. The reasons for doing so were many. Observation could explain behavior that consumers could not themselves articulate or justify; it revealed the symbolic and ritualistic meanings of products; and it was often far more cost-effective than survey research.[28]

In addition, during the 1980s, increasing cognizance about intercultural and transnational differences, continued movement toward greater market segmentation, and the spread of the concept of "corporate culture" all contributed to the idea that useful knowledge came in many different varieties, including qualitative social science. Moreover, as business changed into a "globally-integrated form" that regularly crossed borders and operated in foreign territories, "culture" became a valuable resource and anthropology, in turn, a marketable skill.[29] A heightened demand for cultural competency was likewise a function of the growing emphasis on branding, a practice that gained new vigor in the late 1980s. In contrast to its earlier incarnations, which were more narrowly focused on name and trademark, branding in the late twentieth century emphasized that the core value of a business was less its product or service than what it meant to its customers—aspects that were bound up in image, reputation, identity, design, and goodwill. Anthropologist Timothy de Waal Malefyt explains: "The emergence of new attitudes and approaches to intensify a deeper examination of the consumer and the emotional meaning of brands through lifestyle marketing, relationship building, and experiential understandings of consumption became the very cornerstone of the need for fundamental research like ethnography."[30] Of course, reservations lingered within academic anthropology toward jobs outside the university. Yet some felt that the intermingling of anthropology and business was long overdue, as it finally provided the discipline with a "professional corps of practitioners" akin to psychiatrists or social workers.[31]

To accomplish hands-on, in-depth ethnographic research did not require advanced training, however. It did demand advanced sensitivity to one's surroundings, which could be gained in many ways. For Sharon Lee, these skills were a product of her upbringing. Lee arrived in the United States from Korea at age five, and her family landed in the Los Angeles area. Bouncing around from neighborhood to neighborhood, Lee saw her new homeland through the eyes of a curious outsider who was trying to learn cultural mores. "Every year or two, I would get transferred into these other cultures and one that I didn't really belong in but allowed me to be there," she explained. "I got some early anthropological experience and training just from life experience." After graduating from Claremont McKenna, Lee got a job in account planning at Lambesis, a San Diego–based advertising agency whose clientele included some of the edgiest brands of the 1990s—companies like SKYY Vodka, Guess, and Airwalk. To strategize for these clients, Lambesis subscribed to the few existing youth market reports, but Lee didn't find them useful. "They were not tracking grunge, they were not tracking action sports. . . . It was so vanilla, what was in there," Lee recalls. "And I was like, I don't know where these people are from, who they research here, but they're not covering anything that's relevant to me." So Lee decided to do her own field research. In 1995 she hired DeeDee Gordon, who had worked at Converse, and with her and a small group of others started to investigate their target market themselves. "We literally had paper and pen," Lee explains. "It was this analog process. We would go out, do surveys on the street." They published their findings in an in-house tip sheet they called the *L Report*. Though the approach was experimental and arduous, it worked. Eventually, word of the report spread, with even nonclients clamoring for its insights.[32]

Around the same time, Janine Lopiano-Misdom and Joanne De Luca formed Sputnik, a Manhattan market research company focused on youth trends. In their 1997 book *Street Trends*, they explain the impetus for their company: "Everything about the future and our tomorrow has been planted, molded and nurtured by what is happening in the present. There are no such things as 'futurists'; there are no crystal balls or big secrets to unfold. To get there—to be ready for the big explosion of tomorrow—we just need to look at what is brewing today in the progressive microcultures of the streets—those thinkers and doers who move in individual mindsets, not masses."[33] Despite their disavowal of futurism, Lopiano-Misdom and De Luca took a page from an earlier generation of trend forecasters such as Faith Popcorn and John Naisbitt to envision large-scale trends as driving cultural change. The Sputnik twist came in their reliance upon the "cool" street: their informants were often DJs, club promoters, designers, and the like whom Sputnik recruited to video-record their ideas and experiences. In this way, Sputnik's approach also resembles what was going on in the world of fashion, where street-style photography began to take hold in the 1970s. Under the assumption that the street was a laboratory for new styles, designers began using photographs of people in their everyday clothing to inspire their collections; consumer magazines such as *iD* in London were also starting to feature look books of interestingly dressed people.[34] By the 1990s, fashion forecasting also was enjoying its own cool hunting moment. The process of planning looks, colors, and fabrics for upcoming seasons, which had been in place for decades, began to merge with the bottom-up search for novelty and creativity from the culture.[35] All of these practices reflected a move toward what I call "distributed ethnography," or the practice of ethnographic research across many different sites simultaneously to discover commonalities.[36]

But there was no umbrella term for these practices until the publication of Malcolm Gladwell's *New Yorker* feature, "The Coolhunt," in March 1997. Gladwell, then a new hire under Editor Tina Brown, had published two other notable pieces as a freelancer: "The Tipping Point," about the decline of the crime rate in Baltimore, and "The Science of Shopping," a profile of consumer psychologist

Paco Underhill. Like those previous pieces, "The Coolhunt" married social science to creative storytelling—a hallmark of his pop sociology style. As Gladwell once told an interviewer, "I wanted to mine current academic research for insights, theories, direction, inspiration, or whatever."[37]

The article's central characters are Baysie Wightman and DeeDee Gordon, whom Gladwell calls "the Lewis and Clark of cool." Wightman is a merchandising manager at Reebok, and Gordon works on the *L Report* at Lambesis. Longtime friends and former coworkers at Converse, their jobs require them to stay "in the know" of youth trends. Gladwell recounts some of their expeditions and discoveries. We follow Wightman as she hangs out with black teens in a shopping center in the South Bronx, grilling them for their views on sneaker prototypes. "Baysie is a Wasp from New England, and she crouched on the floor . . . for almost an hour, talking and joking with the homeboys without a trace of condescension or self-consciousness," Gladwell wrote. Gordon, also white, is equally formidable when it comes to cross-cultural translations. Among her claims to fame was convincing Converse to market a sandal after seeing "white teen-age girls dressing up like cholos, Mexican gangsters, in tight white tank tops known as 'wife beaters,' with a bra strap hanging out, and long shorts and tube socks and shower sandals."[38]

The colonial metaphors are glaring, but that Gladwell relies on them so unreservedly indicates both the distance between then and now and the fundamental assumptions of cool's lineage. Not all of that which cool hunters seek comes from poor communities of color; the article also notes that Gordon is infatuated with Pee-wee Herman and that Wightman has a theory about the coolness of Liverpool lads. Nevertheless, cool hunting glorifies difference, which depends on stratification, exotification, and the rigidification of cultural dissimilarity despite postmodern flows and admixtures. Gladwell struggles to articulate this, but he does provide an increasingly circular logic that becomes central to cool hunting's allure. "The act of discovering what's cool is what causes cool to move on, which explains the triumphant circularity of coolhunting: because we have coolhunters like DeeDee and Baysie, cool changes more quickly, and because cool changes more quickly, we need coolhunters like DeeDee and Baysie," Gladwell writes at one point. In another passage, Gladwell compares cool hunting to diffusion research, insofar as it is rooted in word of mouth. He also marvels at "the hermeneutic circle of coolhunting, a phenomenon whereby not only can the uncool not see cool but cool cannot even be adequately described to them." He continues: "It is not possible to be cool, in other words, unless you are—in some larger sense—already cool, and so the phenomenon that the uncool cannot see and cannot have described to them is also something they cannot ever attain, because if they did it would no longer be cool. Coolhunting represents the ascendancy, in the marketplace, of high school."[39]

Despite his gee-whiz disposition, what Gladwell did have his finger on, and what would later make *The Tipping Point* an instant classic, was the incipient fascination with what we now call "virality." The ability for ideas to circulate quickly, widely, and visibly—and for all of us to be participant-observers in the flow of person-to-person influence—does have a magical, mesmerizing quality to it, not to mention an obvious value. Though we tend to equate virality with the web, "The Coolhunt" captured how its seeds were sown before the internet grew to a dominant force. Indeed, what we now talk about as "social media" was built *atop* networks of interconnected people, subcultural communities, and chains of influence that typified industrialized societies in the late 1990s. The tools of cool hunters—the network of hip nodes, lists of interesting things, or reports of cool people—were simply its analog corollaries, its scaffolding. Gladwell also anticipated that corporations and entrepreneurs might want to understand the social in new ways and to intervene in it when and if they could. "The Coolhunt," read charitably, is a prescient take on these developments and an example of the best kind of popular social science.

Nonetheless, Gladwell made errors that benefit his storytelling; like a pointillist, his big picture emerges through a muddle of minor detail. The most egregious liberty he took is that "cool hunting" is his invention, an attempt to find a familial resemblance among those who at best find their stories only partially told and at worst misrecognize themselves. Several of the cool hunters I reached out to during my research remained leery of associating themselves with the term, even twenty years on. It would be easy to find faults with Gladwell's fabling were it not precisely the point. The reification of cool hunting—and, in turn, of cool itself—made it magical and therefore essential. "A company can intervene in the cool cycle. It can put its shoes on really cool celebrities and on fashion runways and on MTV. It can accelerate the transition from the innovator to the early adopter and on to the early majority," Gladwell wrote. "But it can't just manufacture cool out of thin air."[40] It's an observation that reads like a warning. And like an advertisement.

Revolt of the Cool Elite

The influence of "The Coolhunt" was immediate and intense. Gladwell's piece incited an "unbelievable amount of interest" among business leaders and as such increased both the demand for cool hunting and the number of people who identified as cool hunters.[41] Demand for reports like the *L Report* swelled, and major companies—among them Reebok, Nike, Coca-Cola, Nokia, the Gap, and Pepsi—signed up cool hunters.[42] In turn, many people who held jobs in youth market research, consumer insights, trend forecasting, and the like were overnight rebranded as cool hunters, whether their jobs involved the same kind of practices outlined in "The Coolhunt" or not.[43] Even Faith Popcorn, then well established as a futurist, was sometimes called a cool hunter. For a time, the term became a label for anyone who engaged in any kind of cultural prediction.

The tremendous growth opportunity that cool hunting presented was not just for cool hunters. Over the next several years, publications such as *BusinessWeek*, *AdWeek*, *Advertising Age*, *Time*, the *Chronicle of Higher Education*, the *New York Times*, the *Guardian*, and the *Washington Post* covered cool hunting, fascinated by what this strange new practice said about contemporary life and keen to earn the fruits of bandwagon coverage. Ruth La Ferla, writing in the *New York Times*, typified the journalistic characterization. She called cool hunters "anthropologists of the collective vibe who, digital cameras and notebooks in hand, scour the malls, the bodegas and skate parks from Antwerp to Los Angeles identifying youth trends for companies eager to market them."[44] The romance assigned to the job was unmistakable. Cool hunting was quickly becoming to the 2000s what the organization man was to the 1950s or the stock broker was to the 1980s. When sci-fi author William Gibson made Cayce Pollard, the memorable protagonist of Gibson's 2003 novel *Pattern Recognition* a cool hunter, the term's credibility was cemented even further. Pollard, who dressed head to toe in brand-free black clothing and who physically recoiled from bad graphic design, was the perfect balance between human ingenuity and machine-like processing. "'I hunt cool, although I don't like to describe it that way,'" Pollard explains at one point. "'What I do is pattern recognition. I try to recognize a pattern before anyone else does.'"[45]

Even so, not everyone was pleased with the attention. For Matt Marcus, a self-proclaimed cool hunter who also taught a class on the subject at Parsons School of Design, being in the spotlight "destroyed the whole thing, because it created companies and pundits and people, like myself, who are paid to create trends that way. . . . [N]ow it's everywhere." Another cool hunter described the practice as a "significant, if unfortunate," component of his job.[46] Even as more and more people turned out to be cool hunters, it seemed nobody really wanted to be one. Of course, the irony of this was that cool hunting had fallen prey to the same dynamic it was accused of effecting—it had been discovered and thus crippled. As a result, youth, the ostensible target of cool hunting, began to recoil from its overtures, more savvy but also more jaded. "Five years ago if you asked a kid to be in a focus group, he would say 'what's that?'" Will Higham, owner of the Next Big Thing in London, told a *Guardian* reporter in 2003. "Now he says, 'Okay, how much are you paying me?'"[47]

In a few corners, a backlash simmered. Old school market researchers wanted to reclaim their legitimacy and defend their turf. As early as 1998, a reporter at the *New York Times* would write that "though being a cool hunter sounds, well, cool, trend analysis companies consider the term derisive. . . . [C]ool hunting, the firms say, doesn't require sophisticated data analysis of why an item is cool."[48] Irma Zandl, the aforementioned marketing maven, saw cool hunting as a disgrace to her own work, and she frequently issued takedowns. In one story, after interviewing Zandl, a reporter proclaimed that "although some cool hunters continue to prowl, the consensus is that their trade has become uncool, because it resulted in no more than a handful of successful products."[49] A year later, Zandl followed up the reporter's screed. "We never considered ourselves cool hunters—it always struck me as being somewhat of a scam," she explained in 2003. "It's just finally been exposed for what it is: fringe developments that are entertaining for the media to cover but virtually useless for companies hoping to reach critical mass in a timely manner."[50]

That cool hunting aroused such vehement debate was a powerful reminder of the central role of journalists, who were not just informers or storytellers but also cultural framers and commenters, thinkers and influencers. While popular writing had long been powerful in this regard—think of books like Vance Packard's *The Hidden Persuaders* and Rachel Carson's *Silent Spring*—the cool hunting frenzy was part of a bigger shift in the marketplace of ideas, one political scientist Daniel Drezner characterizes as the rise of an idea industry centered on "thought leadership." Generally speaking, thought leadership consists of "big," disruptive ideas that are attached to and promoted by particular people and shared through nonacademic channels such as opinion journalism, conferences, and TED talks. Noting that "the democratization of the marketplace of ideas has made it much harder for traditional public intellectuals to argue from authority," Drezner contends that in recent years, "confident predictions" have seized the spotlight over nuanced critical arguments.[51] Gladwell's blockbuster book *The Tipping Point,* which includes conclusions derived from "The Coolhunt," is a case in point: it provides a simple, revealing, and revolutionary theory of how the world works. Its popularity seemed to prove the soundness of its theory, too—an idea that "tipped." It was easier to issue audacious proclamations than it was to prove them wrong.

Correctives proved especially difficult as activist journalists, public intellectuals, and scholars took up arms against cool hunting. In cool hunting, they found an allegorical foe that confirmed their worst fears about consumerism's overreach. Naomi Klein, for example, devotes a section of *No Logo* to cool hunt-ers, whom she calls "the legal stalkers of youth culture."[52] In *Merchants of Cool*, communication professor Bob McChesney remarks that corporations "look at the teen market as part of this massive empire that they're colonizing," sug-gesting that "teens are like Africa." His colleague, NYU media professor Mark Crispin Miller, agrees, adding in a later segment: "Often there's a kind of official and systematic rebelliousness that's reflected in—in media products pitched at kids. It's part of the official rock video worldview. It's part of the official ad-vertising worldview that your parents are creeps, teachers are nerds and idiots, authority figures are laughable, nobody can really understand kids except the corporate sponsor. That huge authority has, interestingly enough, emerged as the sort of tacit superhero of consumer culture. That's the coolest entity of all."

The concerns of critics like Miller and McChesney were legitimate, if familiar (and, in the case of McChesney, cringe-worthy). Echoing the Marxist-inspired tones of early twentieth-century intellectuals such as Theodor Adorno, they were understandably alarmed at the vulgarities of the culture industries and the ongoing disappearance of authentic cultural spaces. As righteous as these critics may have been, though, their critique was at least somewhat misplaced. The target of their ire was largely the *story* of cool hunting rather than the prac-tice itself. And this story was the product of a shifting ecosystem of influence that redefined who had the right to say what culture mattered. Within this new dynamic, critics who had long ago ceded their cultural station as arbiters of taste and voices of reason lost more of their authority to have a say in how the future unfolded.[53]

Conclusion

Sharon Lee remembers the moment she saw herself in *Merchants of Cool*. She and DeeDee Gordon left Lambesis in 1999 to form their own agency, Look-Look. They agreed to be interviewed for the PBS program without knowing its angle. "When I first saw it, I was like, 'This is bad. This is not good,'" she recalls, uneasy at how Look-Look was lumped in with more nakedly exploitative companies. But miraculously, or perhaps predictably, "the phone didn't stop ringing for, like, two years after. Clients didn't give a shit. . . . I was like, 'We were just painted as these horrible people, and nobody cares.'"[54]

Of all the lessons one might distill from cool hunting, this is the most sig-nificant. *Merchants of Cool* indicted the exploiters of youth culture, but it also encouraged corporations to buy in. It railed against cool hunting, but it also en-dorsed the changing nature of cultural influence and documented young people eager to help companies understand their kind. Above all, *Merchants* validated cool hunting's worldview: a world where the rich and powerful take their cues from the poor, the alternative, and the dispossessed; where journalists with big ideas shape the cultural conversation (much to academics' chagrin); and where everyone seeks validation that they are cool enough. "There are many times when I walked into clients' offices, and they hired me and paid me a lot of money to talk about something about their business, and they would pull me [aside] and go, 'Hey. Is what I'm wearing cool?'" Lee recalled. "And I'm just, oh. I just realized why I'm really here."[55] Cool hunting may have been a short-lived fad, but it indicated a sea change in terms of whose trends—in clothing, in culture, and in ideas—were worth following. And it gave way to a future in which that kind of clout may be the coolest thing of all.

PART TWO

CHAPTER 4

Trends, Inc.

A young man named Tim escorts me into the building through a tiny wooden door. We're on a cobblestoned block near the border of Spitalfields and Shoreditch, two excessively hip neighborhoods in North East London. After squeezing myself and my oversized American backpack through the entryway, I emerge into a verdant atrium, airy and luminous. Along one wall, plants reach energetically toward the light. I later learn that this greenery is a vertical garden, some of it edible; staff can pick their lunch, literally. The potential for "extreme provenance" reaches another height when a tour of the office takes me to the rooftop apiary.[1] The bees' honey, I'm told, gets used in-house to sweeten salad dressings and tea. The IT guy doubles as a beekeeper.

But I'm getting ahead of myself. The bees come later.

I've arrived at the offices of the Future Laboratory, a pioneering London trend forecasting agency that is widely viewed as a global industry leader. Martin Raymond founded the company in 2000, initially conceiving of it as a "think tank" and running it from his East London apartment.[2] Raymond soon joined forces with Chris Sanderson, a marketing and creative professional, and together they forged a business that combined futurist consulting with consumer and market trends research; they also put out a trends magazine called *Viewpoint*, for which Raymond continues to serve as editor in chief.[3] The Future Laboratory now employs more than twenty people and specializes in fourteen different industry sectors, including retail, beauty, luxury, and placemaking.

With more than two hundred clients in its roster, including Airbnb, Condé Nast, Unilever, and Heathrow Airport, the Future Laboratory's work includes tailored consulting (including "bespoke presentations," "foresight programmes," and "curated events"), as well as a subscription-based editorial platform called LS:N Global.[4]

In 2016 I met Hannah Robinson, a woman in her twenties who has been at the Future Laboratory since 2010. At the time, Robinson was LS:N Global's visual editor. Robinson studied at the London College of Fashion, where she developed an interest in image making, psychology, and semiotics. Her first position with the Future Laboratory was picture intern, and she has since worked her way up. With her training in fashion, one might expect Robinson to have landed somewhere like WGSN, perhaps the world's best-known fashion forecasting company. Yet Robinson feels that the Future Laboratory allows her more latitude to explore a diversity of interests. "At Future Laboratory we're really more interested in looking at how one sector impacts another and looking at things with a more long-term view," she explains, countering the singular focus and short-termism that typify fashion.[5] In-house, staff refer to this process as "cross cultural analysis," which entails researching different sectors for themes that resonate through them all.[6]

The purpose of all this work is "working out what are the new behaviors that are going to impact on consumer's decision making, and how is that going to impact brands, lifestyle, thinking about things in a broader sense," Robinson explains. The operative word is *new*: in a world where nothing stands still, the job of the Future Laboratory is to identify shifts, decipher them, and package them so they are stunning, provocative, and utilizable. "Our role is separating all of these stimuli and saying, 'This is what you need to know, this is what you actually need to understand and think about,'" Robinson explains. This may at first blush not seem like a very taxing job—perusing one's environment, observing interesting things, developing generalizations. Yet the attention to detail, flexibility, and the ability to tune into one's environment are hardly work just anyone can do. "You need to really be able to go into a space, and decode it, and look at small elements that perhaps other people wouldn't notice," she comments.[7] Trend forecasting takes a certain je ne sais quoi.

Stated most plainly, the work of trend forecasters is to observe and explain trends. Forecasters use trends to reveal to clients the world that is unfolding around them; trends indicate the directions in which they should prepare, strategize, and lead. Forecasters find trends through their hypersensitivity to information, their curatorial acumen, and their ability to connect tiny changes to the broad shifts that frame human motivation, desire, and interaction.

Trends are a sort of stereogram of culture: illusory, ever changeable, and emerging only through committed surveillance. Forecasters hone skillsets to detect these changes as they unfold, to see where the world is heading by making sense of the random, the overwhelming, the seemingly miscellaneous. The ability to do this goes by many different names—intuition, foresight, prescience, futurism—but whatever it is called, it arises from picking up what others might not and having the ability to interpret those discoveries.

Considered from another angle, though, the work of trend forecasters is not about finding trends but about producing them. Trend forecasting is performative. Like marketing in general, trends function "pragmatically to 'move things forward', to make judgements about what to do next; to guide what information is valuable and why; to stabilise realities so that actors can generate at least partially shared understandings, coordinate their activities and take action to materialise imagined markets."[8] In other words, the production of trends is more than a process of enacting and circulating influence; it does more than simply hold sway over what decision makers think and do. At companies like the Future Laboratory and elsewhere, trends are commodities, the outcome of forecasters' labor. They result when an observation turns into an insight that suggests a particular pathway for innovation. Selling trends requires telling convincing stories about change, as well as developing efficacious and credible instruments to detect and measure it. Trend forecasters must create the conditions for their own existence, packaging and commodifying not just cultural change but also the very idea of cultural observation.

This chapter details the complex processes through which contemporary forecasters see, build, and market trends. Forecasters tend to talk about trends as something out in the world waiting to be discovered and to share what tools might be used to locate them. In contrast, I start from the premise that the contours of trends emerge as trend forecasters observe them. I don't think that there is nothing new under the sun or that finding commonalities among cultural happenings is make-believe. Nor do I want to suggest that forecasters fabricate their analyses out of thin air and overlay them onto the world to serve their own or their clients' agendas. Rather, I want to show how trends function as a window for seeing the world, a framework for assessing the world, and a template for taking action in the world. Additionally, trends supply a comprehensive habitus for forecasters' work, informing their behavior, directing their professional ways of being, and justifying their existence. By understanding how trends transform from observations into products, we can see that trend labor operates reflexively to necessitate itself and recursively to bring the world it imagines into being.

Seeing Trends

In *The Trend Forecaster's Handbook*, Martin Raymond writes of Cassie, an imaginary forecaster whom he uses to explain how to go about observing, sorting through, and learning from one's cultural environment:

> Cassie uses her "forecaster's nose" to search for a pattern, to sense that something new is in the air. On recent trips to Los Angeles, London, Buenos Aires and Madrid she noticed a growing number of wholefood and organic food outlets in parts of these cities where she wouldn't normally expect to find them. They were also selling seasonal and locally produced products, with pictures of the people who grew them stamped on the packaging itself. Meanwhile in Frankfurt she travelled in a taxi that ran on hybrid fuel, and while in Tokyo visited a store that looked like it had been made from recycled pieces of wood. . . . All these things are fragments, rarified bits of "stuff" drifting about in the ether and in Cassie's unconscious. She senses a pattern here, anomalous shifts that tell her something is afoot. But what?[9]

"But what?" is the million-dollar question. It marks the difference between a collection of curious notes and the germs of a trend. Cassie must not just find interesting tidbits in her environment but also decipher how they fit together and determine which ones signal a meaningful social shift. In his book *Anatomy of a Trend*, Henrik Vejlgaard explains the distinction. "A trend is not something that *has* happened," he insists, "but rather a *prediction* of something that is *going to* happen in a certain way."[10] The job of a trend forecaster—or "trend sociologist," as Vejlgaard prefers—is to make these kinds of judgment calls.

On its surface, Vejlgaard's definition is conventional and widely echoed among other forecasters. For Cecily Sommers, a futurist consultant based in Minneapolis, "trends are how we define themes and patterns of change"—an elegant definition that meshes well with Vejlgaard's.[11] If we work under the assumption that preparing for the future is the best way to stay competitive, then these "themes and patterns of change" establish a context for purposeful invention. "Trends [are] the fuel that powers innovation," explained Marie Stafford, European director of the Innovation Group at the London branch of JWT Intelligence, a futures center attached to big-name ad agency J. Walter Thompson. "What enables you to innovate is understanding what the trends are and how they're changing the world." She continues:

> A trend we wrote about [in 2015 was] the Elastic Generation—which was about consumers in their fifties and sixties and how they're a really important consumer group that has been, you know, a little bit neglected, a little bit ignored by

advertising, but they're actually quite dynamic and have a lot of financial clout. [There's] this perception I find that, you know, that's kind of done now . . . but in my mind trends evolve. They don't just fall off. They don't expire on the 31st of December. I think of them as living and breathing things, and they change. [We] did a review of the ten-year anniversary of our trends group, looking back at trends we'd already looked at. And, you know, so many of them are still relevant.[12]

Though forecasters routinely conceptualize trends as tools to anticipate the future, Stafford's remarks make clear that trends are not merely useful for looking forward. Forecasters may use trends to facilitate looking backward in situations that necessitate retrospectively accounting for the accuracy of their work. Trends are also central to how forecasters explain the present. Consider Stephan Paschalides, founder and CEO of the Brooklyn-based Now Plus One, a company whose very name emphasizes its presentism. In Paschalides's words, his company partakes in "insight emergence" at the "edge of tomorrow," with the aim of positioning "clients at the forefront of culture to explore trends and insights up close." Paschalides is not the only forecaster I spoke with who preferred to think of trend work as compulsively fixated on "next"—a time just a tad ahead of right now—as opposed to some approaching but murky future. "Calling yourself a futurist and claiming that you can give the forecast for the next five, ten years seems a little unrealistic," he explained.[13]

Regardless of these definitional and temporal quarrels, trends serve a similar purpose. Trends create ways of *seeing through* cultural information. They are foundations upon which forecasters construct stories about where culture is going—whether it will get there tomorrow, in six months, or in fifteen or fifty years. Kiwa Iyobe, a freelance trend consultant in London who began her career working for Faith Popcorn, explained that at BrainReserve, trends were "the lens through which you were taught within the company to look at culture," thereby becoming the architecture of a forecaster's thinking.[14] As trends may be a prism through which forecasters do their work, they are also the product of that work.

The basic technique for seeing a cultural trend involves three steps. First, forecasters digest cultural information in abundance. Second, that information undergoes a filtering process in which forecasters study it for relevance and patterns. Finally, forecasters organize these patterns so that they tell a story about the world. Though these steps may both unearth new trends and revise old ones, forecasters do not work with a limitless number of trends at any given time, and there is some variance among firms as to what a manageable number of trends is. Faith Popcorn's BrainReserve works with seventeen trends, for instance, while Sparks & Honey and JWT Intelligence are often monitoring over a hundred.

Forecasting operates both through and because of information overload. "One of the primary drivers for [our work] is the morass of information that we're all faced with," said Hayley Ard, then head of consumer insights at Stylus, a London-based trend firm. "In this information age that we're firmly embedded in, there's more and more of a need for curation and steering people toward the right insights at the right time."[15] Scott Lachut of insights and trends company PSFK voiced similar thoughts, noting that having "theoretical access to information at your fingertips" does not necessarily equate with being able to navigate it. "Some people just don't have the time or interest to go out and figure out what is interesting," he continued, and it is this deficiency that PSFK services.[16] Max Luthy, director of trends and insights at TrendWatching and based in New York, likewise understood the impetus for his work not as a lack of information but as the opposite. "Clients aren't like, 'I don't have enough information,'" he explained. Instead, they say, "'What information relates to me and what do I do with it?'"[17]

Media studies professor Mark Andrejevic coined the term "infoglut" to describe the exponential rise of mediated information that, paradoxically, threatens our ability to feel comprehensively in the know. "At the very moment when we have the technology available to inform ourselves as never before, we are simultaneously and compellingly confronted with the impossibility of ever being *fully* informed," he notes.[18] The current moment transcends "information overload" insofar as it is not simply that we have readier access to more facts, news, statistics, opinions, and images than ever before. What constitutes information also continues to balloon as areas of human and nonhuman experience such as emotions, sociality, biology, and culture increasingly come to be thought about and treated as essentially informational.[19] The informational turn—especially the conversion of culture into information and the datafication that corresponds to it—is a precondition for the existence of trend forecasting. Forecasters understand culture as information in order to claim mastery, expertise, and relevance.

Drawing an equivalence between culture and information also dictates how forecasters engross themselves in culture. Forecasters use the term "desk research" to describe the process of immersion in mediated cultural information. Desk research is common to many business fields, and in the case of trend forecasting two points are worth emphasizing. First, desk research is one of the primary research methods that forecasters employ; at some firms, it may be the only method used for a particular project. A second point about desk research is the large amount of information forecasters overview to do their jobs. Desk research may involve daily reading of hundreds of news sources, including magazines, newspapers, websites, newsletters, and social media; consuming visual content such as movies, videos, and Instagram feeds; or listening to music, podcasts, and other audio. Over time, these habits can become reflex-like. "Part of it is literally building intuition. . . . It's the same thing as when you're constantly reading and scanning things," explains Dan Gould, formerly of Sparks & Honey and now at Google working as human truths manager. "You're building this kind of muscle memory for what's happened and where things are so when you see a new thing, a new signal, whatever that might be, you can build that off what you already know."[20]

As Gould's comment suggests, digesting cultural information involves continuous processes of judgment. Forecasting requires making associations: between bits of found culture, between those bits and ideas, between ideas and particular clients, and between all of the above and brands. Andrejevic's observation that infoglut demands "shortcuts for managing large amounts of information without necessarily having to delve into, engage with, or even understand it" relates to both the process of filtering information for trends and the trends that are the end result.[21] Forecasters internalize what to look for in order to create timesaving information management strategies for both themselves and their clients. These processes, which are both conscious and unconscious, rely on the strategies of *pattern recognition* and *salience*. The first is about seeing connections among heterogeneous things, while the second involves focusing on making those connections useful.

Pattern recognition is a familiar idea within the study of culture. Chapter 1 already explored how the idea of culture as a tableau of interrelated behaviors first achieved prominence with Ruth Benedict's 1934 *Patterns of Culture*, a book also responsible for popularizing the notion of "culture" now commonly associated with anthropology. In the following decades, the idea of cultural patterns grew in importance across the social sciences. Writing in 1961, British sociologist Raymond Williams remarked, "It is with the discovery of patterns of a characteristic kind that any useful cultural analysis begins."[22] While seeking out patterns is in many ways a fundamental component of cultural research, within the business sector cultural pattern recognition tends to reference "design thinking," one of the most influential business ideas of the 2000s and a trademark of Tim Brown, CEO of renowned design firm IDEO. Arguing that "design is now too important to be left to designers," Brown explained in his book *Change by Design* (2009) that "the mission of design thinking is to translate observations into insights and insights into products and services that will improve lives." Design thinking relies on "synthesis, the act of extracting meaningful patterns from masses of raw information." Synthesis is more than simply data crunching; for him, it is "a fundamentally creative act."[23]

The term "pattern recognition" is also significant within the natural sciences, as the idea of finding patterns was essential to early discoveries in astronomy, physics, statistics, and many other fields. Contemporary pattern recognition is especially relevant to machine learning, concerned as it is with "the automatic discovery of regularities in data through the use of computer algorithms and with the use of these regularities to take actions such as classifying the data into different categories."[24] It is interesting, then, that forecasters routinely mention pattern recognition as a basic competency for their trade—one that is not only required for success but also inherently human.[25] Some forecasters suggest that pattern recognition is so thoroughly human that it cannot really be taught; it is like having perfect pitch. Others don't go quite so far but will argue that someone who possesses the quality innately will always excel beyond someone who doesn't. "Pattern recognition is not easy for everyone," noted Piers Fawkes, founder of PSFK. "There are people who are faster at it and more perceptive."[26] Unsurprisingly, trend forecasting tends to attract people who understand themselves as naturally curious and extremely observant cultural omnivores who possess skills that machines could never replicate.

Pattern recognition may either drive or follow the trend discovery process. At JWT Intelligence, for instance, Stafford and her team work deductively, using pattern recognition to corroborate their impressions. "When we think we have kernels of an idea, we'll go off, and we'll do desk research, we'll talk to experts, and then we'll do research with consumers as well and see if we can see patterns in all of that data that support the idea we have," she explained.[27] But pattern recognition can also be more of an inductive process. At the beginning of this section, we saw how "Cassie" began to see trends in her environment by recognizing patterns. Arguably, she would have been open to "seeing" whatever her environment produced, though by roaming the world's affluent global cities in search of consumerist novelty, she was primed to encounter it. Moreover, visiting cities such as Los Angeles, Frankfurt, and Tokyo increased the likelihood of her stumbling across sameness. Cassie didn't find herself in suburban Canada or rural China; she went where taxis would take her.

Pattern recognition strongly correlates with salience, another important issue that shapes how forecasters perceive the world. Salience refers to the processes that guide forecasters as they determine whether an observation or a connection is useful. Many considerations shape whether a forecaster deems a trend salient, including the needs of a particular client or project, the norms of the forecasting company in question, the interests of a forecaster, and the leanings of the physical and discursive sites where research occurs. Of course, not everything can be salient. Forecasters must negotiate a balance between bringing their unique perspectives to their work and countering their own preferences, between working within what makes sense for clients and telling them hard truths. While these issues certainly come to bear during the strategy phase of trend forecasting, they begin perceptually. For example, Gould, the Google employee, described a type of "cognitive bias" that could move forecasters toward "giving importance to this thing just because they are kind of into it."[28] Similarly, at Sparks & Honey, staff are encouraged to think beyond the bubble of New York City, about clients' customers who might be less affluent, educated, or open-minded. "Our philosophy is to remind people constantly you are not the target audience," explained Sarah Davanzo, then chief cultural strategist. "Remove your bias from [the process]."[29]

As important as it is to eliminate one's prejudices, "bias" is not so easily done away with when the raison d'être of trend forecasting is to imagine a future in which trend forecasting continues to retain its relevance. By this, I mean something more than the simple fact that trend forecasting rarely questions the basic premises of the global consumer capitalist order of which it is also a beneficiary. More endemically, trend forecasting concerns finding "opportunity," no matter the future. There is always the potential for a client to devise a profitable response. What this betrays is an abiding optimism that frames how forecasters tend to perceive the future and how that future depends upon not just change but also continuity.

To take a simple example, in 2017 many forecasters found themselves contending with the sudden dominance of populism, nationalism, and protectionism—a development that most forecasters did not anticipate, despite their futurist orientation. The reasons why some "missed" this rise is complicated and is one of the topics I'll develop more in chapters 5 and 6. For now, it is enough to point out that forecasters embraced this new state of affairs, seeking to help brands position themselves to weather a new era. In a 2017 report on the disappearing American middle class, for instance, the Future Laboratory argued that in many instances "celebrating the everyman is more effective than aspirational advertising"; wise brands need to embrace "the New Heartland" and "consider how to immerse your brand in the culture of the flyover states."[30] In other words, not even Trump could undermine the power of branding.

Seeing a trend is a multidimensional endeavor that balances learned skills with inborn dispositions, external phenomena with internal drives and vocationally shaped motivations. Forecasters have internalized modes of perception and valuation that render the world an orchard of circumstances and trends the choicest, ripest fruits. The next order of business is turning them into something delectable.

Building Trends

Halfway through JWT Intelligence's May 2017 report, *Food + Drink,* sits an image of a hand pouring brown powder from a packet into a porcelain coffee mug. The powder is Four Sigmatic's Mushroom Hot Cocoa; the package claims that it's "dark and spicy," fortified "with cordyceps." The drink exemplifies a food trend called "Hack Snacks," where "products that stimulate and have natural and self-optimizing credentials are the order of the day." Alongside the report's other food trends—such as photogenic "Insta-Serves," programmer-friendly "Valley Foods," and brand-curated "Food Journeys"—JWT's report explores how food and beverage companies are responding to environmental pressures, regulatory changes, and shifting consumer attitudes. "The scale of the challenges facing the global food and drink industry seems immense, but there is cause for optimism," the report states. Greater attention to health and well-being from policy-makers, restaurateurs, food entrepreneurs, and consumers can reconfigure the food market in ways that savvy companies can latch onto. With cordyceps, whatever those are.[31]

Food + Drink reflects how forecasters at JWT perceived the trends in their environment. Its goal is not just to document what already exists, though. With this report, JWT aspires to shape how others view their surroundings, to advocate for how the world could be. Raw trend information must transform into credible theories, compelling narratives, and measurable outcomes. Stated differently, forecasters must *build* trends through rigorous methodologies and persuasive communications.

Armed with observations from their environment about promising trends, forecasters still have much to do. Trends require packaging to be believed, communicated, and sold. Packaging includes names and stories, data and evidence, images and formats.

One way in which forecasters package trends is by turning them into metrics. British sociologist David Beer defines a metric as a "form of data through which value can be measured, captured, or even generated."[32] Especially lately, scholars interested in metrification have focused on the spread of quantification as a means through which people understand themselves and the world around them. Numbers certainly matter when it comes to measuring trends; forecasters are ardent users of statistics, surveys, Big Data, and other tools. However, forecasters also devise an array of qualitative metrics that "aim to establish a constellation of characteristics, stabilized at least for a while, which are attached to the product and transform it temporarily into a tradable good in the market."[33] Trends establish categories through which cultural change may be systematically correlated, anticipated, and valued.

For example, consider how Scott Lachut of PSFK explains the systematic method through which a trend is discovered: "In our process, we wouldn't see one individual signal and say, 'Oh, this is interesting, that means something.' There has to be enough velocity behind that so there's a mass of similar [examples] that are starting to shape an idea. By virtue of that, there seems to be some robustness behind that process. . . . Because when we present the trend, we present supporting evidence in the sense of 'here's a bunch of examples that show how this is manifesting within the marketplace.'"[34] Piers Fawkes, founder of PSFK, describes the method that underlies this process as "grounded theory analysis."

> I went and saw a classically trained market researcher maybe a year or two years into the commercialization of my business. And I said, "This is how I do it. I gather all this data, do patterns, talk to experts," and he said, "There's a name to that approach. . . . It's called grounded theory analysis." . . . And to date we still use that theory throughout everything we do. I think you will find there are different ways people are identifying trends. I don't know if there's a right way or a wrong way. . . . We only go through this way because we argue that it's robust. It's based on a volume of data that gives you—I won't say statistically, but at least a robust analysis.[35]

Both Lachut and Fawkes, in touting the "robustness" of their methodology, are likewise making a claim that a trend is a cultural metric. Using a method that is more empirical than a hunch or an opinion, forecasters understand common themes across diverse, largely qualitative data sources as proof that a trend exists. Varied examples "add up" to or "cluster" to suggest a trend.[36] That the data may be highly variable is a strength that suggests the comprehensiveness of the method rather than that examples have been culled, curated, or cherry-picked. This "proof" helps to build the case for a trend.

Els Dragt, Dutch trend forecaster and author of *How to Research Trends* (2017), refers to the process of measuring a trend's existence as "validation," writing that validation "is about diving into each cluster and [finding] more information related to each trend theme." To validate a trend, a researcher seeks out additional evidence of a trend's existence, including digital traces, images, text, or objects. Dragt advocates following a checklist of questions to ensure validity, including "Why is this trend happening right now?" "Where can you see this trend happening already?" and "What consequences can this trend have on our future quality of life?"[37] Questions such as these not only allow the extent of a trend to be measured but in turn permit the trend to measure culture.

Many forecasting firms also lean heavily on visual analysis. Figure 1 shows one of Future Laboratory's trend boards, a method that brings trends to life

Figure 1. The Future Laboratory trend board. Image courtesy of the Future Laboratory.

through groups of images, sticky notes, and key phrases. The Future Laboratory strongly advocates a visual approach to evidence, notably maintaining "visual" analysts and researchers in addition to those who focus on "data." Raymond also suggests that the budding forecaster find a way to keep track of cultural evidence visually, noting that for any would-be forecaster, it is "important to establish a 'den' or area in your house, room, lecture hall or college research lab, where you can paste, post and capture all this 'stuff' in a visual way."[38] Showcasing a variety of images together is eye-catching; "reading" them in tandem draws from a range of traditions in visual studies, including anthropology, cultural studies, content analysis, and semiotics.[39] But beyond deciphering the images for what they *say,* the assemblage also acts as a metric that gives weight and validity to the observation. One can't help but see commonalities when the images are collected together.

Trend forecasters maintain that trends travel at different speeds along different trajectories, affecting different populations of people along the way. Some burst swiftly into the mainstream, while others idle at the margins; some stay geographically confined, while others rapidly crisscross borders. To interpret these distinctions requires additional levels of metrification. Patrick Lodge, of the London-based firm Breaking Trends, shared with me the inner workings of the company's trend matrix, the method his firm uses to grade trends:

> We grade the trends depending on whether they're local, i.e., they're just going to affect people in the M25 [the London Orbital Motorway] area, or the Eastern

Seaboard of the US, or whether they're global trends, i.e., they're going to affect the majority of the human herd in developed economies. [Temporally] we grade trends in five different ways. What we call a horizon trend, that would be five years out. Then we have, coming in a bit, there's an emerging trend, and there's a breaking trend, and there's a maturing trend. Maturing trend is probably three months, or it has kind of hit the mainstream. Then there's peaking, which is sort of done and dusted. . . . Then we also have like a device to denote whether it's major, i.e., it's going to affect most people in most developing economies. Or if it's medium, it's just going to affect maybe quite a specific group. If it's minor, just maybe really early adopters or even just the very, very niche kind of subset of people.[40]

The trend matrix, which Lodge also described as "weighting" trends, is predicated in part on the idea of diffusion. Following the classic understanding, certain populations of people become aware of novel cultural developments prior to others; these people then spread innovations to everyone else. At Breaking Trends, this idea assumes geographic connotations, with the M25 in London and the East Coast of the United States representing nodes where cultural innovation often takes hold. Linking trends to preexisting assumptions about the world—for instance, that urban dwellers live "faster" or more innovatively than rural folks, or that early adopters are more open to novelty—allows the company's system to appear rigorous and measurable while also deeply qualitative.

Other companies categorize trends hierarchically. A common way of doing this is to define macrotrends, megatrends, or parent trends, inside of which faster-moving dynamics (usually identified as trends or microtrends) exist. To give an illustration of how this works, figure 2 shows the parent trends for TrendWatching as of March 2017. Note that parent trends are highly abstract and general; therefore, they are widely applicable to a variety of cultural developments. Other, faster-moving shifts are cataloged as subsets or specific manifestations of parent trends. In December of every year, for instance, Trend-Watching issues five trends for the next calendar year. One of 2017's anticipated trends was "Worlds Apart," referring to the destabilizing geopolitical shifts that continue to ricochet around the globe. As TrendWatching advised, 2017 would be a year in which "purposeful brands will find renewed opportunities in helping people understand their changing relationship to home—be that their nation, city or neighborhood." They linked this trend to the parent trend of "Remapped," described as the "epic power shifts in the global economy."[41]

Parent trends, megatrends, or macrotrends provide a steady metric against which the constant churn of cultural change can be measured. "We would consider macrotrends more as drivers, so, you know, the big shifts," explained

Figure 2: TrendWatching Parent Trends

Trend	Description
Status Seekers	The relentless, often subconscious yet ever-present force that underpins almost all consumer behavior
Betterment	The universal quest for self-improvement
Human Brands	Why personality and purpose will mean profit
Better Business	Why 'good' business will be good for business
Youniverse	Make your consumers the center of their YOUNIVERSE
Local Love	Why 'local' is, and will remain, loved
Ubitech	The ever-greater pervasiveness of technology
Infolust	Why consumers' voracious appetite for (even more) information will only grow
Playsumers	Who said business had to be boring?
Ephemeral	Why consumers will embrace the here, the now, and the soon-to-be-gone
Fuzzynomics	The divisions between producers and consumers, brands and customers will continue to blur
Pricing Pandemonium	Pricing—more fluid and flexible than ever
Helpfull	Be part of the solution, not the problem
Joyning	The eternal desire for connection, and the many (new) ways it can be satisfied
Post-Demographic	The age of disrupted demographics
Remapped	The epic power shifts in the global economy

Note: These trends are taken verbatim from the 2016 website of TrendWatching.com.

Stafford of JWT Intelligence. "They're kind of powering microtrends or what are driving them along."[42] At Sparks & Honey, the top-level trends are known as "elements of culture," which provide a "full taxonomy" of the world. Sarah Davanzo described the process this way:

> Every ninety days we review all of our trends. Elements of culture is the whole mindset, but within that, there are microtrends. You know, the bursts, the shorter thing. The macrotrends, which are maybe changeable within the year. The mega-trends are the actual cultural shifts that are taking place, right? And how many can there be? How many can we actually manage is actually the point. So, as you'll notice, we actually have more megatrends than we have macrotrends right now because the megatrends are rather accepted shifts that are taking place. You could say they're trends, but they're slow moving, kind of much more global, much larger reach. And they're in fact permeating many aspects of life. The macrotrends are changing much more rapidly, and therefore we have to keep our eye on the ball. And we happen to have five categories of macrotrends that we track regularly.[43]

There is great variety in terms of how forecasters determine the speed or spread of a trend. But one method that is common is ethnography, especially distributed ethnography. Distributed ethnography refers to doing ethnographic work in many different sites to find continuities and similarities. The corroboration of a trend in multiple sites becomes a metric in the same way as noted above with cultural artifacts: the wide replicability is evidence that a trend has "legs."

TrendWatching relies heavily on a coordinated system of distributed ethnography. The company employs a global team of spotters called a trend insight network (TW:IN). Spotters are located around the world, hunting for locally based innovations.[44] Spotter inputs then meld with what analysts are able to surmise from their base offices of London, New York, and Singapore or their affiliates in Lagos and São Paolo. For instance, if a certain development is coming in from Asia, office analysts will ping the network to see if it's also occurring in other parts of the world. "With some trends, they'll come pouring in, and sometimes they'll come pouring in more from South and Central America than they will from Asia," Luthy remarked.[45] Trend networks such as TW:IN are meant to provide a low-cost way to span the world, but they require vigilance and management. Nia Christy, who manages the network at TrendWatching, explained to me that such networks are often more concentrated in certain parts of the world than others and that spotters need to be constantly reminded to focus on local rather than global phenomena—a point I will return to in the next chapter.

While not every company has an extensive network like TW:IN, many invest resources in internationalizing their perspective. Some enlist international experts to weigh in on cultural developments. Others coordinate excursions to other countries where clients can immerse themselves in unfamiliar, stimulating surroundings. In the next chapter, I will address more broadly the implications that such cosmopolitanism has on trend forecasting as both an economic and a political project. For the time being, let me make the more general point that under these processes, global cultures become a kind of metric in themselves. If a forecaster can demonstrate that the same dynamic is happening around the world, that serves to affirm its credibility.

Trend research is constantly evolving. A number of companies and freelance trend professionals are pioneering unique methods, many of which are aimed toward the possibility of someday automating trend discovery. For instance, when I spoke to Sem Devillart, a freelance trend specialist in New York City, she was developing a method she referred to as "mapping." The idea is not so much geographical as it is thinking in terms of a matrix or grid. "I started to develop maps that were based on associations," she explained. For example, "if yoga rises, if yoga is successful, imagine yoga as a planet, okay? It has satellites. That means if this gets strong, if yoga gets strong, then tea will rise compared to coffee."[46] With such maps, Devillart contends that it might be possible to find a cultural "atom," a distinct unit that, like the physical atom, opens up a field for a "science" of cultural prediction. If it were possible to find something about culture that would tell you whether a phenomenon would catch on or not, you could then build software to analyze these elements, implant them into cultural developments, or perhaps synthesize them.

If this idea feels implausible, be mindful that many trend firms are beginning to use artificial intelligence, data mining, and machine learning to reinforce their qualitative and more classically quantitative methods. The result may be systems that "know" that something has the likelihood of becoming a trend, even if they aren't able to say why. At the time of this writing, much of this work remains experimental. Few firms have large amounts of capital to pour into such initiatives, and those that have invested in this area still rely on humans to do qualitative interpretation. Often, claims made about the efficacy of artificial intelligence are overblown—not just in trend forecasting but everywhere. Despite this, AI tools are sexy, cutting edge, and extremely marketable. I expect things will continue to move in this direction, especially if companies like Google and Facebook devote resources to broadening such initiatives either in conjunction with trend forecasters or on their own. In addition, development is happening in universities to complement what's going on in industry. Justien Marseilles, a Dutch futurist who has taught at the University of Applied Science in Rotterdam, is one person who is working with students in design and information science to develop computational systems that can collect "weak signals" and "clusters of change" in the hopes of being able "to measure out [if there is a] chance that cluster is already emerging."[47] The implications of such developments are gigantic if difficult to fully foresee.

Trends structure how forecasters communicate. Using inventive turns of phrase, catchphrases, portmanteaus, and other tricks of language, trend forecasters translate the information they have digested into a sharable, persuasive form. Their phraseology often anchors the stories they tell about the world to procure and maintain business, as well as how they talk to each other.

For example, Sparks & Honey's 2016 report, "UnMoney," explores "how our very concept of money is evolving, and describes how the system designed to manage its movement is ripe for disruption." The term "unmoney" intends to remind us that what we now take for granted as money—bills in our pockets, change in our purses, entries in our checking accounts—is "simply a representation of a transaction about to take place, completely dependent upon our belief that it has a value." Once the notion of money returns to its basis in exchange, almost anything can be considered valuable and may even become a form of value thanks to new technologies like cryptocurrencies and blockchain. The report calls this the "quantum economy," noting that "every moment of the day assumes a new value that lives beyond the moment itself." Or, put even more starkly "tomorrow, everything will have a value. Including you."[48]

With names like "UnMoney," "The Moonshot Economy," "Big Tent Branding," "Frontier(less) Retail," and "Roboromance," it is easy to ridicule trend naming as the kind of corporate doublespeak that marketing and advertising professionals trade in as a matter of course.[49] As *The Economist* put it in 2010, "Consumer watchers . . . constantly coin annoying neologisms, which they would doubtless call 'annoyologisms.'"[50] Some of my interviewees also voiced cynicism about this tick among their colleagues. Rather than find things that are truly novel or illuminating, "we're packaging a lot of things that have been happening in culture for at least ten years," noted Katharina Michalski, at the time a freelance forecaster in London.[51] For others, names played a more central role. "One of the reasons we come up with these new names for these papers is so that it's value free," explained Edie Weiner, who is the founder of the Future Hunters and who has been working in futurism since 1969. Committed to maintaining "objectivity," the Future Hunters uses new words in an effort to prevent clients from reflexively rejecting an idea out of hand. In addition, Weiner explained that her company "makes up words" so it can "lay the groundwork for the newness of the thought."[52] The argument goes that new words require clients to be imaginative as they attempt to make sense of something for which there is no precedent. Davanzo, formerly of Sparks & Honey agreed: "If we do not have a name for it, we can't have an intelligent conversation one-to-one or with our clients, and so then we're talking at odds."[53]

The Future Hunters maintains a glossary of terms and phrases it has coined since Weiner's original consultancy, Weiner, Edrich and Brown, began in 1977. Among the list are some common terms with long histories and multiple claimants, including "biopolitics," "leapfrog" (as in when a developing country skips over a phase of technological progress), and "virtual reality." Others, like "prifecta," "mediapeds," and "comployment," are unfamiliar. While it is beyond my interest to debate the accuracy of this glossary, its existence attests to the centrality of "thought leadership" to trend forecasting. As I mentioned in the last chapter, thought leadership, or the idea of inventing and owning a groundbreaking idea, has become central to many sorts of businesses in recent years. As Shepherd Laughlin, then director of trend forecasting at JWT Intelligence in New York, reasoned, "Everyone has more of an interest in being a mouthpiece for new and disruptive and radical ideas."[54] Inventing new terms to describe cultural dynamics is therefore a way of not only generating thought but also branding it, since a distinctive label "helps your audience to remember and communicate with others about a trend."[55] In the most successful instances, these labels may also reify a cultural development in a manner that works recursively to render the world congruent with the forecasted idea.

One particularly noteworthy example of thought leadership is Faith Popcorn's "cocooning," one of the trends she identified in *The Popcorn Report*. Journalists credited Popcorn with coining the term in the 1980s, when it described a "growing tendency on the part of city dwellers to stay home and surround themselves with comforts, rather than confront a complex, AIDS-infested, nuclear-threatened society."[56] "Cocooning" grew in popularity as it resonated with other themes of 1980s America—a time when cultural commentary lamented the existence of "couch potatoes" who did nothing but order merchandise from catalogs and channel surf. The term likely also legitimated a practice without a name, which then allowed more people to identify with it. Merriam-Webster added this usage to its dictionary in 1986. Since then, it has become a legendary instance of the power of forecasters to seed an idea into culture.

More recently, "normcore" tells another, more suspect aspect of trend-naming conventions and thought leadership. In 2010 Greg Fong, Sean Monahan, Emily Segal, Chris Sherron, and Dena Yago were recent college graduates early in their marketing, design, and PR careers when they stumbled across trend materials like reports and decks, which are presentation materials.[57] The genre was confusing but also mesmerizing, so the group decided to try their hand at making their own. Working under the moniker K-Hole, "we wanted to discuss how the worlds of art and commerce were borrowing and stealing from each other," explained Yago. As a result, K-Hole's reports became a medium to blend, play with, and comment on the trend business and its intersections. K-Hole published three reports that developed a strong following in the art world, but it was one they published in late 2013 that changed the arc of their project and brought them mainstream attention.[58] That report, entitled *Youth Mode: A Report on Freedom*, used the term "normcore" to describe a move "away from a coolness that relies on difference to a post-authenticity coolness that opts in to sameness."[59] By early 2014, "normcore" had grown into an all-purpose label for "studied unfashionableness," with K-Hole's services in high demand by some of the most prominent consumer brands.[60] "We didn't set out to coin 'normcore,'" Yago explained, noting that they wanted instead to explore "when does a branding become art and art become branding?"[61] Nevertheless, the power of naming to congeal and circulate marketable ideas overpowered any efforts at critique, aesthetics, or play. Normcore won, but not without losing something.

The above anecdotes showcase how new words prime trend perception. They also suggest how heavily forecasters and the clients they serve rely on storytelling. Trends themselves are storylike, but stories are also the way that forecasters relay strategies. "So much of it comes down to narrative," Luthy of TrendWatching explained. "That story that you end up telling your client, the way you explain how it's relevant to them and how it applies to them. And I think that's something we're good at—saying, 'This is what the opportunity is.'"[62] With his colleagues Delia Dumitrescu, Henry Mason, and David Mattin, Luthy coauthored a book called *Trend-Driven Innovation*, which among other things exemplifies the storytelling process. The book argues for the importance of thinking about trends within the "Expectation Economy," which is an "economy of ever-accelerating customer expectations, applied ruthlessly to every purchase decision, experience, and moment of attention."[63] Customers primed on expectation compare experiences not only within a sector, the authors argue, but also across sectors. "In the expectation economy, Macy's is in competition with Singapore Airlines," Luthy explained.[64] The TrendWatching team suggests that brands maintain competitiveness by looking to trailblazing businesses for inspiration, aided by TrendWatching's methods and proprietary data.

The Expectation Economy is a compelling trend story meant to generate business, quiet uncertainty, and steer future action. It constructs an uncomplicated vision of the world that quickly results in a mandate for acting within it. At the center of this action is the practice of trend forecasting itself. Whether the Expectation Economy or any other trend has value depends on the ability for forecasters to translate their perception to clients who trust them to provide insight about the future that might otherwise elude them. What scholars Timothy Clark and Graeme Salaman say about consulting in general therefore reverberates here: "Management consultants [are] story tellers attempting to create a reality for their audience (i.e. clients) which captures their imagination and commitment. . . . [If] the modern manager is beset with 'information anxiety' and doubt, then the consultant's success lies in the apparently confident grasp of, and dominance of, these ambiguities and uncertainties which he or she can resolve and dissipate through concise, economical and resolute texts and talk."[65]

Selling Trends

The 2016 IAB Forum, an interactive marketing conference in Italy, invited Australian-born, New York–based futurist David Shing to address the group on the next frontier in their profession. Shing, who is better known by the nickname Shingy, works at Verizon Media, where his title is digital prophet. Small and sprightly, he wore a flecked black suit and sported a haircut reminiscent of a

Flock of Seagulls video. During the half-hour speech, he darted from side to side and topic to topic while a gigantic screen hanging behind him displayed complementary video and graphics. The screen read "TECHNOLOGY CHANGES BEHAVIOR NOT NEEDS" as Shingy opined that "our needs are rooted in the DNA of humans." Later he told the crowd, "You are in the business of sight, sound, and motion," and each of the words appeared behind him on the screen, one after another. "To do what? Create emotion. Why? Seventy-five percent of purchases today are made by emotion." The word MOTION became EMOTION as a bright blue letter *E* materialized.[66]

Such is the magic of Shingy.

Shingy is divisive: you take him either not very seriously or very seriously indeed. One of those in the second camp is his employer, Verizon Media, where he earns a six-figure salary. Likely in that camp too are the numerous organizers of gatherings across the world where Shingy has delivered keynotes. Shingy's talks are long on vision and short on specifics, which might be a criticism were it not for the fact that many people find him dazzling, rousing, even a muse.[67] What are his methods? Where are his data? Who can say. He is one of a kind.

In the world of futures, though, Shingy is also *of* a kind. The outer reaches of trend forecasting begin to approach divination, a sort of hocus-pocus for the executive set. Futurists can command handsome wages for providing imaginative predictions and motivational advice; a number of people I spoke with admitted that this amounted to a significant source of revenue. For others, that these types walk among them is an embarrassment. More than one forecaster spoke to me, usually with a hint of scorn, about the "gurus" and "entertainers" in their midst; many wanted to distance themselves from "crystal ball"–style approaches or were quick to point out that what they did was more evidence-based.

Still, approaches like Shingy's exist and flourish for a reason. As I have argued, trends allow culture to be interpreted as a flow of measurable forces that lead toward the future. However, to become useful, trends must become sellable products that generate client opportunity. Prophecy is just one example of a larger dynamic in which trend knowledge is sold as cultural strategy—and one way in which forecasters position themselves as avatars of futurism.

Cultural strategy is an oxymoronic notion, since it presumes the possibility of strategy that is somehow *not* cultural. Yet it rests upon very old foundations. According to English sociologist Don Slater, culture "has generally been understood as covering all that is expelled from a society that abstracts formal rationality from concrete specificity; the very term 'culture' is therefore an artifact of the early modern split in which the world is understood as increasingly governed by formal rationality and market money calculation."[68] Despite this long-standing separation between "economic" and "cultural" activity, businesses have long made use of cultural forms to enhance their position within the marketplace, even though culture rarely conforms to the dictums of economic rationality. Most obviously, advertising, marketing, branding, and design are commonplace cultural technologies that influence how goods and services enter, circulate, and obtain value within marketplaces. That said, they have never been perfect adjuncts for cultural knowledge, seen on the one hand as perversions of culture due to their instrumentality and on the other as irrational, problematic, and unpredictable.[69]

Culture therefore remains elusive within businesses—which makes it a mythical source of competitive edge. At many points in the modern history of business, commenters, advisors, and executives have made efforts to take culture "seriously." These calls have spawned a variety of approaches: from organizational culture to consumer ethnography, from Ernest Dichter's motivation research to Leonard Berry's relationship marketing, and many more in between. It seems that no matter what businesses do, though, cultural considerations never adequately influence day-to-day operations; someone can always come along to demand "more" from culture. For example, Grant McCracken's 2009 book *Chief Culture Officer* is a manifesto on the importance of companies reckoning with "the world outside the corporation, the body of ideas, emotions, and activities that make up the life of the consumer." He continues: "It's not that the corporation hasn't *tried* to take account of culture. It's resorted to the advertising agency, designer, consultant, cool-hunter, and guru. Worst case, someone says, 'Let's see what the intern thinks.' But culture is too important to be left to an outsider (or a twenty-year-old). When there's $1.4 billion at stake, it needs a Chief Culture Officer . . . to supply cultural intelligence as a matter of course."[70]

The irony of McCracken's commentary is that he has made his name carrying out the sorts of cultural interventions he here disparages. And while a few companies have followed McCracken's suggestion to add an executive-level position focused on culture, his remarks about the centrality of "cultural intelligence" have had far more traction. The idea of cultural intelligence originally referred to the ability for a manager to be sensitive to and deft within business environments that are not culturally uniform.[71] Today its use is more in line with what McCracken intended: it refers to the ways in which companies excavate culture to gain insight, build knowledge, and create strategy. "You have people in the C Suite that are now struggling to stay abreast of where the world is going in order to create a competitive advantage," noted Terry Young, founder and CEO of Sparks & Honey. "And I think that what it all adds up to is knowledge.

And that whoever is the owner of knowledge and that can stay ahead and own that is going to be the winner."[72] Sparks & Honey and other trend forecasters position trends as conduits to "winning" knowledge and themselves as knowledge brokers whose mastery of trends and track record can make the difference between a successful future and an uncertain one.

In this sense, trend forecasting acts as management consultancy. In corporate America, consultants came into existence near the turn of the twentieth century because the complexities of contemporary business required specialized skills such as accounting, engineering, and law that businesses did not possess in-house. By the 1930s, these "management engineers" had exploded in number, and a new generation of companies, including stalwarts like McKinsey, provided guidance on management, as well as avenues through which to share knowledge across sectors legally.[73] In the middle decades of the twentieth century, consultants of this kind—now known as "management consultants"—specifically took on the job of propagating "isomorphic" corporate structures within industries.[74] Later, during the 1960s and 1970s, as corporate structures became increasingly uniform around the world, management consultants invented "strategy consulting," positioning themselves as knowledge brokers "able to master, manipulate, and extend novel realms of complex knowledge."[75] Consultants actively produce knowledge for which they must find suitable markets. Driving this, at least in part, is the "faddish nature of so much management thought," which compels companies to be constantly in search of new ideas about management, production, organization, and communication.[76]

In the trend business, a central mechanism for the dissemination of strategy consulting is the report—which, as I noted above, is also a key communication device and product. Several kinds exist. Many trend forecasters create on a regular basis general topical reports, which they sell individually and offer on a subscription basis to clients. The reports often cost at least a thousand dollars; subscriptions, which can include access to exclusive content and other perks, can run as high as hundreds of thousands of dollars per year. Several forecasters also offer more regularly updated content free on their websites, via apps, or through newsletters; the write-ups are sometimes kernels for reports. "You might write a blog post about something that's the first example of a change," noted Ard from Stylus. "Then in our reports we gather together trends in a more kind of analytical way."[77] The content of these reports is a mix of striking visuals, interviews with experts, statistics and figures, and information that piques ideas, sometimes underwritten by a corporate sponsor. At PSFK, for example, the June 2017 report, *Consumer 2020*, argues that consumers will "lose their digital threshold" as they embrace mobile, internet-enabled technologies in more terrains of their lives. Brands must learn to see the "consumer as a platform," the report argues, because "the consumer sits atop a personalized network of data that helps them make informed decisions and control their experiences," for example, new developments in AI that read faces at social gatherings to determine the music selection. The report ends with a series of "challenges to meet" and "strategies to succeed."[78] Of course, the final section includes heavy plugs for Cisco's Digital Network Architecture, or DNA, as a solution.

Reports like *Consumer 2020* are categorical examples of corporate social science, industrial knowledge parallel to yet distinct from academic research. Corporate social science operates under what geographer Peter Taylor calls a "'double hermeneutic': as the research practice affects the objects of study, the latter are simultaneously subjects that can find their own meaning in the research and can react to alter the findings."[79] In other words, trend reports and other forms of corporate research aim to study, sway, and extend the processes of corporate capitalism; as Taylor notes, the mimicking and "capture" of social science is just another manifestation of corporate seepage. The überstrategy of these reports, then, is to legitimate the trend business as a valid, useful, and timely resource for social research. This serves the auxiliary purpose of discounting academic social research, but it also fills a gap that university-based researchers do not, cannot, or are not inclined to fill.

A second strategic purpose of these reports is to create actionable outcomes. Reports may identify a new market or point of sale, propose responses to social changes, or alert their readers of technologies, platforms, or consumer behaviors that are relevant for their businesses. Forecasters are careful to share only the most pertinent information. "We never really wanted to be a place where you're just like, 'Here's a thousand ideas a day that come from everywhere,'" explains PSFK's Fawkes. "There's sort of a filter, a subjective filter, that's applied . . . through our reports and in the types of topics we choose."[80] That being said, even the most discerning suggestions have to bump up against client inertia, short-termism, and workaday routines. "How do you implement [a strategy] when everyone else is trying to make their numbers?" noted Janet Siroto of BrainReserve. "Someone brings you in as these visionaries, but everyone else is [thinking], 'What am I doing this quarter?'"[81]

The above underscores that despite the attempt to make reports carriers of actionable goals, one of their central purposes is to be informational and promotional. Strategy begins with education, guidance, and inspiration. Reports, it follows, should be easily understood but awesome, vibrant but graspable. Yet these are oppositional objectives. On the one hand, they complicate a report's ability to simply grow into strategy. On the other, they enhance its capacity as public relations—generating attention, establishing expertise, and advertising a trend firm's creativity and range. Moreover, because trend research is laborious and expensive to produce, it must serve multiple purposes, even if those purposes conflict. At the extreme end of things, what political scientist Daniel Drezner notes about consulting firms applies here—that much of their work "should be viewed as marketing rather than analysis."[82] When created for general client use, research, knowledge, and strategy are less a game plan than bait to lure clients into further services.

Ideally, trend knowledge comes to serve as the basis for an ongoing advisory relationship that will result in better cultural strategy. In their book *Cultural Strategy: Using Innovative Ideologies to Build Breakthrough Brands*, Douglas Holt and Douglas Cameron argue that cultural strategy is the key to astute cultural innovation: "Strategy is a blueprint that guides action. But strategy is usually conceived in highly abstract generic terms. In conventional innovation strategies, the more specific and contextual directives are left out because such nuanced details are considered to be outside the domain of strategy. But these abstract strategies are of no use for cultural innovation. Since cultural innovation is about locating a specific historic opportunity and then responding to this opportunity with specific cultural content, cultural strategy must be tailored to these more specific historical and contextual goals."[83] This is a telling passage. On the one hand, it acknowledges the nonscalability of cultural strategy, which is grounded in qualitative research that is necessarily specific, contextual, and tailored. On the other hand, it implies that once such a customized approach is engaged, it is continuous; the landscape is ever changing, and the need for newer, better strategy never ends. The trend business follows the logic of cultural strategy in its bid to vend its services. Trends are general, but client needs are particular, and only through personalized advice can a client determine the best way to proceed. The rhetoric of personalization overlaps with that of the future and the perspective that culture is idiosyncratic, multitudinous, and alive with change. Combined, they justify the need for constant advisement.

Aware of the perpetual need for their services, a number of trend forecasters told me that they aspired to teach companies how to bring preparedness for the future and sensitivity to trends in-house. In these instances, they don't want to sell tools so much as training, and they prefer to position themselves as educators and doers rather than simply knowledge suppliers. Offering educational services is a way for forecasters to assert relevance and differentiate themselves within the marketplace. Jacomine Van Veen, an independent trend forecaster based in Amsterdam, has based her career around trying to bring useful knowledge into companies. She explains how the knowledge that trend professionals generate "should not end up in a drawer," echoing a common refrain among the industry that trend reports are often underutilized. "I get frustrated when I'm just writing up stories and telling things and I have the feeling that it's just inspiring people for half an hour and that's it," she continued.[84] Janet Siroto of BrainReserve agreed that razzle-dazzle only goes so far. "We don't go to a client and say, 'Robots are coming, the end of humanity is coming, your driverless car will actually be a mobile home where a nomadic generation will go from location to location,'" she explained. "We apply our future insights to get at what's going on with the consumer and how it applies to [the client's] category and their business."[85]

The desire among some trend workers to have a lasting impact is ironic, given that they are in a business dedicated to constant change. Moreover, what counts as "application" is difficult to surmise, especially for forecasters who ultimately may not be at the table when real decision making takes place. When relevance is pinned to convincing others to follow cultural currents toward the unknown, applying strategy will always involve risk, change, and uncertainty, which are costly in all senses of that word. Yet in a world where the future weighs heavily upon the present, the need to feel somehow equipped is real. Trend forecasters take advantage of the fact that there is a demand not just for customized approaches or high-level research like trend reports. Sometimes, all clients want is highly general, lower-stakes transfers of information, such as webinars, conferences, clinics, and presentations.

And here is where we return to the more prophetic aspects of trend forecasting. Making sweeping generalizations about future trends for a general audience almost obliges the repetition of platitudes. Doing so in a performative context, like a keynote address, is an invitation for the forecaster to personify futurity, which even in the staidest contexts welcomes pageantry. The conflicting strategic purposes of trends work against one another as forecasters attempt to square the best of both worlds. "Most foresight firms, even most trend firms, come in and give a phenomenally interesting presentation about all the stuff you should be aware of," explains Don Abraham, a futurist I met while he worked at the Futures Company. "And you sit back and go, 'Holy cow, what do we do now?' And you go back to your day job. That's what often happens."[86] Abraham hit upon an important if ugly truth. Trend gurus are, in some ways, the purest embodiment of what trend strategy is supposed to do: convince the audience that they are unprepared for the future.

Conclusion

Trends are commodities made up of stories about the future. Trend forecasters create them through techniques of trend perception, sorting the world into patterns that suggest crucial, unavoidable changes. Trend forecasters' expertise balances the mystique of intuitive understanding against a data-driven mastery of exorbitant information. Though their services are unique, they are part of a seemingly ever-growing battalion of consultancies that provide corporations with know-how and vision that, for whatever reason, they do not produce sufficiently within themselves.

There are many reasons why trend forecasting flourishes among management consultancies, brand strategists, and other types of advisement. For one, the trend forecasting industry plays an active role in creating the perception of a world overrun with change. While far from the only actors engaging in this creation, for them, doing so is an existential matter. Unless they can convince their clients that trends are ways to manage information overload, competently measure the future, and strategically intervene, trend forecasting ceases to matter. Trends are performative insofar as they usher into being the conditions for their existence, which forecasters then position themselves to address. Trends provide an illusion of control in the face of precariousness.

But the trend industry is performative in a second way. In a perfectly corporate, infinitely digestible, exhilarating yet safe fashion, it models the look and feel of futurity. Trends are the scripts through which forecasters conduct their professional lives and manifest their professional identities. It justifies Shingy's haircut, it explains the gorgeous imagery that fills trend reports, and it rationalizes why companies like the Future Laboratory have an in-office beekeeper. As much as the business of trends attempts to manage the future, it must also maintain its allure, mystique, and wonderment. Trends are ways of seeing and understanding, measuring and assessing, communicating and acting. Most of all, they serve to distinguish between those who know and those who don't know—those who show the way to the future and those who, if they can even find it, are just hoping that they will fit through the door.

CHAPTER 5

Global Futurity

On a criminally lovely June day, I sat down with Reinier Evers, founder of Trend-Watching.com, at a canal-side café in Amsterdam. We have met for a drink to discuss his professional background but quickly develop a loose and amiable banter awash in jokes, asides, and musings. We somehow wind up philosophizing about universal theories of human history. (Doesn't everyone?) Boats drift dreamily along the water as the sun's heat intensifies; Evers bears the brunt of it, seated across from me on the sunny side of the table. He squints, leans back, takes a sip from his glass. "Culture is another thing I'm just done with," he says. "In the end, it's deeply uninteresting."[1]

From a man who has spent much of his working life in the business of anticipating culture, I find this a provocative statement, to say the least. I press him. "So, you mean the notion of having traditions that need to be preserved?" He demurs. "Whenever you have a group, it is always defined by which group you are, and therefore which group you are not, which always ends up in animosity," he responds. "I find it deeply childish." He goes on: "I'm getting way more into Indian philosophy and the mix of Buddhism and Hinduism, where it's all about you, and that's it. There is no God or culture or whatever, it's just you. I feel like if there is one thing that we can learn from Asia, outside of Asia, [it] is that kind of thinking."[2]

I'd argue that Evers is less indifferent to culture than pragmatic about it: he has an abiding faith in its transportability and mutability. Dutch by birth, he's an avid traveler who has called London, New York, and Amsterdam home and is as comfortable discussing hot spots in Porto as he is deal making in Shanghai. TrendWatching, the company he founded in the early 2000s, similarly reflects utilitarian pluralism: branches in Singapore and São Paolo, trend scouts in Cape Town and Moscow, and a faith that the next big thing could surface from any horizon, cross any border, and conjoin a diasporic web of internationals. When he started the company, Evers decided not to say on the website where the company is located. "Everyone assumes we're in the US or the UK," he explains, a lilt of sly laughter rising in his voice. "Then we start getting invitations—like, the board of Tesco in the UK. I'm still fairly young, so they're in shock, and then they find out I'm Dutch, and they're double in shock." He smiles.[3]

For TrendWatching and its peers, business assumed this shape out of necessity. Trends are worldly. Though we tend to detect them within our immediate environs, it is travel that confirms that a development taking root is not just a local phenomenon or a tick of our own observations but a bona fide shift, something with legs and magnitude and power. Trends do not stay confined to their communities of origin—if they did, we'd call them something else. And though, as one scholar notes, "transcultural trends have been the norm rather than the exception, both in the past and today," in our contemporary world, with easy transport and abundant media, these processes never moved as fast or as visibly.[4]

In spite or perhaps because of such worldliness, the business of trends is place-bound. It rests on the assumption that newness comes from somewhere. Of the many kinds of knowledge trend forecasters peddle, one is sophisticated, encyclopedic comprehension of differences between places, their people, and their habits. Rootedness matters; it is the canvas against which forecasters draw conclusions about change. The future comes into focus through the traffic between the city and countryside, the hub and its outskirts, the inside and the outside. Even if the world feels more closely knit than ever before, the markets into which trends enter abide by national borders, physical topographies, language barriers, regional customs, and political realities that are distinct, if fluctuating. What's more, the trend industry operates within the asymmetries that exist among and within nations, regions, and peoples—power dynamics that help to determine what trends are, how they look, and whether they spread.

To untangle the relationship between cultures and the circulation of trends around the world, this chapter explores how the people, places, and practices of the trend industry exemplify what I have come to understand as "global futurity," which refers to the interrelated beliefs that shape how trend forecasters comprehend and thereby facilitate the transnational movement of trends. Global futurity also frames the geography of the trend industry, defining its centers and outposts, its zones of work and play. Global futurity therefore is both descriptive and prescriptive for the trend business. It is a way of seeing and acting in the world, and as such it has power to create and privilege futures that uphold its values and neglect or obviate those that do not.

At the core of global futurity is an abiding faith in globalization, or the notion that the world is deepening its cultural and economic interdependence. Globalization has long been a central component within neoliberalism as corporations seek out international markets while also experiencing increased competition from beyond their borders.[5] What distinguishes the trend industry's take on globalization is its forward momentum, or the contention that globalization is where the future resides. Even given recent political backlash, the widespread assumption is that the future will be more global and that the job of those invested in the future is to bring this globality into existence. Globalization, therefore, is not just the inevitable effect of the passage of time but a self-serving goal and a destination that render some people, places, and things as "more global" than others.

Another major component of global futurity is its "proactive optimism," which takes for granted that the future will be better and that it is the mission of trend forecasters to highlight and accelerate toward that goal. As with globalization, proactive optimism is not exclusive to the trend business; it is in some ways the spirit of late capitalism, especially the tech-inflected version that resonates with the utopian solutionism known as the "Californian ideology."[6] Yet such pervasive and interventionist positivity is more than just a disposition. Thanks to the predictive nature of the trend business, proactive optimism that purports to describe is as frequently attempting to control the course that change should take. Moreover, such changes often privilege the very people and places already anointed as ambassadors of the future, maintaining the dichotomy between sites that determine the future and those that merely follow it. Proactive optimism is the element of global futurity that allows elite parochialism consonant with the imaginaries of the urban centers of developed consumer economies to masquerade as simply "the order of things."

A final irony of global futurity lies in its dependence upon stratified futures. As my research connected me with forecasters from several countries, in a panorama of settings, I came to understand that "the world" for forecasters includes some locations, some people, and some developments to the exclusion, ignorance, and even avoidance of others. Since trends depend on developments that conform to forecaster ideologies, and chief among those is the persistence and advancement of consumer capitalism, "the world" of the trend business exists primarily where wealth exists already or can be developed or withdrawn. Furthermore, because trend forecasting assumes both enduring difference and susceptibility to change, maximum value derives both from places that "produce" difference and those that readily consume it. Ultimately, the business of trends exacerbates these contradictions, thriving on the tension between cosmopolitan flux and fixed localism even as it also attempts to obliterate this distinction.

Call the setting for this chapter "the world," though two sites, the Netherlands and Dubai, form the backbone of my analysis. On the surface, one could hardly pick two more different locations: one a water-rich nation steeped in tradition and history, the other a young desert metropolis actively seeking to (re)write itself into the global narrative. I'm also keenly aware of how my chosen focus reproduces some of the biases I want to critique; my understanding of how futures are taking shape in many of the most underprivileged parts of the world is minimal at best. I focus on the Netherlands and Dubai here because of these issues, not despite them. Both places are centers of capital; thus, they are voracious customers of futurity and central to the global flow of trends. For this reason, they are ideal settings in which to witness trend forecasting in action and to understand the way global futurity shapes how forecasters imagine the future and for whom.

Dubai: Globalization in Motion

Fifty feet ahead of me is a futurist. At least that's what I suspect. It's a Monday morning in November in Dubai, and burning sun makes the glass and metal buildings that flank this stretch of Sheikh Zayed Road gleam like gold. I'm staying just across the street from the Hotel Jumeirah Emirates Towers, the site of LaFutura, an annual gathering of trend and future professionals. Even so, after ten minutes of wandering—across a footbridge spanning a multilane highway, through an immaculate subway station packed with people of every hue, and around a seemingly endless construction site—I am lost.

Then, I see him.

White man, somewhere in the neighborhood of fifty years old. He's dressed in jeans and an untucked button-down shirt, with a fashionable bag slung over one shoulder. He looks out of place, though with a better idea of where he is going than I have. Quickening my pace, I decide to trail him. He leads me down a long bend of sidewalk, into an underground parking garage, up a staircase, into a building, and through a complicated maze of lobbies, walkways, sliding doors, eateries, and retail establishments. Finally, I catch up to him and introduce myself, and yes, we are headed to the same place. We enter yet another lobby, where a small sign reading LAFUTURA directs us down an escalator into a lower level. At its bottom there are perhaps sixty people milling about and sipping tea and coffee. It's a sea of white middle-aged Europeans. The babble is largely in English and German. Men outnumber women two to one.

Welcome to the future.

Since its first convening in 2010, LaFutura has traveled to some of the world's most vibrant cities, including Amsterdam, Helsinki, Berlin, New York, and Singapore. That its 2017 gathering is in Dubai has a feeling of inevitability; an organization that dubs itself the "Global Trend Network" belongs here in this most global of locations. Here, *global* and *future* are synonymous. The global is the future because it represents the plane of possibility; like the future, the global is at once boundless and manageable, reachable and elusive, quotidian and utopic. Where better to harness a feeling of global futurity than here, where more than 80 percent of the population is foreign-born, at the site of the World Expo 2020, in a city that Thomas Friedman, imagining the region post–Arab Spring, called the "Manhattan of the Arab world"?[7]

The relationship between the global and the future certainly predates twenty-first-century Dubai. Globalism has been important within futurism since the postwar period, when wide-scale and long-term problems, from overpopulation to nuclear war to environmental degradation, aroused the concern of and cooperation among an international network of futurists.[8] Jenny Andersson and Sibylle Duhautois, sociologists based in France who study governance of the future, write that "the idea of the future itself is central to forms of globality in the post-war decades." The argument they make is twofold. As a practical matter, trend extrapolation and ecological foresight helped to document the interconnectedness of the globe; future possibilities appeared most clearly at the global scale. The future was important imaginatively, too—a potential tomorrow where today's problems might find resolution. Andersson and Duhautois also point to the "fundamental utopianism in futurism, and in many ways that utopianism referred to the possibility of salvation by shaping new forms of action on the world level."[9] If human beings could influence the future of the world, the thinking went, they could also work together to change it.[10]

This classic version of global interest in the future is not what greeted me at the bottom of that hotel escalator. Futurism bent on addressing "world problems," as Andersson and Duhautois conceive of them, stands at some distance from the corporatized variant that I am calling global futurity. Rather than emerge from the idealism of international cooperation, global futurity is a product of globalization, that fin de siècle buzzword describing the political, economic, technological, and cultural interdependence among and the competi-tion between the world's nations. The utopianism that underlies globalization is market-based rather than intergovernmental—although, as I'll soon explore, it requires complicity on the part of government actors. Amid the popularization of the internet and the rise of digitization; the lowering of trade barriers and the empowerment of international bodies like the IMF and the World Bank; and the movement of people, goods, and information across national borders, global futurity envisions a future of unfettered corporate possibility and consumer freedom. In this landscape, the trend business exists to exploit, cohere, and direct change. LaFutura's program promotes that "200 leading futurists and trend spotters will come to Dubai to address future challenges" in coordination with "strong partnerships" across UAE government and business interests. It is a type of intervention that is designed for corporate players and that privileges access, deals, and the world-making power of entrepreneurialism. And it is one where, as is still the case in many corridors of power, white men continue to predominate.

Over its reign, globalization has incurred deep criticism, including from those who observe both its failure and a backlash manifesting in growing inequality, reactionary populisms, and the resurrection of national borders.[11] At the same time, globality itself has not lost its sanguine gloss, even if its architecture is under question. Globalization continues to benefit from the association with positive values such as betterment and tolerance, especially as inflected by inventiveness and enterprise. Anthropologist Anna Tsing explains that "glo-balization draws our enthusiasm because it helps us imagine interconnection, travel, and sudden transformation"—words that have remained true since she wrote them in 2000. Tsing also notes, however, that globalization "also draws us inside its rhetoric until we take its claims for true descriptions."[12] Our con-temporary understanding of globalization describes not just actual processes or observable shifts but also *beliefs about* and *faith in* those processes and shifts. Global futurity emerges within this transference, making globalization a goal and a destination no matter what. Without it, the future has no place to go.

Participants at LaFutura Dubai are therefore agents of and players within global futurity. LaFutura started with the intent of being more than just a con-ference. The mission was to become a clearinghouse for trend professionals worldwide and an organization that would guide the industry toward growth and legitimacy. "I was wondering, '[Are] there any other trend people in the universe?'" explained Nils Müller, LaFutura's founder and owner of TrendOne, a top German trend agency that he started in 2002. After identifying a few possible connections online, Müller decided to "invite them to an association event, like an industry event for futurists and trend people."[13] The first LaFutura, held in Berlin, had one hundred participants. Since then, the annual gathering has become part trade show, part industry conference, with attendance split between trend professionals and their clientele. Müller's dominance over the organization means that it is heavily German; Adidas, Deutsche Bahn, and several other high-profile German companies sent representatives. There was likewise a strong expat contingent of Europeans currently living and working in Dubai. North or South Americans were few and far between. While there were a few people from Asia, and many of our hosts were from the Middle East, I encountered no one from the African continent at all.

The first day's program consisted of a "Trend Journey," a series of talks and on-location tours meant to expose participants to how the future has taken root in Dubai. Who better to accomplish that task than Noah Raford, the chief operating officer and futurist in chief of the Dubai Future Foundation (DFF)? Raford holds a doctorate from MIT and has a background working with NGOs and governments on scenario development, strategic foresight, and other futuring tools. He helped Dubai develop DFF, which began operations in 2016 with the mission "to play a pivotal role in shaping the future of strategic sectors in cooperation with Dubai government and private sector entities."[14] DFF coordinates with all twelve ministries of Dubai's government to support futurist programs. DFF also oversees several projects, including the Museum of the Future, a space scheduled to open in 2020 that will encourage interaction with immersive, speculative, and design futures; the Dubai Future Accelerators, a challenge-grant program that funds international teams to develop futuristic innovations; and the Mohammed bin Rashid Center for Accelerated Research, an institute that underwrites "moonshot" projects such as space settlement. Raford explains to the LaFutura audience that despite the stereotype of government being slow and uninspired, "entrepreneurial" and "visionary" governments can spur innovation, growth, and foresight rather than impede them. He shares a slide showing a photograph of Sheikh Mohammed bin Rashid Al Maktoum, the prime minister and vice president of the UAE and the ruler of Dubai, looking hopefully off into the distance. Another slide quotes him: "The future belongs to those who affect [*sic*] radical change, not those who make gradual improvements."

For me, listening to Raford speak triggers a momentary flash of future shock—a jumble of wonder, disbelief, confusion, excitement, and fear. The velocity of change feels careening, unstoppable; his images dazzle, and his words mesmerize, even as the question "why" pinballs around my head. We see prototypes for the Museum of the Future; hear about the construction of the world's

Figure 3. The world's first 3-D printed building, in Dubai, UAE. Photo by the author.

first 3D-printed building (which we later visit; figure 3); and learn about plans for government innovation, like the mandate that 100 percent of Dubai's government transactions be conducted via blockchain by 2020 or that a quarter of all vehicles must be self-driving by 2030. Following his talk, Raford cedes the floor to representatives of several Future Accelerators projects, who add to my sense of vertigo. Reforestation of the desert? Check. Enormous, dehumidifier-like machines that suck moisture from the air and transform it into potable water? Wait, what? It's a TED talk on overdrive, a civic sales pitch extraordinaire, a pageantry of the impossible made possible—or at least prototypable. All of it is subsidized by the largesse of the Dubai government.

As the day's Trend Journey continues, it becomes clear that in Dubai, "the future" is a justification for action. This amounts to more than lip service about caring for the next generation or being mindful stewards of the planet, more than pontificating from an Elon Musk or a Ray Kurzweil. The official line—coming directly from spokespeople for the government, which overlaps with and is often indistinguishable from private enterprise—is that that which can lay claim to the future should be attempted, no matter the expense. No idea that embraces futurity should be deemed out of reach or ludicrous. As a result, Dubai is replete with grand experiments that wear the future like a bejeweled crown. Even more, Dubai utilizes "the future" as a globally competitive currency, a way to attract notice, money, and minds. From such a vantage, world leadership is determined by who innovates fastest, bets biggest, and disrupts most profoundly.

This assertive presentation of Dubai as a zone of global futurity where the future itself is the product is recent. That said, Dubai is no stranger to serving as a backdrop for capitalist fantasy. Since the late 1990s, Dubai has symbolized the zenith of globalization, drawing both the admiration and the scorn of commentators around the world. Building on its history as a strategic port city and buoyed by the modest yet still lucrative oil reserves of the emirate, the city of Dubai rapidly developed during the 1990s, attracting foreign investment, industries such as banking and tech, and immigration from South Asia, the Middle East, and Western and Eastern Europe. By 1999 the city was well known for its shopping and tourist attractions, many of which were over the top.[15] That same year, the world's first "seven-star" hotel, the Burj Al Arab, opened; celebrities began to flock to Dubai to frolic on its beaches and luxuriate in its lavish amenities. Ever since, the city has maintained a reputation as a carnivalesque playground for the world's well-to-do, a place to make money and exploit life's excesses, and an ever-expanding checkerboard of construction sites, free zones, and *Guinness Book*–worthy feats of engineering. There's a notorious underside, too: Westerners jailed for holding hands in public, rooming with someone of the opposite sex, or engaging in suspected gay activity; slavery-like conditions at labor camps; human trafficking, especially for sex workers; and lax environmental regulations.[16] The spectacular clash between the visionary and the vile is what led Mike Davis, author of *City of Quartz*, to proclaim Dubai to be a "monstrous caricature of futurism."[17]

Dubai is a city with its own culture and problems where residents go about their lives in commonplace and unremarkable ways that are often invisible to casual tourists and even vested researchers. It is not a democracy, though it has a sizeable welfare state; one cannot become a citizen of Dubai without lineage going back generations. In this and many other ways, Dubai is not just a passive receptor of the forces of globalization. Many of its hallmarks have been rejected outright, while others have been adopted from the ground up as a way for Dubai to distinguish itself and compete on the global stage.[18] Yet the Dubai on display for the attendees of LaFutura is largely one that accommodates Western imaginations, one that seems eager to mirror back a generic version of the future, distinguishable only by the fact that it is arriving so expeditiously. Ahmed Kanna, writing in 2011, contended that "only those characteristics of the ruler, state officials, and state institutions that [urbanists] recognize as similar to their own—neoliberalism above all but also an assumption that they as actors are exempt from politics and history—are elevated to the level of cultural qualities evidencing the Gulf's modernity."[19] Global futurity is a strategy for being seen, where visibility depends on already embracing and reflecting consumerist values.

This mimetic quality contributes to the sense that Dubai is less a place than a nonplace, an anthropological anomaly that lacks its own culture and that feels, as *New Yorker* writer Andrew Marantz once asserted, "more like an architect's rendering than an actual built environment."[20] For lunch during LaFutura's Trend Journey, we eat tacos, quinoa pilaf, and tiramisu on an immaculate plaza in Dubai's Design City, a walkable office park dotted with colorful sculptures and fashionable stores but very few actual people. That afternoon, I join a group that tours the regional offices of Coca Cola, where a jovial, blue-eyed American offers us Fanta-flavored slushies, something that (I guess?) exemplifies the company's regionally informed innovation. Later, we take a charter bus down a smoggy highway to another office park (this one in Internet City) and meet more go-getters, who spin tales of their killer technologies inside neutral conference rooms. Are we in Tel Aviv? Tallinn? Mumbai? Mexico City? We're still in Dubai, of course, but where we are appears to matter less than what being here might enable us to do. And the stories of what can be done in Dubai are convincing. Many attendees are enthralled and visibly envious, intensely aware that they could never pull off such bombastic projects back home, where bureaucracy, complacency, and democracy get in the way. Forecasters and their global partners clearly envy the capacity of Dubai to be at the center of bold action, even if what gets sacrificed are the mechanisms to preserve localism, effect compromise, or prevent colossal mistakes.

Dubai has invested heavily in future-forward initiatives as the emirate prepares for a postoil economy.[21] That, in sum, is the allure of future-focused globalization: it transforms the future into terrain for the competitive exercise of power. Dominate emergent markets, preserve and increase capital accumulation, achieve a prominent place in the international hierarchy: despite the hopefulness that often accompanies talk of the future, globalization renders its goals synonymous with those of the present. The trend industry aspires to participate in and guide such processes, not to question whether this should be the future's destination.

Globalization also means that global futurity itself will circulate around the world, with trend forecasters among its envoys. LaFutura 2018 took place in Shanghai; the 2019 gathering will be in Lisbon. As ideal as Dubai may be for futurist fancy, global futurity demands that the future keep moving.

The Netherlands: Cultures of Optimism

Daan Roosegaarde does sublime things with light. There's the light that emits from the sidewalks he has fashioned through Amsterdam, shimmering in blues and greens that hark back to Van Gogh's *Starry Night*. There's Windvogel, the smart kites with radiant strings that draw energy from the wind; the glow of the dikes across Afsluitdijk, whose surfaces have been outfitted with reflective panels modeled on butterfly wings. Roosegaarde, a Dutch artist, designer, and futurist, is one of the keynotes during the second day of LaFutura, and the audience reacts to his presentation physically. People sit up straight, overflowing with attention and energy. They ooh and aah and gasp. They whisper to their neighbors. They smile and clap and snap pictures. His knack for awe is particularly acute when he recounts the story of "smog-free" diamonds. With the support of the Chinese government, Studio Roosegaarde built a tower in a park in Shanghai that acts like a giant vacuum cleaner, sucking up smog from the air. The resulting soot can be pressed into diamonds, which sell for 250 euros apiece. Roosegaarde holds up a ring, a simple silver hoop set with a cube-shaped gem. The stone is clear but for a dark, polluted center. The crowd goes wild.

A Dutch designer with the ear of powerful world governments and an eye toward the future, Roosegaarde has built a worldwide reputation as "Dutch boy wonder of innovation."[22] He champions the view that design should not just create beautiful objects but also solve problems. "Cities have become machines that are killing us," explained Roosegaarde in a 2017 interview with the architecture and design magazine *Dezeen*. "Good design, good luxury is not about a Louis Vuitton bag or a Ferrari, it's about clean air, clean water, clean energy."[23] His work crackles with proactive optimism, the gospel of global futurity and one of the cardinal assumptions that makes trend work possible. Proactive optimism means harnessing control of the future for the good. It means considering anything within human imagination as possible. And it means the future becomes a scene of unlimited opportunity and staggering greatness. Trend forecasters peddle proactive optimism because it infuses their work with a sense of purpose, momentum, and righteousness. They not only show businesses how good the future can be but also become ushers toward that future.

Today's proactive optimism originates deep within the history of Western thought. For example, the notion of human progress—itself a secularized version of Christian ideals about the perfectibility of humanity, the meaningfulness of life, and inevitable advancement toward the ideal—first became central to modernizing societies in the wake of the Enlightenment. French philosopher Alain de Benoist argues that it was then that "the hereafter is reconceived as the future, and happiness replaces salvation." The resulting "scientific optimism" sutured progress to the interests of the ruling class.[24] Optimism, it follows, may be thought of as a by-product of progress that aligns with and cements market values. British intellectual Terry Eagleton goes further, arguing that "optimists are conservatives because their faith in a benign future is rooted in their trust in the essential soundness of the present. . . . Only if you view your situation as critical do you recognize the need to transform it. Dissatisfaction can be a goad to reform. The sanguine, by contrast, are likely to come up with sheerly cosmetic solutions."[25] I will forestall a full discussion of the conservatism inherent to optimistic future imagining for the time being. It is enough to say that optimism is not just a psychological disposition or a market driver but also a "theory of politics" that accompanies and presumes political realities such as free market democracy.[26] As such, in its proactive iteration, it more than promotes positive outlooks. It justifies intervention into the world, claiming the mantle of benevolence and betterment.

Proactive optimism is especially technologically deterministic. In Silicon Valley and its global corollaries, proactive optimism lends itself to what writer Evgeny Morozov calls "solutionism," an ideology that "[recasts] all complex social situations either as neatly defined problems with definite, computable solutions or as transparent and self-evident processes that can be easily optimized."[27] Titans of technology perennially make claims about enhancing our lives through this app or that gadget and in the process transforming human capacities such as sharing and attention into currencies that underwrite their platforms.[28] Trend forecasting sometimes falls prey to this kind of techno-optimism, especially in light of the overlap between innovative tech companies and the hungering newness that animates trends. But I want to go further in my argument. Proactive optimism is what allows trend forecasting to produce the future as a desirable, necessary good. In turn, the trend business exports proactive optimism from the people, places, and positions that manufacture it to those sites that must buy into it. While proactive optimism may appear like a neutral perspective on future imagining—or at least one with only positive effects—it is better understood as a form of soft power, a way to refashion the world in the image of the powerful corporate and geopolitical interests that have the most to gain from global futurity. It doesn't follow the future so much as actualize it.

To see how proactive optimism becomes practice, we might look to Roosegaarde's homeland of the Netherlands. When it comes to the business of trends, one is never very far from the Netherlands; both "the future" and "trends" are major Dutch exports. The Dutch are quick to tell you that theirs is a tiny country, less populous than several of the world's megacities. Still, the people of that low country do not think small. Their influence has long stretched around the globe, from the Dutch East India Company to Royal Dutch Shell, from Rembrandt to Rem Koolhaas. Today, the country boasts an absurdly high concentration of future professionals. Max Luthy, an Englishman who works with Reinier Evers at TrendWatching, once joked that in Holland there are "more trend agencies . . . than there are post offices." I can't verify that assertion, but the Dutch are widely revered in trend circles and can rightly call themselves the global epicenter of the trend business.

Among Dutch trend professionals, there is a heightened awareness that their trend business is unique. "Holland has this name of being good in trend watching," explained Nanon Soeters, one half of the respected Dutch trend-watching firm ROZENBROOD. "What I'm hoping for is that trend watching is going to be something godlike, something like Dutch design, something we're famous for."[29] That Li Edelkoort, one of the world's most famous trend forecasters, happens to be Dutch adds appeal—Edelkoort is known for her mysterious, almost religious trend proclamations. The connection between the Netherlands and trends is far more widespread, however. "Dutch people are considered to be designers and constructors of both physical and social environments," explains one Dutch trend report. "If we envision a shared future, we directly start implementing it."[30] Lieke Lamb, of the husband-and-wife team Trendsverwachting, agreed with this view. "Holland is a knowledge economy," she explained; the Dutch "[have] always been good at giving advice to other people."[31] For Els Dragt, a prominent trend forecaster and author of the book *How to Research Trends*, the country's history as a center of trade and immigration makes it especially gifted in this field. "Because we're a small country, you always have to be very open to other cultures and other people," she explained, adding that "there are quite many [Dutch] trend forecasters [who] are also worldwide working in an international group for such a small country."[32] Mark Schipper, another forecaster and trend educator, noted that in the Netherlands, "you are sooner confronted with barriers to overcome and [called upon] to look differently and to look at what's happening. . . . As a small country, you always have to look at other countries, what's happening, and how it affects us."[33]

From these observations, we might conclude that future-mindedness emerges from knowledge of the world and an intimate familiarity with difference. The argument goes something like this: being small means less capacity for stasis, confrontation with difference means more comfort with change, and both together add up to an improved ability to imagine the future for others. These points strongly suggest a sense of entitlement to the future, in keeping with the solutionist facets of proactive optimism discussed earlier. They also point to a link between proactive optimism and cosmopolitanism. According to Brazilian anthropologist Gustavo Lins Ribeiro, cosmopolitanism encompasses "a desire to construct broad allegiances and equal and peaceful global communities of citizens who should be able to communicate across cultural and social boundaries forming a universalist solidarity." Ribeiro continues by arguing that cosmopolitanism tends to thrive among elites, for whom it serves as a "metaphor for mobility, migrancy, sensitivity and tolerance to otherness, independence from specific authorities, and transcultural and transnational realities and claims," standing against "xenophobia, fixity, parochialism, restricted sovereignty, and allegiance to a motherland, or a nation-state."[34] It is no wonder, then, that cosmopolitanism is the ethos of transnational capitalism, an expression of the globalizing sensibilities that see the promise, and profit, in rapid change. Sociologist Craig Calhoun argues that "cosmopolitanism—though not necessarily cosmopolitan democracy—is now largely the project of capitalism, and it flourishes in the top management of multinational corporations and even more in the consulting firms that serve them. Such cosmopolitanism often joins elites across national borders while ordinary people live in local communities. This is not simply because common folk are less sympathetic to diversity—a self-serving notion of elites. It is also because the class structuring of public life excludes many workers and others."[35]

Cosmopolitanism is a prerequisite for imagining optimistic and proactive futures that might transcend their place of origin and result in broad-based change. Cosmopolitanism is also a luxury, one that tends to be enjoyed among those for whom it does not threaten their way of being. And cosmopolitanism often is most comfortable for those who have the power to dictate the pace, direction, and nature of change. Rarely during my travels was the Netherlands' cosmopolitanism related to its history as a colonial power or its extensive slave trade, both of which helped to make it the powerful, diverse country that it is today.[36] The point here is not to single out the Netherlands or suggest that the nation is somehow unique from any number of countries with colonial pasts, my own included. Nor is it to deny the real gains that can come from multiculturalism and openness to change. With that being said, to say that the Netherlands is a "hidden superpower" that "for centuries . . . had benefited from its exposure to the outside world" demands acknowledgment of the source of those benefits and how they fuel the futures that emerge today.[37] Global futurity derives from the affordances of the past.

How the Netherlands utilizes the natural world also informs contemporary trend work. Many trend professionals I spoke to referred to "the water" to explain why their people have focused so much attention on the future; I came to understand this as something of a running joke or a cliché. Nonetheless, it wasn't an empty reference. The Netherlands is a country stolen away from the sea, with extensive waterworks, windmills, and dikes, which keep the low-lying land dry and habitable. Expertise about managing water has made Dutch engineers desirable advisors around Europe for centuries. Foresight in environmental management also pertains to the oil and gas industry, of which the Netherlands is a global leader. Royal Dutch Shell, a binational Dutch/British corporation founded in 1907, was among the first to experiment with scenarios as a method of anticipating and planning for future change in an effort to "incorporate political and general risks in upstream investment evaluation."[38] Though Pierre Wack, the person most often associated with Shell's scenarios, was French, many Shell employees were involved, meaning the method has been impactful within the Netherlands, especially as people with familiarity with it at Shell left to take jobs elsewhere. All of this suggests a strong environmental basis for Dutch futurism, where environmentalism is just as much about controlling the environment as it is caring for or protecting it—an especially important point in light of climate change.

In Holland the most convincing feature of global futurity and the proactive optimism that underwrites it is how much the Dutch trend industry has confidence and faith in itself. A widespread conviction in the necessity of affecting the future translates into a robust trends industry, which is taken very seriously, makes abundant use of its platform, and takes pains to regenerate itself. Dutch futurists and trend watchers are prominent in many arenas in a way that outpaces many other countries. I met futurists who worked not only with major corporations and fashion houses but also utilities, government services, scientific bodies, universities, and more. The Dutch Future Society, a professional organization for futurists founded in 2013, brings together these various strands; even the World Future Society struggles to do the same. It is one example among many of the move to professionalize and elevate futurism, foresight, and trend watching as the Dutch answer to global futurity.

In another example, on the third Tuesday in September, the people of the Netherlands mark Prinsjesdag, the day on which the political and budgetary priorities for the next year are declared. Prinsjesdag takes place in The Hague, the seat of the nation's government, and has become a grand multiday event packed with festivities and infused with symbolism. Thousands of people line the streets to watch the processional of the Golden Carriage, one of the country's most precious artifacts, as it makes its way from the royal palace to the parliament. Once arrived, the monarch reads the *troonrede*, or "throne speech," which is a formal address from the monarch to the people about what lies ahead.

The trend industry has a September tradition too—less august, but a tradition all the same. Its tradition is the release of the TrendRede, the "trend speech."

Started in 2011, the TrendRede is produced by a small but prominent group of trend professionals. "The results of our annual measuring of societal developments and summary of developing insights find their way to many organizations and are increasingly contributing to new policies," they write in the 2016 edition. "For this we are happy and grateful. Over the next few years we want to actively help bridging the gap between vision and practice."[39] Though perhaps a clever marketing stunt, the TrendRede is also a powerful symbol of the place of trends on the Dutch national stage. While many forecasting companies around the world put out year-end or summary reports, few attach them so prominently to national priorities. In the Netherlands, the TrendRede is considered the "State of the Union for trends," as Caroline van Beekhoff, one of the contributors, explained.[40] It is also a venue for trend forecasters to share their off-the-record knowledge. "We heard so much inside information, which we couldn't use," explained Richard Lamb, one of the TrendRede's founders. "But indirectly we can use it [by] telling, 'Hey, this is the way the Netherlands probably will go, and this is what Europe is doing and so on.'"[41] Proximity to the seats of power is an especially good way to understand and influence how the future might unfold.

Education in the Netherlands may also come to embrace proactive optimism amid a push toward the wider adoption of trend and futures methods. Erica Bol is a pioneer in this work. She is the deputy director of Teach the Future, an international organization that believes that "students of any age can learn to think critically and creatively about the future and develop the agency to influence it." When I spoke to Bol in 2018, Teach the Future was embarking on Futures Education Pilot NL, a first-of-its-kind program to "integrate futures thinking in [the] curriculum" in the Netherlands at the primary, secondary, and teacher education levels.[42] Bol explained how critical it is for futures education to be seen not just as job training but also as a skill that students can take with them in their professional and citizen endeavors. "It should be something that you use in whatever you're doing," Bol explained, with the goal to nurture the next generation of trend professionals and future thinkers. If funding materializes, similar programs may be duplicated in other parts of the world.[43]

Carl Rohde, a cultural sociologist, is another trend educator who has been very successful in not only growing the domestic trend industry but also spreading it around the globe. Beginning in the late 1980s, Rohde began developing methods for studying how cultural mentalities changed over time. At the time teaching at the Utrecht University, he brought those methods into his university courses. Rohde also developed a consulting business, Science of the Time, and continued to teach his methods both in the Netherlands and outside it. Several forecasters who are prominent in the Netherlands today had him as a professor. Today, Rohde not only consults but also runs the International Coolhunt

Project, a multinational program that instructs students and teachers on cool hunting methods; he has been particularly active in China. Rohde also teaches in the Netherlands at the Fontys Academy for Creative Industries at Fontys University in its Lifestyle Studies program, where students can focus on trend forecasting. The program enrolls twenty-five hundred students, many of whom end up working in the industry. "I raised my own competition," he stated. He also elevated the regenerative role of education more generally and its capacity to act as a node of global futurity.

With Fontys and other programs producing so many graduates every year, Dutch trend specialties are becoming ever narrower. Trendslator's Hilde Roothart, one of the country's most respected trend professionals, told me that she had recently heard from an aspiring trend watcher who wanted to work on Christmas trends; Roothart advised the title "festive trend watcher" instead as a way of finding work all year long.[44] But the story is telling, and it is one that many in the Dutch trend industry feel acutely. Trend watching "is a very crowded field," noted Farid Tabarki, founder of the cutting-edge trend agency Studio Zeitgeist. Crowdedness is also why trend thinking seems to be increasing its reach throughout Dutch society, even becoming an asset the Dutch can bring to their international interactions. "I and my colleagues have a really important role to play [in] making this as transparent as possible and try to be as communicative as possible on the things we see," he explained, adding that he has been recently working with the Dutch Ministry of Foreign Affairs, the Dutch Embassy in Moscow, and the University of Applied Sciences in Rotterdam.[45] Tabarki is also a columnist for *Het Financieele Dagblad*, the Dutch financial journal, where he uses his perspective on trends and the future to cover everything from lifestyle issues to education to European politics.

It is important to stress that proactive optimism does not mean blind idealism or enthusiasm for every development. Many of the forecasters I met in the Netherlands were deeply aware of problems at home and abroad. I'm also aware that pitching clients, taking on consulting work, and scheduling speaking gigs often invite a sunny perspective, even if spreading possibility and hope is also contingent on spreading anxiety. The point is that the members of the Dutch trend industry have acquired a reputation for being as good as anyone at seeing, planning, and enacting futures. A trend-centric, profuture perspective holds a prominent place in Dutch society, with no signs of abating; it is also a skill set that Dutch forecasters aspire to market internationally. For sure, preparedness for and agility with the future bring along with them many perks and possibilities, and the degree to which these techniques can be democratized within the Netherlands is a good thing. For the time being, though, Dutch trend forecasters are in a class apart.

The World: Stratified Futures

Tom Palmaerts is thrilled.

Palmaerts, a preeminent Belgian trend forecaster with the Brussels-based firm Trendwolves, has taken the stage during the second day of LaFutura in a dark, windowless ballroom on the lower level of the Hotel Jumeirah Emirates Towers. He is broadcasting a video of Moon Ribas, a Spanish artist. Ribas has a seismic monitor implanted in her arm that allows her to feel tremors in the earth's crust. She translates these sensations into dance. Because Ribas can sense even the faintest tremors, Palmaerts explains, she possesses a preternatural awareness of the constancy of change in the environment. The expected unexpectedness, the anyplaceness, of these seismic events is a metaphor too luscious for Palmaerts to pass up. Trend professionals must become more like Ribas, he explains. They must seek out tiny ripples, feel the quakes before anyone else. He advocates that forecasters pursue these perturbations, these "thrills." He shares some examples of what thrills him: South African fashion designers doing daring things with denim, Belgian craftspeople fusing artisanship with tech, German composers who make music not for falling asleep but for sleeping.

There is not yet a wearable device that can pinpoint exciting cultural developments; no implant can anticipate that a cultural happening will take off or where it will take root when it does. Ribas may embody, quite literally, a hope for how forecasters might someday track global culture, but the message she imparts is not simply to do as she does. She inspires because her project is predicated upon the inevitability, naturalness, and persistence of global change. Trend forecasting on a global level requires similar rationale: an unflappable belief that global culture is like our planet's surface and is in constant motion. The job of the trend forecaster is thus analogous to that of a seismologist, but with an important twist. Yes, forecasters must monitor, reveal, and warn about change the world over, but they must also productively channel it. Their job is to find and produce the future.

And like any good seismologist, the trend forecaster knows the fault lines.

If global futurity is a lens through which trend professionals see the world, what appears through it has refracted to spotlight certain features. An accent on globalization privileges interdependence and competition, drawing forecasters to celebrate the sites most welcoming of reconfiguration. Optimism as a modus operandi allows forecasters to industrialize the production of interventionist futures and promote sanctioned forms of disruption. In sum, the global trend industry appears to rest on the assumption that the future, as multiple as it may be, is broadly headed in one direction. As such, some locations are much closer to the future than others.

The final element of global futurity, then, is that of stratified futures. William Gibson, the Canadian American science fiction author, is most often credited with the idea that the future is "unevenly distributed"—visible but piecemeal, scattered about the present. The idea is fundamental to both the concept of a trend and the trends business. In her book *The Signals Are Talking: Why Today's Fringe Is Tomorrow's Mainstream*, American futurist Amy Webb puts this idea suc-cinctly: "The future doesn't simply arrive fully formed overnight, but emerges step by step. It first appears at seemingly random points around the fringe of society, never in the mainstream. Without context, those points can appear disparate, unrelated, and hard to connect meaningfully. But over time they fit into patterns and come into focus as a full-blown trend: a convergence of multiple points that reveal a new direction or tendency, a force that combines some human need and new enabling technology that will shape the future."[46] A future that arrives all at once would be neither foreseeable nor malleable, and the business of trends depends on both. Trend forecasters seek out harbingers of the future in the form of innovation; forecasters then collect those harbingers and create patterns with them (see chapter 4). Yet even as tremors of innova-tion render certain environments thrilling, others are comparatively at rest. A trending future must be defined against something, be it the mundane status quo, a regressive backwater, or simply an unappealing development. Taking the idea of diffusion of innovation to a planetary scale means that some people and their pockets of cultures reflect the future more thoroughly, consistently, and satisfactorily than others. Forecasting purports to seek out these places, wherever they might be. In practice, however, there are structural and ideological reasons why the future must be conceived of as stratified to be comprehensible. Without omniscience, the future can be found only where it is pursued.

How might a company identify trends across the entire world? Any pos-sible method for doing so is sure to be cumbersome, expensive, and flawed. As noted in chapter 2, trend forecasting has always been in part about information management, with forecasters reading and synthesizing excessive information for clients. The internet makes taking these practices global much more pos-sible than it might have been in earlier eras, and several companies are actively working to employ social media, AI, and Big Data to these ends (see chapter 4). Regardless, seeking out trends remains a taxing and very human process. Original research eats up time and resources. "One of the real difficulties that we face is having enough funding to be able to do research in multiple markets," explained Marie Stafford of London's JWT Intelligence, speaking about how her company manages globality. "We usually restrict it in how many markets we can survey in, purely because of the cost."[47] Trend companies make choices about where they allocate resources, establish satellite offices, or seek out opportunities, and this inevitably means choosing certain locations over others. In addition, the trend industry is itself a culture industry, making geographic aggregation a central aspect of its structure.[48] Forecasters tend to live in places that are rich in entertainment, the arts, immigration, and technology—precisely the features they tend to gravitate toward when establishing additional outposts.

As I noted in the last chapter, the trend industry has attempted to address the problem of its geographic concentration through "distributed ethnography," or the method of doing empirical work across multiple sites to glean patterns. Distributed ethnography manifests in a few different ways. Most obviously, trend forecasters are keen observers, the type of people to take in stimuli from their environments and assimilate them wherever they might be. The same skills may be utilized in both domestic and foreign environments. Some companies take this a step further, offering their clients trend tours or treks, which are guided visits to one location usually centered around one theme. Kiwa Iyobe, a Japanese American based in London who worked for BrainReserve in the early 2000s, often led the company's treks in Japan even after she was no longer formally employed with the company. "Because I spoke Japanese, I would go out there often and do presentations and do trend treks where I would take a group of executives out into the field," she explained. "I did things like package design, future of eco, sustainability stuff, . . . depending on what they were trying to accomplish and for what brand."[49]

For many companies, a big part of their distributed ethnography efforts comes in the form of trend scouts or "spotter" networks. Related to practices of observation, surveying, and fieldwork that became mainstream in market research in the 1980s and 1990s, scouts are (usually) unpaid volunteers who track innovations where they live and relay them back to the main office. In the context of global trend hunting, the volunteers promise a method to discover "raw" trend data at a level of intricacy and a scale otherwise unfathomable to produce. Trend companies commonly promote their networks as hundreds or even thousands of people scattered to the farthest reaches of the globe—a symbol of the company's dedication to global futurity.

In all its forms, distributed ethnography often falls short of its ideal, beset by problems both practical and ethical. The issues are particularly evident if scouting networks are put under scrutiny. For instance, consider the extractive nature of trend scouting, where the express goal is to round up cultural developments from all over the world, "process" them in centralized global hubs, then farm them out to clientele everywhere. On the one hand, we can hardly fault the sincere attempt at diversification these techniques represent; without them, many companies would have far more limited perspectives. On the other, interesting cultural developments are often reduced to their simplest terms and then circulated abroad, where they become subject to unequal power relationships not only among countries but also between an individual country's classes or castes. For instance, when in 2018 TrendWatching highlighted the construction of celebrity architect James Law's O-Pods, or "tube homes," in Shenzhen, China, the company lauded them as an affordable housing solution for the city's growing population of young workers. TrendWatching's coverage is only a capsule, and it shares very little about the local context that might help to unpack this development—for instance, what is driving young workers to Shenzhen in the first place, how the local population has responded to the development, or the politics of Shenzhen, which also happens to be home to one of Apple's most notorious subcontractors. The localism of this trend quickly crumbles under the weight of its capacity for circulation. The conditions that have given rise to it matter less than the fact that it is catching on.

There are other ways that spotter networks forsake the localism that supposedly necessitates them. Despite the desire for them to span the globe, many companies find their networks concentrated in certain countries or regions, affecting the kinds of observations that emerge. Nia Christy, who is TrendWatching's head of global insights and is based in Singapore, explained that though one of her job duties was to build up the company's scout community in the Asia Pacific, she found it "really hard" and has since come to rely more on "partnerships with different stakeholders." She provided a few plausible explanations. Trend forecasting is nascent in Asia, with quantitative market research still dominant; trend forecasters who live there tend to work in the international offices of companies based in the United States or Europe. As a result, trend forecasting isn't well known in the general population, and it can be hard to convince people to volunteer for a service that doesn't provide "tangible benefits out of it except the community." She added, "I think it's the mindset."[50]

A brief detour to the continent of Africa helps hammer home this point. The burgeoning youth population and growing middle class have caught the attention of global trend forecasters such as Stylus, JWT Intelligence, and TrendWatching;[51] narratives like "Africa Rising" have helped to attract international investment across a range of sectors. Even so, Africa has relatively few developed economies and only a handful of homegrown futuring businesses. The small number of trend/futures professionals I was able to locate in Africa tended to fall into one of three categories: those focused on fashion and design;

representatives from or scouts for companies based in other parts of the world; or those who worked for government, universities, and the public sector and used trends as an element of strategic foresight more generally. Mphathi Nyewe, a futurist in Johannesburg, explained that in his country of South Africa the futures industry is "still in infancy," though demand for tools and insights is growing, as are professional networks.[52] Katindi Sivi Njonjo, a futurist in Nairobi, explained to me that her job is "to make futuring systematic and conscious in the public and organizational spheres"—vitally important, "because we often tend to act after the fact to manage crisis instead of deliberately anticipating probable occurrences and taking contingency measures."[53] This is not to say that trend work is not useful; instead, its utility so far seems to be primarily in addressing pressing issues and concerns, as well as farming out select insights to beyond the continent.

Indeed, there is something distinctly Western about trend forecasting, or at least the style of it that prevails in the industry now. Beyond that, the differences among the countries and cultures of Asia or Africa make it difficult to grasp and generalize about, especially for an industry that is relatively small yet purports to be able to have global reach. Yet Christy's point about "benefits" deserves further attention. That scouts are unpaid at many companies clearly impacts their recruitment, retention, and management and no doubt informs what kind of work can reasonably be expected of them. Consequently, some function less as embedded ethnographers and more as outsourced laborers doing their own desk research, sometimes even reading the same international news sources that home office employees are reading. What is the use of having a trend scout based in Jakarta or Accra if all that person is doing is reading *Wired* in English?

The above dynamics and tensions also make it very hard to dispel the idea that certain regions are more generative of trends than others—an opinion I found common, though not universal, among those I interviewed. In part, the viewpoint arises from the same logic that governs distributed ethnography in general, namely, that locations have unique cultures and that deep knowledge of those places results in worthwhile insights. Lourenço Bustani, a Brazilian forecaster based in São Paolo, explains that trends can manifest in cultures in a variety of ways depending on who is influencing and who is being influenced. "Emerging economies might mimic cultural trends from the United States, for example, in an aspirational sense. Those same trends can be the root cause for fundamentalist groups to want to wage war against the United States," he explains. "Having said that, there are parts of the world that are known for having a strong contribution in distinct fields: Scandinavia for design, for example. Asia for technology. USA for arts and entertainment."[54] It seems that the reputation of various countries and their dominant companies serves as both a useful shorthand and a limited lens for understanding what emerges there.

We can see the same dynamics at work at TrendOne, Müller's German firm, where they purport to use eighty scouts speaking twenty-two languages to track innovations across the world. Based on the insights of this multicultural group, Müller told me definitively that half of all global trends come out of the United States. When I asked him how this could be, he explained that "we are looking for really new startups, not copycats. Really new things. New technology. New business models. New marketing and service innovations. That's what they scout."[55] I have not figured out how a trend scout might differentiate between the "really new" and the "somewhat new" and whether the longevity of said innovation matters in determining its trend-worthiness. Similarly, if the metrics for determining a trend are measured by marketing and service innovations, which themselves are defined in a certain way, they might likely privilege the United States over other countries. But what the TrendOne example indicates is a certain amount of lock-in, where despite the widely echoed idea that trends can emerge anywhere, the industrial mechanisms of trends concentrate hierarchically and scarcely. Henrik Vejlgaard, a Danish forecaster and author of *Anatomy of a Trend*, was adamant on this point. "Trends can happen anywhere in the world, but if they are to be a global trend, they go through London, New York, and/or Paris or Milan or Tokyo," he explained. "That's just the process, the way it is, and I don't have any opinion about that as such."[56] Other forecasters made similar observations. "There are certain centers where new things are happening," explained Max Celko, a Swiss forecaster based in Germany. "The main metropolitan areas—London, Berlin, New York, LA, San Francisco—and then, you know in Asian countries have hubs, South America has hubs."[57] These same locations tend to be the places where trend forecasters live, where conferences tend to convene, and which then come to exemplify the centers of the interesting things happening all over the world.

Seen through the lens of global futurity, trends are little more than those cultural developments that pass effortlessly through the world's premier urban centers. Furthermore, trends of this ilk privilege an attenuated view of the world—one created by and for trend forecasters and their peers. Anita Chan's argument about the tech industry is relevant here; she notes that "rarely does anyone have to justify . . . that the digital futures imagined by select populations of engineers, designers, and innovators of new technologies in elite design centers can—or should—speak for the global rest."[58] As hotbeds of globalization and purveyors of proactive optimism, these elite zones also secured their position as the places where the future will crop up first. They top the pecking order of stratified futures, in part because they do the work of stratification.

The idea of stratified futures also means that leading spaces demand cultural resources from beyond their borders. Forecasters who work in and for those most "advanced" sites must pepper their futures with outtakes from the global rest just as much as they must look to new territories into which to expand and replicate. Even more, they require foils against which to compare themselves. I never had any forecaster tell me that a certain city or country was not worth exploring, but they almost didn't have to. It was more common that many places—rural, conservative, remote, disconnected, underdeveloped, or highly regulated places—could not be seen at all.

Conclusion

It's late on the final night of LaFutura, and I'm on my third glass of wine at a beachfront club nestled in one of Dubai's swankier neighborhoods. Chill electronic music wafts through the air. Appetizers and snacks float by—asparagus risotto, pommes frites, bruschetta. I chat affably with other conferencegoers about the news of the day, our post-LaFutura travels, our cultural differences. Then comes that point in the night where someone decides it would be a good idea to go in the water. Why not? The Persian Gulf expands nearby, and at this hour it is nearly waveless. Kicking off my shoes, I walk in until the water is at midcalf. The Burj Al Arab rises theatrically in the distance.

I can't believe this is my life.

At this moment, I can't say that I *dislike* global futurity, cradled as I am in comforts of the trend industry at its most divine and gracious. It feels worldly and chic to be buzzed in a country with Sharia law, to be telling jokes about Angela Merkel with Germans, to be debating the relative merits of different long-haul airlines. But I am also keenly aware of the privileges that brought me and others here now. I can see how far Dubai's world has bent to accommodate ours. If tonight represents some version of the future—both the means and the ends of trend labor as such—there is nothing inevitable about it. Quite to the contrary, powerful insiders and persuasive outsiders embrace this future at the expense of so many others. They embrace it because it is comfortable and familiar, because it does not require their sacrifice.

As a participant in and enabler of global futurity, the trend industry finds itself caught inside vast paradoxes. On the one hand, the business depends upon the continuing disappearance of barriers around the world and the constant flow of innovation and change that are the hallmarks of globalization.

The creation of global sameness at a breathtaking scope and pace is an essential ingredient of excitement that the future holds. At the same time, trend forecasting must constantly seek out and reproduce global difference not just to make for delightful presentations and sellable futures but also to ensure the kinds of inequalities that allow the future to stay "unevenly distributed." The trend industry is part of a hypercapitalist structure that bolsters belief in the possibilities that the future lends, often with technological solutionism as the core. But the problems that aren't corrected through proactive optimism, or the ones created by it, must be addressed by other means that tend not to fit into futuristic idealizations. All kinds of political, environmental, social, and economic problems go unaddressed via the global futurity that trends peddle. The trend industry often promises a wonderful global future, but one that may not help the people who need it most.

Will there be a day when trends can expand to fit all the world's directions? What would it look like if everyone had a chance to participate in the creation of their futures—not just as colorful detail but as full participants? I can't help but think of Quinsy Gario, an artist I met in Amsterdam who is the most visible figure behind the country's Zwarte Piet is Racisme (Black Peter is racism) movement. Zwarte Piet is a black servant who accompanies Sinterklaas (Saint Nicholas) during the country's annual Christmas celebration; he is typically portrayed in blackface, and many Dutch celebrants also wear blackface during the event. In 2011 Gario wore a T-shirt reading "Zwarte Piet is Racisme" to the festivities in Amsterdam; he was assaulted and arrested. Since then, he has been involved in spreading awareness about racism in the Netherlands through art, performance, television appearances, and campaigns. A former student of Carl Rohde, Gario explained to me that trend methods can act as tools creating possibilities for social change, connecting people around the world and building transnational movements.[59]

That's a future that deserves a chance to take hold.

CHAPTER 6

Eventful Futures

In 2015 an Afronaut wandered the streets of New York City, searching for clues. His suit included the latest gadgetry from his time, otherworldly gizmos designed to help him breathe, eat, and communicate. He arrived on a mission to create representations of blackness for a time that lacked them. On his journey through his past and our present, some of the people he encountered marveled and gawked, pointed and questioned, scratched their heads. Others just got it. One child pointed and yelled: "A black astronaut!" One older gentleman, after some back-and-forth, cheered him onward.

Where some saw a puzzle, others saw a possibility.

The Afronaut was a project of Ayodamola Okunseinde, a Nigerian American artist and educator based in Brooklyn. His art commonly grapples with themes of reclamation: projects that explore how black people can recoup the past, reenvision the present, and (re)imagine and intervene in the future. Another ongoing project is the Iyapo Repository, a collection of "future artifacts" designed to teach present-day viewers about what the future might hold, created with fellow artist Salome Asega. The project began with holding speculative design workshops in low-income black communities where participants brainstormed their future hopes, dreams, and needs. The most viable of these ideas became prototypes. Okunseinde shares with me an image of one: a therapeutic suit designed to soothe the "cultural trauma crossing large bodies of water"—a clear reference to the Middle Passage. Another participant desired a necklace that would "alert people to negative vibrations" radiating from "geolocations where black bodies have been actually killed." Trained at Mason Gross School of the Arts at Rutgers University and the Parsons School of Design, Okunseinde asserts that not everyone enjoys regular opportunities to imagine their future. "When it's a person of color that hasn't had the opportunity and literally cannot see their future beyond, like, Tuesday" it can be difficult to get them to think of an abstract time, of long-term needs. "The way that some of these individuals grew up, they cannot," he explains, trailing off for a moment. He collects his thoughts, begins again. "Asking them to create something of the future, of their future, one person drew a sneaker."[1]

The Afronaut and Iyapo Repository incarnate Afrofuturism, which at the time of this writing is not only a method and mechanism of future imagining but also a bona fide trend reverberating across popular culture. The signs are unmistakable. Movies like *Black Panther* and *Hidden Figures* spin stories about black futures of yesterday and tomorrow. Musicians such as Janelle Monae, Flying Lotus, and Thundercat toy with black soundscapes that are at once computational, irreverent, and intergalactic. The images and visions flow from South African fashion to black manga enthusiasts; the opportunities grow from black venture capitalists to black algorithms and black code. On another level, though, seeing these developments as some kind of trend misunderstands, mistakes, and even exploits their radicality. Trends presume that culture's significance comes in its spread beyond its community of origin. Afrofuturism, less interested in adapting white futures than in imagining uniquely black ones, would surely carry on regardless of added attention. Moreover, corporate embodiments of futures such as trends contend with what Afrofuturist scholar Lonny J. Avi Brooks calls "the weighted language of colonial expansion, exclusion, conquest, and erasure for imagining the dilemmas of racial identity."[2] We could also ask whether a nation with rampant police profiling, rising income inequality, and a resurgence of white supremacy is moving toward an Afrofuturist reality or if exposure will simply expedite its subdual.

As the previous chapters have shown, trends are powerful tools for seeing and realizing the future. Trends justify social exploration and excavation wherever they appear by indexing, documenting, and incubating leading-edge culture. Because of these characteristics, trends have come to prescribe corporate action and intervention. As we've seen, companies and other entities use trends to "future-proof" their decision making, to imagine new products and services, and to perform futurity on both the national and global stages. However powerful they may be, though, trends are limited heuristics baked with assumptions about social interaction, temporality, and cultural change.

The trend commodity is a private creation that is predicated upon leaders and followers, imitation and co-optation, and a constant, obsessive hunger for the next and the new. Though elastic enough to accommodate differing speeds of change, trends necessarily and incessantly look forward; the time of trends is linear and rarely historical, even as it is often iterative, cyclical, and recursive. And the emphasis on constant change limits the ability to see and account for cultural persistence. Tom Vanderbilt, writing about the "cultural blindspot" of futurism, observed, "We expect more change than actually happens in the future because we imagine our lives have changed more than they actually have."[3]

Corporate trends have certain inherent characteristics; "cultural blindspots" suggest that those characteristics might be accentuated not just because of what trends are but also because of who generates them. In a 2015 piece about the lack of women in futurism, journalist Rose Eveleth recounts a telling anecdote: a futuristic film from the 1960s anticipated early twenty-first-century office gadgetry with prescience yet failed to show any women working.[4] One would hope that cultural trend forecasters might avoid the glaring oversights that bedevil other kinds of futurists. Those who work expressly with culture necessarily must consider social phenomena, human behavior, political developments, and cultural subgroups even as they wax about the potential of new technologies, new businesses, and new ideas. Beyond this, forecasters are largely a progressive bunch—open-minded, curious, and urbane, with a genuine optimism about humanity's potential and the promise that can come from change. Yet trend work is still susceptible to homogeneity and tunnel vision. As labyrinthine and intertwined as culture is, trends charge ahead, leaving behind those continuing to fight entrenched battles, those unable or unwilling to "catch up." Trend forecasters are overwhelmingly white, which informs how the industry conceptualizes "future" and "change." Dependence on the fruits of hyperconsumerist capitalism means that trends generally extend rather than question privilege. And perhaps because trend professionals tend to see themselves as objective or at the very least agnostic about the future, trend work tends not to possess a social consciousness beyond the most anodyne notions of progress and betterment. One prominent trend watcher once told me that objectivity is necessary in order to see the future clearly. But I would counter that if the future is less a product of objective facts than subjective will and situated power contests, then anyone with a stake in it must imagine and act to bring their vision into existence.

I have spent this book exploring how trends work to strategically foresee and plot our increasingly consumption-driven future. In a quest to marketize future prediction, trend forecasting seeks not only to quell but also to celebrate and accelerate change and uncertainty. At face value, it might seem as though these features might also connect trends to political change, that is, change that alters social relationships, redistributes resources, or otherwise improves social life for the less fortunate among us. Yet I argue in this chapter that trends enacted as commodities are better considered orthodox implements for future imagining. Though superficially progressive, the goal of trends is apolitical or even antipolitical; it is to envision a future that keeps the fundamental structures and relations of the present intact. If we want to envision a truly visionary future—not one decreed through the puissant charge of disruption but one arrived at through the resolute work of struggle—then we need to radically rethink how trends behave, where they come from, how they travel, and whom they are for.

To make this argument, I had to do this broadening work myself, moving away from the privatized output of the trends industry and into the public activist futures of art galleries, classrooms, community groups, and more. My lodestar on this journey was Afrofuturism, which theorist Lisa Yaszek has described as a "larger aesthetic mode that encompasses a diverse range of artists working in different genres and media who are united by their shared interest in projecting black futures derived from Afrodiasporic experiences."[5] One of the objectives of Afrofuturism, according to theorist and filmmaker Kodwo Eshun, is to acknowledge how power "functions through the envisioning, management, and delivery of reliable futures." To undermine those power structures, Afrofuturism instead works with what Eshun calls "counter-futures."[6] Counter-futures transcend and decenter whiteness and white supremacy; they dare to tinker with history and to contemplate a future that upends the present's foundational assumptions. It is in this spirit that I explore how trends may or may not direct toward what I call "eventful futures," futures that bring about substantive political change.

Even as I delved into the manifestations of Afrofuturism, I did not find any black trend forecasting agencies. The number of black trend forecasters and futurists is relatively small, at least among the trend industry in the countries this book has explored. It was also much more difficult to find trends when their shape was not prescribed and packaged, much more challenging to locate futurists who recoiled at the label. But futures, futurists, and trends I did find, but only after I cast aside my expectations. What I found broke with the orthodoxy of corporate futures, where revolution can sometimes be little more than a gussied-up status quo. What I found demanded that I puzzle through to possibility.

Trends without Events

The JWT Intelligence "weekly roundup" for the week of March 30, 2018, screams with signals of social change.[7] Three models—two black, one white—snarl and pout at the camera, their sinewy bodies beautiful and fluidly gendered. The stories in the newsletter are equally defiant: tales of vegan makeup, gender-neutral retail, black culture jamming, accessibility emojis, plus-sized fashion. The roundup perfectly aligns the company's year-end forecast for 2018, in which one of the trends was "intersectionality." Published the previous December, the report from JWT announced: "From tech companies to traditional corporations, organizations are under pressure to improve diversity and inclusion in their hiring, but the layered challenges associated with achieving this are coming to the fore. Meanwhile, thanks to politicized generation Z and the mainstream feminist movement, lazy, sexist images and limited representation are increasingly being called out publicly. Media brands hoping to appeal to a younger audience have to embed values of diversity, intersectionality and inclusion in their philosophy from the get-go."[8]

As much as we might praise JWT for its awareness, in a sense there's little startling about the declaration. Today, we've come to expect companies to embrace brand activism, corporate social responsibility, and issue-oriented marketing. Especially amid diminishing faith in government and rising citizen protest, corporations are increasingly compelled to take a stand on a wide variety of issues—a phenomenon that trend forecasters participate in and encourage. Academics such as Sarah Banet-Weiser and Roopali Mukherjee would likely argue that JWT's activities smack of corporate opportunism; in a 2012 critique they note that when businesses champion causes, "social justice transforms into yet another strategic venture to secure the corporate bottom line."[9] For the trend industry, the fact that trends so often derive from subcultures, fringes, and other sites on the cultural margins means that when trend firms talk about them, they often appear overtly political. Yet awareness of confrontational, unfamiliar, or radical culture has never directly corresponded to any political prescription. Underground music, funky clothing, and countercultural practices easily lose their edge.[10] The same holds true when considering trends. Even if adhered to, an ascendant trend can float into many kinds of space, can boomerang backward or fold upon itself, can be evacuated of meaning or filled with its opposite. Especially regarding topics related to racial inclusion, often "racial difference is the source of brand value celebrated and marketed as diversity," and "visibility and recognition at the level of representation [affirm] a freedom realized by applying a market calculus to social relations," as sociologist Herman Gray put it.[11] In short, intersectionality may be revolutionary today and compromised tomorrow.

My objective is not to rehash these well-worn criticisms of co-optation and corporate politics in general. Businesses embrace issues for a variety of motives, sometimes in good faith and other times for reasons we might rightly question. Moreover, what businesses do is a priori political, regardless of their explicit intent. Nonetheless, when the output of the trend industry concerns demands for rights, recognition, and resources, what happens? Are trends equipped to radically depart from the world as it is? Might they be able to usher in the future as it should be?

For all the rhetoric of disruption, revolution, and innovation that circulates among trend forecasting circles, the capacity of trend commodities to challenge social relations, redistribute power, or attend to unfulfilled needs is at best unproven, at worst improbable. Sociologist William H. Sewell used the word "event" to describe such profound transformations of social life: events are "sequences of occurrences that result in transformations of structures."[12] Robin Wagner-Pacifici, also a sociologist, follows a similar line of argument in her 2017 book *What Is an Event?*, where she notes that "events are so disorienting and uncomfortable" in part because they transpire in an undefined way.[13] Trends do the opposite. They seek to assuage incomprehension and instability through defining and incorporating happenings as they happen. They may ride or rev up changes, but in their economics and means of circulation, their range and their demands, they tend—nay, *intend*—to work within existing or fathomable structures. In both these senses, trends promote change without events.

Let me elaborate on what I mean beginning with an observation from Lonny J. Avi Brooks, a futurist academic with extensive experience in participant observation at the Institute for the Future in Palo Alto, California. He observes that "while visionary in the domains of technology, most forecasting firms do not foretell of radical departures from, or represent a fundamental break with, the continuities of capitalism."[14] The same insight holds true for trend work. Staying tethered to the fundamentals of market capitalism makes sense for an industry that wants to profit off the here and now, even if it uses future speculation to do so. Moreover, capitalism is neither intrinsically evil nor uniformly practiced— certainly, trend forecasters foresee abundant changes in how the mechanics of business will proceed into years to come. But the incapacity on the part of many trend forecasters to seriously question mainstream economic assumptions (the imperatives of growth, the need to appease Wall Street, the tenets of private property or ownership, to name just a few) underscores the positionality of their futurism and highlights a central premise that is seemingly too big to question. Many forecasters might, for example, imagine fundamental changes to how individuals share their data with companies but not the disappearance of data markets or the abolishment of encroaching notions of individual data "ownership." Such a deeply held core belief raises numerous questions about how transformative the trend industry is willing to be, about whose priorities it serves, and about where and how it looks for signals of impending shifts. Trend forecasting frequently operates in the service of a future in which all but the most privileged among us are incapable of doing anything but comply.

Additionally, trends do not transcend the conditions of their production, a quality that exacerbates what political scientist Jodi Dean has called "communicative capitalism." Communicative capitalism is "the proliferation, distribution, acceleration and intensification of communicative access and opportunity," in which "communicative exchanges, rather than being fundamental to democratic politics, are the basic elements of capitalist production."[15] Under communicative capitalism, communication is increasingly understood as an end, diminishing the terrain of political agency while also serving profit motives. Applied to trends, this means that something other than an imperative for social change motivates their circulation. We should never assume that the point of identifying political or progressive trends is to bring society closer to realizing them. Instead, the priority of such trends is to serve the trend industry in general, which must digest and distribute newness as a condition of its continued existence. Highlighting "progress" is therefore not significantly different from highlighting any other kind of development and may hasten its neutralization. In the end, all of it exists to *inspire* corporate action, which is not the same thing as continuing, furthering, or perpetuating social action.

For an example, consider *Cassandra Daily*, a newsletter published by the Cassandra Report, a consultancy and trend shop with headquarters in New York, Los Angeles, Melbourne, and London. Like many of its peers, Cassandra regularly publishes a newsletter that explores a wide range of topics: eco hotels, poetry in advertising, no-waste grocery stores, hipster laundromats, and the like. The newsletter is free of charge and primarily exists to generate attention, establish domain over a sector or development, and entice readers to subscribe to the firm's proprietary content. An April 2018 edition of *Cassandra Daily* featured the following item: "In the era of #MeToo and #TimesUp, young people have more concerns over sexual consent than ever. New apps aim to quell some of those concerns by recording consent from each party before they engage in intimate activity. While critics contend that such tech is contributing to The Sexual Mehvolution, proponents attest that it's helping create a more progressive society for modern men and women."[16] Certainly, Cassandra's trend spoke to its moment. Credible allegations of sexual harassment and assault felled numerous high-profile men over 2017 and 2018, magnified by the swell of popular feminism, legislative battles over women's rights, and continued contestations around gender roles and expression. For Cassandra, newly minted apps LegalFling, Sasie, and We-Consent, which in varying ways allow users to express their comfort level with sexual activity, seemed to perfectly illustrate the shifting context around sexual relations. The onset of what Cassandra calls the "Sexual Mehvolution" established a novel and potentially threatening context that demanded a reflective response from brands. As Cassandra notes in the description of the wider trend on its website, decades of abundance of sexual information and opportunity have backfired, leaving a generation uncertain about and sometimes uninterested in utilizing the sexual license that older people had fought so hard to obtain.[17]

Is this a positive or negative development for the future? Are apps the answer to the problems of sexual consent? Is this a way forward or a movement to rebel against? Where Cassandra stands isn't clear, for two reasons. First and most crudely, though the newsletter write-up of these apps is free to all, Cassandra's "Sexual Mehvolution" is a proprietary trend, inaccessible except to those who pay its costly subscription rate. Calling attention to this might seem like an unfair point. One can hardly expect Cassandra or any business to sustain itself by giving away its products for free. Having said that, sharing information via its newsletter mostly serves the objective of circulation itself: it does not require response, and the "action" it most immediately demands (subscription) serves the company rather than the issue. Yet if the changing nature of sexual relations will profoundly affect businesses at all levels, it needs to be taken seriously not just by those who are able to pay for that understanding.[18] These issues transcend mere competitive advantage and veer toward corporate social responsibility, as knotty as that concept may be. We should ask: When is a trend so important, so vital, that its content deserves to be shared widely with the populace? When does the business of profiting off what might be monumental social change serve to thwart the possibility of that change? And if the nuts and bolts of strategic future planning happen in the closed boardrooms and bespoke research of private companies, how is it possible to have any sense of accountability to the public?

The second reason why Cassandra's stance on sexual consent is not clear has to do with accountability. Accountability facilitates social change. It allows us, as consumers and citizens, to ascribe responsibility. It demands that powerful forces answer to the demands of the present and the mistakes of the past. Such accountability can be difficult if not impossible to find within futures work. I took up this issue with Don Abraham, who at the time was an executive at the Futures Company.[19] We were discussing the idea of "accuracy," or how a firm could be held responsible for the forecasts it offered its clients. "Basically, there is no accountability," Abraham explained, noting many futurists struggled with this problem. "At the end of the day, if I do a project today on 2025, you're not going to be in that seat in '25, and neither am I."[20] Though he wasn't talking about political action per se, the observation is telling. Business changes quickly, institutional memory evaporates, and priorities shift in competitive landscapes—all dilemmas might quash even the best intentions. These are also dynamics that work structurally to undermine the possibility of following through with deep change.

Another reason why trends aren't transformative "events" concerns whether companies conceive of their trends as corresponding to some overarching sense of values. For sure, some forecasters openly express a commitment to "progress" broadly construed. Piers Fawkes of PSFK explains, for example, that at his company "we have a high purpose which is about inspiring our audiences to make things better"—and he includes within that technological innovations in both retail and social activism, such as foster care, women's sexual expression, and volunteering.[21] Other companies express values in a more tacit way. I encountered many firms that never overtly articulated what they stood for but sent a clear message through their focus on topics such as diversity, gender equity, and environmentalism as opposed to prominent but reactionary social forces such as white nationalism and antiqueer sentiment. Yet equally common were forecasters who expressed a discomfort with the idea that their work had a position on the changes afoot. "Change in and of itself doesn't have an agenda," noted Cecily Sommers, a Minneapolis-based futurist; she added that she considers it her job to explain the positive and negative potential of any development.[22] Some went even further. Faith Popcorn succinctly espoused a typical belief: "The trends are the trends." She continued, "People will say, do you think you create trends? No. I think sometimes we can accelerate it, because we let people know about it so they recognize it, but we don't create them. We observe them, we have a unique way of capturing them."[23]

In the eyes of many forecasters, what drives trends are not values—that is, an overarching sense of where society should be going or what changes really matter—so much as ubiquity, or the sense that something is simply there. (Surely this is the case with Cassandra: while it is not clear whether the "Sexual Mehvolution" and its corresponding apps resonate with the company's values, what is clear is that it qualified as a hot-button issue.) And here is where we can return to thinking about how communicative capitalism might contribute to the "eventlessness" of trends. In writing of politics under communicative capitalism, Dean asserts that popularity and abundance are widely believed to be manifests of political will—and that the success, efficacy, or importance of any communication is determined not by the response but rather by its "popularity, the penetration and duration."[24] The same logic binds trends insofar as they are both an effect of popularity and an instrument to amp up popularity. From here, two points follow. As the Popcorn quote above illustrates, trends can feel gravitational rather than willful (simply "what's out there"), thereby abdicating forecasting of its political responsibility in advancing (or not advancing) a particular social dynamic. But the opposite can hold true as well. The circulation of trend information is not a substitute for action or change, but it can take on the appearance of political action, extending not only to trend forecasters but also to the companies they serve. Companies of all kinds can use trends to cosmetically gesture toward their solidarity with progressive futures, even if in other ways they subvert it, even if they move on before those changes are really achieved, and even if their acts of unity do the work of defusing deeper, more eventful changes. A company can support feminism or gender neutrality in its marketing and product offerings while still paying women, transgender, and nonbinary people less, for example.

Automation provides another set of contradictions. It's an issue of ongoing concern to workers and companies the world over, and one that is clearly political though by no means clear-cut. In their 2016 *Workplace Summit Report*, the Future Laboratory grappled with these thorny issues. "Whole areas of employment will fall victim to the march of the machines," they explain, noting that occupations traditionally filled by men, such as long-haul trucking and delivery, could be displaced by the advent of driverless cars.[25] Though the issues raised by artificial intelligence have in no way been solved, at best the Future Laboratory has delivered mixed signals on the issues in its publicly available trend reports. Two of the reports from 2017 show the divide: on the one hand, a report on middle America explains that automation "bears some of the responsibility for hollowing out the middle class and contributing to the class divide," whereas another briefing from the same year calls automation "good for creativity" and encourages business leaders to "educate [themselves] and [their] employees about the upsides of at-work automation."[26] Their other reports more or less cheer the inevitability of artificial intelligence, robots, and more. Though trend forecasters routinely encourage their clients to take a stand, it seems forecasters themselves are reluctant to back many controversial developments outright, save for those firmly tech-driven.

Change, we must remember, is *opportunity*: opportunity for new services and products, opportunity for new techniques and processes, and, importantly for trend forecasters, opportunities for new business. I was strongly reminded of this when in June 2018 I attended the Future Hunters trend summit, where one trend elaborated upon the idea of "the new earthly epoch" in store because of climate change. "While it is human nature for people to be scared by all of this, it is less about whether this reality is good or bad . . . it simply is," the report notes. "We have to contextualize what is happening, consider positive adaptations that humanity is already making, and consider the implications."[27] Some might find this position antithetical to their politics, especially when the possible implications include activities that are themselves environmentally destructive or ethically questionable, such as mining the sea floor, drilling in the Arctic, and colonizing the moon. It is precisely the ability to remain agnostic about change that allows trend forecasters such as the Future Hunters to seize these opportunities when taking a position might not. Business demands that forecasters use trends to convert the future into capital.

I've already mentioned that trends are property: owned and developed, circulated through reports and conferences, marketed and sold for high sums to clients in need of insurance against risk. Despite the fact that reports may communicate unsettling information, by and large they reflect corporate priorities. Trends not only reflect what behooves trend shops themselves but also represent the demands of the businesses they serve. Common priorities include a focus on practicality and utility, an emphasis on prespecified audiences, and a circumscribed outlook that dictates what elements of the future come within view. To use a simple example, at the Future Laboratory a company-wide focus on certain sectors (e.g., retail, beauty, and luxury) means that the trends employees look at tend to be those most pertinent to that business sector. At other companies, priorities may mean focusing on affluent clients, certain racial groups, or segments such as Generation Z and women. One forecaster, for instance, shared with me that very few clients take any interest in income brackets below $60,000 per year and recalled another only interested in customers with more than a quarter of a million dollars in wealth. Even if such boundaries make sense given a company's short-term targets, it restrains what it's possible for trends to do. The trend-driven future is held hostage not just to corporate elitism but also to class inequality.

Another working assumption I encountered among trend forecasting is that trends are unidirectional, moving from leaders to followers. When a forecaster asserts, as in the above case with automation, that businesses must disrupt or be disrupted,[28] trends function less as tools than as mandates, corralling activity into a finite scheme of possibility determined by one's peers. Such a trajectory also affects the political potential of trends. Assumed unidirectionality may reinforce economic and social hierarchies, as it does when the disadvantaged become source material for ideas that are then monetized by and for social elites (e.g., craft brewing, drag, protest, and hip hop). Yet leading and following do not always work this way and do not always result in hierarchies in the traditional sense. Rather than traversing social boundaries, "leading" and "following" often levitate in the highest of social registers. For instance, many trend companies use what businesses are doing to develop their trends, valuing not only the innovations of small-scale startups but also bets taken by successful big companies, visionary CEOs, and the like. The Volkswagens of the world want to be the Teslas; Steve Jobs is the idol of lesser-known executives; and a retailer like Bloomingdale's conceives of its competition not just in other big department stores but among pop-ups and e-retail, airports and automobile manufacturers. Leading and following come to equate with peer-to-peer knowledge sharing, competition, and cooperation, which the trend forecasting process facilitates and encourages. The result can easily resemble a selective merry-go-round, where companies exchange with one another to affirm a shared worldview and the righteousness of the future they codesign.

Unidirectionality connects with the premise that trends are temporally linear. Despite the fact that there are many ways to understand and experience the passage of time, trends hammer home the relentless drive forward and project our own temporal conceptions into tomorrow. Trends participate in the overall presumption that time is moving faster—an assumption so deeply embedded in contemporary life, accepted by champions and critics alike, that it often goes unnoticed. Sarah Sharma, in her book *In the Meantime: Temporality and Cultural Politics*, argues that this view of temporality serves powerful interests: "It is not speed per se but the explanatory power of speed that . . . has the undue effect of preparing more and more sites for the institutions of modern power to intervene in bodies in increasingly invasive and inequitable ways."[29] A world that plays by the rules of trends labels anyone who does not, cannot, or chooses not to keep up with them as insufficient.

All told, trend commodities are a cultural form that can gesture toward politics but usually fall far short of delivering the kinds of "events" that add up to substantive change. Even when they do connect to moments of significance, forecasting "tends to squeeze out the messiness" of cultural change, which allows change to often remain incorporated in some semblance of existing structures.[30] In a sense, there is nothing problematic or unexpected about this, insofar as we expect that the future should be indebted to its past. Yet when trends resemble or mimic radical progress, they can become a poor substitution for the kind of change that would really alter social relations. And they can fail to include visions of the future that do want to incite such challenges.

Eventful Futures

"Black people have always afforded futurity, especially in a Western context," explains Florence Okoye, a British technologist and one of the organizers of Afro Futures_UK.[31] Black liminality, doubleness, and in-betweenness anticipated modern and postmodern experiences of identity—this is why Paul Gilroy, channeling Toni Morrison, calls blacks "the first truly modern people."[32] Or consider the mining and appropriation of black culture by white that has persisted within American culture since the dawn of minstrelsy in a bind that Eric Lott, in a poignant phrasing, called "love and theft."[33] From the thrill of black music or dance to contemporary neoliberal fascination with the development potential of the African continent, blackness exists often as premonition, even as white power structures oppress and undermine black people. Beyond this, black people still tend not to be considered a necessary part of the future. As a child, Okoye remembers being "really aware" of the "lack of narratives about the future or futurity that [accepted] black people existing in the future," she explained.[34] In the future, humanity is supposed to transcend or get over race.[35] This is surely disappointing to anyone who wants to see people who look like them participating in the future. Discovering a musician such as Janelle Monae and a novelist such as Malorie Blackman allowed Okoye to see what black futurism could be, and her interest grew. In 2015, having learned about the concept of Afrofuturism, Okoye helped organize Afro Futures_UK, which held its inaugural gathering in Manchester, England. One hundred and fifty people showed up, many of them from outside England. Suddenly, what had felt like an isolated interest presented itself as a formidable force. "There's a real power in actually naming things," she explained.[36]

For Okoye and many others, Afrofuturism acts as a principle guiding creative thought, action, and imagination. Coined in 1993 by Mark Dery to reference the connections between black music and science fiction, Afrofuturism enjoys a wide range of manifestations, although most center around two general goals. The first is to celebrate and amplify the presence of black people and black ways of thinking in science fiction, technology, and speculative arts.[37] Though very much an active contemporary movement, this strain of Afrofuturism often claims black creative productions from earlier in the twentieth century as precursors, including the music of Sun Ra, the science fiction of Octavia Butler, and the Black Arts Movement. Second, Afrofuturism serves to respond to and correct the frequent erasure of race in futures. This perspective on Afrofuturism acknowledges how dominant ideas of the future understand race as "primitive" and superfluous to a transhuman/posthuman tomorrow.[38] As race becomes an artifact of "history," those who are racialized are omitted from the future; Kodwo Eshun argues that "the powerful employ futurists and draw from the futures they endorse, thereby condemning the disempowered to live in the past."[39] The two impulses of Afrofuturism interrelate in ways that are both symbiotic and antagonistic. Black people projecting themselves into the future undoes some of the harm effected by their absence. Yet even as black people contribute to the very conception of "futuristic" for all people, blackness continues to be effaced in ways that representation alone cannot solve.

One central difference between Afrofuturism and the kind of futurity that proliferates in business contexts is Afrofuturism's deep focus on the continuity between the past, present, and future. Moor Mother Goddess, writing in the 2015 anthology *Black Quantum Futurism*, explains that "our past futurism, the hopes and dreams of our ancestors, act as important metaphysical tools that serve as agents to help one discover hidden information in the present time."[40] One of the objectives of black futures is not to erase, abandon, or disrupt but to reclaim and repair; the past is a constant passenger in future endeavors. Technology in this sense is not just a tool to build toward a new and different future. It can also recover the past. In her book *The Social Life of DNA,* sociologist Alondra Nelson takes this view of DNA technologies, which in creating a technological blueprint for self-discovery "allow us to try—or try again—to contemplate, respond to, and resolve enduring social wounds."[41] Black scientists, technologists, and entrepreneurs use tech to create "cutting-edge solutions to age-old injustices and yearnings," believing that the future is never about simply the march forward.[42]

Afrofuturism is not the only way for black people to be in the future, and not all black people who are interested in the future define themselves as Afrofuturists. Moreover, the success of the film *Black Panther*, as positive as it has been, also has inserted Afrofuturism into the mainstream in a way that has altered its meaning and diluted some of its impact. Nonetheless, Afrofuturism brought me toward a deeper understanding of the politics of trends. First, it allowed me to think through how black futurism in general and Afrofuturism in particular possess distinct methods, ontologies, and publics that often don't overlap with the assumptions and mechanisms of the dominant trend and futures industries. Second, it pushed me to contemplate the circumstances under which black futurism could bring about eventful futures not only via what we might call political change but also within the trend industry.

In the remainder of this chapter, I'll explore these questions through three cases that dovetail or are in conversation with Afrofuturism: local Afrofuturist activism in Philadelphia; an Afrofuturistic tech conference in New York City; and a "game jam" in Heyward, California.

CASE 1: TIME CAMP 001

"EXPERIMENT 1:

1. Seat yourself or stand in front of the mirrors in a darkened room with a small, flickering light, such as a candle or a flashlight. Create a vacuum in the room by sealing it from excess light and sound coming from outside the room. Stand two mirrors upright to form a right angle. Take a small clock, and place it in front of the mirror before you. Set the clock ten minutes fast.
2. Repeat the words Who am I, where have I been? Into the mirror over and over until you no longer recognize the words.
3. If you take each reflection to your left as the past and reflections to your right as the future, and use each reflection to signify one day, you can see yourself yesterday and yourself tomorrow, or as far ahead or behind you as you wish. Your images in the mirror should morph, the further back or forward you look.
4. To conclude the exercise, count backwards from ten. When you get to 1 you will be fully back in the present."[43]

There are about two dozen of us, mostly black and brown folks, sitting cross-legged or sideways or kneeling inside the echoing main gallery of Philadelphia's Crane Arts Building. The workshop we're attending is called "Dreaming Social Justice: How Dreamwork Transforms Futures." Facilitators Sheree Brown and Asia Dorsey radiate blissful, centered energy of the kind that my type A, hardened East Coast, categorically nonheady self can only rarely approach. Brown and Dorsey are here to show us how to tap into ancestral knowledges and our collective imagination, how to dream a more just future into existence. Dreams are "egalitarian magic," we learn; they allow us to travel in time and space, to sense and experience the wisdom buried in the universe. There are candles burned, silences observed, silences broken. In one exercise, to practice collective dreaming, they ask whether any of us has a dream we can remember and would be willing to share with the group. Someone volunteers, recalling a near nightmare of being chased by a mountain lion through a dense wood. A lively conversation ensues:

"Can you hear the mountain lion?"
"Did it ever catch you?"

"Were you afraid?"

"Did you feel as if you knew the mountain lion?"

"Maybe, just maybe, the mountain lion was you. Maybe it's all of us."

I don't really "do" mountain lion, but I am trying to keep an open mind. The workshop is part of Time Camp 001, a small Afrofuturist gathering combining art and music with workshops, discussions, and meditations. The organizer, Rasheedah Phillips, is known in local and transnational Afrofuturist circles as a boundary-spanning polymath whose work includes visual art, writing, community organizing, and law.[44] Her organization, Black Quantum Futures, is the sponsor of this and other local Afrofuturist projects in recent years. Phillips, a housing attorney, also runs Community Futurism, a related initiative that employs futurist ideas to explore gentrification and displacement in North Philadelphia. Speaking recently about her work, Phillips explained wanting to use "art as activism by asking participants to imagine the future through literature, remember the past through oral history and preserve the present through visual documentation."[45] Phillips's work illuminates what futurism is when its goals are local rather than global, egalitarian rather than wealth seeking, and organic rather than slick and instrumentalist. "The main thing with me doing Afrofuturism," she notes, "is helping to look at time as a cycle and use that and the past for change. How can I use those cycles in a way that is more powerful for me to change my future?"[46]

In the United States and much of the rest of the West, the power centers of mainstream future imagination—including science fiction, military, governmental and corporate planning, and futurism and futurology—have generally been the province of white men. White men founded organizations such as the Institute for the Future and the World Future Society, and they continue to dominate the membership rolls of the latter; public pronouncements about the future tend to come from well-known white male entrepreneurs such as Richard Branson and Jeff Bezos. The whiteness inherent to hegemonic future thinking dovetails with the overarching assumption of whiteness in technology, which is increasingly seen as the main driver of future change. Joel Dinerstein, an author and curator, has pointed out that technology "as an abstract concept functions as a *white mythology*" that is intrinsic to the practice of thinking about progress and the future for white people.[47] What this means is that whiteness, especially white masculinity, fundamentally shapes the logics, questions, and motivations of "the future." Futurist journalist Rose Eveleth contends that "when only one type of person is engaged in asking key questions about a specialty—envisioning the future or otherwise—they miss entire frameworks for identifying and solving problems."[48] It's a good point, one that I will address more in depth in the next section. But the problems of homogenized future imaginaries go beyond how problems are approached and solved and extend to what kinds of futuring are legitimized and what kinds are not.

Consider the example of space exploration, at the time of this writing a common topic among trend forecasters and futurists. Whether the goal is commercial space travel, development on the moon, or mining Mars for natural resources, futurists tend to see space as a vast domain ripe for discovery. In 2016, for instance, I saw Canadian American entrepreneur Bob Richards of Moon Express give a talk at the World Future Society meeting in Washington, DC. Richards spoke excitedly of moon expeditions as the realization of his childhood *Star Trek* fantasies. Trend forecasters have also tapped into the opportunities taking off in space; JWT Intelligence noted in June 2018 that "luxury space travel" could be a new frontier for innovation.[49] (Never mind the $55 million price tag, affordable to only the wealthiest of the superwealthy.) Ebullience over the limitless possibilities of space, as well as the growing amount of capital investment, crowd out discussions about who "owns" space, the spiritual aspects of space, and what the upsides and downsides could be to further human interference. Unchecked future imagination of this stripe ends up as a kind of conquest, ignorant of the social, political, environmental, cultural, and cosmic consequences of its actions.

What this points out is how white masculine fantasy—whether about unrestrained space exploration, frictionless social interaction, or servile technology—commandeers "the future," normalizing its interests and methods. We may see men like Jeff Bezos, Elon Musk, and Bob Richards as narcissistic and arrogant in their plans for space, but we don't dismiss them. We *can't* dismiss them—their social position demands that they be taken seriously. On the contrary, in its epistemology and its enactment, the version of futurism that Time Camp 001 and Community Futurism represent has not been embraced as a legitimate form of future imagining. For many, including myself at first, it appears to be less serious. Why? The importance of this style of Afrofuturism therefore is not solely in the work it is trying to do for its communities. It importantly demonstrates how diversifying the ranks of futurism or trend work is only a partial solution to the problem of making the future amenable to all people. In addition, we also need to reconceptualize whose future we care about. We need to shift our perception of who may claim the mantle of serving "the human race" and what "serious" thought about the future should comprise.

Phillips's brand of Afrofuturism raises additional questions about how to see and identify trends. To the degree that I can call her work trend-driven (my language, not hers), what animates it are the sorts of problems that rarely make it into professional trend reports and splashy keynotes. Her work likewise fails to conform to those logics.[50] Her goal is to address gentrification and dispossession, the changing complexion of Philadelphia neighborhoods, rising income inequality, and worsening public services. Signals might be the appearance of a new storefront or the shuttering of an old one, higher bills for internet access, another longtime neighbor who moves to New Jersey or Delaware, or fewer community gathering places. We don't clearly have a class of innovators; the term "disruption" feels inadequate, mistaken. Collected together, there is a problem to solve and a future into which actors could interject, with money or protest or capital investment or different policing practices or community involvement. Market solutions? Those exist, too, but they are of the sort that hover out of sights of the "consumer insights" through which commercially driven trend firms make their decisions.

For many reasons, the trend industry is not set up to solve these kinds of problems, and perhaps it never will be. However, I do think that its tools can be repurposed and reassembled—merged with other styles of futuring, put to radically different ends—to increase the likelihood of eventful futures.

CASE 2: AFROTECTOPIA

In her 2018 book *Algorithms of Oppression*, Safiya Noble underscores the oft-forgotten point that "mathematical formulations to drive automated decisions are made by human beings." Continuing, she notes that rampant "racism, sexism, and false notions of meritocracy" in Silicon Valley and other technology hubs contribute to continued discrimination against black people in tech in the form of "technological redlining," which shapes black encounters both online and off.[51] Reframing Noble's points in terms of futurism, we might say that the biases of the present infuse and curtail the future. As tech futurist Amy Webb notes, "Structural racism, xenophobia, homophobia, and sexism [are] being inadvertently coded into the systems that will eventually interconnect with all of our daily activities."[52] Taken together, the racism that undermines black digital experiences is both actively enforced and passively perpetuated. Addressing both demands more diversity among the people who are involved in tech decision making.

Of course, trends are not synonymous with technology, and they are not only tech-driven. Yet discussion about the future is often interwoven with tech, and I encountered abundant interest in and concern about the future among black technologists. I wouldn't go so far as to say that this is representative; as I suggested in the previous section, the concept of "futuristic" imparts a certain bias that can deter or preclude black people from identifying with it.[53] Instead, I would say that the linkage between black futures and tech is as material as it is symbolic. It speaks to a passionate desire to recognize technology as racial and to use tech, widely construed, as a tool of expression and action. In his book *Distributed Blackness*, André Brock goes further, examining the possibilities of "blackness as technology": what it means not only to think about blackness as an instrument of modernity but also to place black culture and practice as the default assumption of technological activity. While he cautions against "Black cultural beliefs in technology as 'progress' . . . even those developed by Black people for Black people," he still acknowledges the potent sway of technology as a liberating, libidinal modality.[54]

These issues were at the forefront of my mind as I went scouting for trends at Afrotectopia, a two-day symposium held in March 2018 at New York University. The conference, in its first year, was a production of graduate students in the Interactive Telecommunications Program (ITP), a program for students interested in the creative application of communication technology. "Afrotectopia is entirely about setting up the black community for success in the future by building a community of people that can build with one another now," explains Ari Melenciano, the festival's founder and an ITP grad student.[55] More than 250 people, most of them black, participated across two days of panels, workshops, performances, and keynotes. The topics and presenters were wide-ranging. I learned about activists using virtual reality to make visible the legacy of violence against black and brown people, including a project aimed at removing the statue of Columbus from New York's Columbus Circle. I watched an interactive music and dance piece about black hair; I heard two black venture capitalists discuss how they make investment decisions in socially conscious ways. And throughout, there were animated discussions about the possibilities of black algorithms and black code, the need to diversify existing tech spaces and build indigenous ones, and the need to define blackness not through the experience of suffering but through the promise of reclamation.

There was not express talk about trends at Afrotectopia, at least not any that I heard or participated in. The event's engagement with tech and the future proved instructive anyway. Sustained confrontation with the paradoxes of technology meant that no idea for technological innovation proceeded without concern for its possible social consequences. "Practical" also took on a different valence; though it often concerned commercial opportunity, it also necessarily embraced long-term spiritual, communitarian, and equality needs. For example, economist and engineer James Felton Keith delivered the final keynote of the conference, on data ownership for black people. He adamantly argued that blacks needed to embrace ownership to display their worth on data markets and that through the use of technologies like blockchain, black people could finally be compensated for their cultural contributions in online spaces. Predictably, the discussion about "ownership" and black subjectivities grew heated, making for a lively discussion about copyright, slavery, socialism, and discrimination. Though there was no conclusion, the important point is that this conversation happened reflexively in the presence of the people who would be most affected by it. Afrotectopia provided a clear indication that there are different types of future practice and that taking the time to discuss the social impact of a technology should not be an afterthought.

After Afrotectopia, I spoke to Kendra Clarke, vice president of data science at Sparks & Honey, about how she saw race affecting the tech issues behind trend work. Clarke was one of the few quantitative researchers I spoke with, but many of the issues she faced in her job paralleled those raised by folks on the qualitative side of things. Especially pertinent to the current discussion was Clarke's insight that the shape of trends depended upon who was doing the looking or the building—issues that business pressures and plentiful data often worsened. "Because of the need to produce tolerable results quickly, we're at a point where we have to trade precision [for] accuracy, and these are decisions that we make all the time," Clarke explained. And when most of the people who do this work are men who think of themselves as simply there to write code, it's easy for shortcuts to disproportionately affect women, people of color, and other disenfranchised groups. Problems arise "when you're not actively thinking about populations that are not necessarily your own," Clarke added.[56]

The potential pitfalls that may threaten data science extend to all kinds of work within tech and likewise apply within the wider industry of trends and futures. There are no statistics on who carries out trends work, and my own research on trend forecasting cannot claim representativeness in a statistical sense. I encountered several trend shops that are making concerted efforts to have diverse staff, and I also met plenty of women, particularly white women, at all career levels. That fact did not change my observation that men tended to make more presentations and be more visible, even at companies with plenty or even majority women on staff.

People of other racial and ethnic backgrounds proved markedly more difficult to locate than white women, however, especially in the upper ranks; some firms simply had no people of color working there beyond support staff. Furthermore, I sat through many futurist and trend gatherings where I was the only or one of an extremely small number of black people. Not all this lopsided representation is unique to the trends or futures industry, of course. In America, very few sectors have managed to transcend the racial bias that permeates our society. Across Europe, the dynamics of race relations differ, but racism, xenophobia, and homogeneity persist. Since the field of trends is so murkily defined, and so many people stumble into it by chance, it is harder to know how to pinpoint and rectify the so-called pipeline problem. Regardless, a field where entry is deeply aided by social relationships, chance opportunities, and professional leaps of faith demands more deliberation and intentionality to diversify, not less.

Particularly, several forecasters explained to me their fervent belief that diversity facilitates seeing the future. "If you have nothing but privilege and have never really had to question your present circumstances, I think doing forecasting work is harder for you," explained Jason Tester, a gay white man who is a research affiliate at the Institute for the Future.[57] MJ Petroni, another queer futurist who is founder of the San Francisco–based consultancy firm Causeit, agreed: "Futurism is always about asking questions about . . . or foreseeing paradigm changes. That is, of course, always situated in the person who is doing the observing or participating. When you have a lot of straight, white, male, Christian, background-of-privilege perspectives, that's a set of perspectives . . . but it's not the only perspective. It's not the right perspective inherently."[58] In explaining how that belief affects whom Causeit employs, Petroni gave an answer that is worth quoting at length:

> We often look for people who have existed in lots of different worlds, and in walking back and forth between these spaces and never being fully at home, they learn a lot about the unspoken rules and assumptions and codes and values that exist. At the same time, because they become at home in traversing all of those things, they develop a native skill set in connecting the dots and translating and reformulating their own identities or questions in response to radically changing circumstances. So we tend to look for people like that and work with those people.[59]

Petroni's ideas are very attractive: that creativity, pluck, and a propensity to see the world differently emerge from those who have spent their lives navigating ill-fitting social structures. Unfortunately, what I encountered in the offices, conferences, and networks of the trend industry suggests a field where such wisdom is not taken to heart very often. There are notable exceptions. Sparks & Honey, a company that has made concerted efforts to diversity in terms of age, race, nationality, and gender, impressed. That said, even there, there is more to do. Anywhere, it's possible for diversity to act as window dressing that obfuscates deeper issues such as pay equity, lack of opportunity, chances for promotion, intraoffice politics, and many other issues.

Which brings me back to Afrotectopia, technology, and trends. What if we envision trends less as harbingers for the future waiting to be excavated and more as contrary practices that, in their innovation, forge new and more inclusive ways of being? What if technologies are not so much the gadgets built for us that reshape our world but also the abilities we bring to the world, based on who we are and how we live? The Afrofuturism on view at Afrotectopia, its goals and its challenges, are reaching toward eventful futures. Eventful futures must recognize the significance of human agency and the reality of human bodies, the affordances and the limitations of technology, and the importance that change not be encouraged just for its own sake. As Joel Dinerstein has observed, "Over two centuries, technology has piggybacked onto social progress by creating the *rush* of change without social improvement."[60] To nurture eventful futures, trends and other future-invested industries can begin to use technology toward social change—rather than assume technology *is* social change—and can also invest in the technologies of identity that all of us possess. "When it comes to technology, we are still learning to think outside of the terms of all or nothing," notes feminist futurist Sarah Kember. We should see technology "less as an independent agent—that will either supersede us (in intelligence, in the evolutionary stakes) or act as a panacea on our behalf—and more as a co-constituent of what we call human—a form of agency that we work and are simultaneously worked with."[61] All of us are instrumental parts in whatever and however technologies emerge.

CASE 3: GAME JAM

The final Afrofuturist case occurs at the nexus of games and pedagogy. Games have enjoyed a long history in mainstream futurological practice. First adopted in the military during World War II, fictive tools like scenario planning and role playing were considered both strategic and persuasive, useful in helping planners imagine the enemy and articulate their positions.[62] In the subsequent years, games and other playful forms spread across many industries, sometimes specifically for planning purposes, while at other times employed as a way to tap into creativity and build a more freewheeling work environment.[63] In education, while games have long been used to practice skills or reinforce information, more recently educators have used immersive gaming as a unique way to simulate environments and promote critical thinking.[64]

Lonny Avi Brooks and Ian Pollock are professors at California State University–East Bay (CSU-EB) who have been at the forefront of Afrofuturist experiments in gaming. Since 2015 CSU-EB has been sponsoring quarterly Game Jams, events where participants create playable games over a short period of time under a set of guidelines. Since 2017 Brooks and Pollock's twist on the format has been to target a subset of the Game Jam specifically at low-income and students of color, infusing the sessions with futurist thinking. They call these sessions Minority Reports: 2054, with the goal of having students think about what their communities might want or need in that year.

As Brooks has written, games "can facilitate novel memories of black alternative futures that step beyond dystopias."[65] Game playing can act as a kind of "futures therapy," allowing students to think not just of more hopeful tomorrows but also of ways for their own speculations to take root in the real world.[66] The educational potential of such exercises is vast. In discussing the use of science fiction in education, Kurt Squire and Henry Jenkins explain that the genre provides a template for "thought experiments" that can seed future aspirations and innovations.[67] In mimicking speculative fiction, Brooks and Pollock not only give the students an opportunity to think differently but also "literally jam the normal conversation of what we think of as alternative futures," Brooks explained.[68]

In 2017 Minority Reports: 2054 was dedicated to revising the futurist game *The Thing from the Future*, originally created by futurist and Carnegie Mellon professor Stuart Candy. *The Thing from the Future* is traditionally played as follows:

> Each round, players collectively generate a creative prompt by playing a card game. This prompt outlines the kind of future that the thing-to-be-imagined comes from, specifies what part of society or culture it belongs to, describes the type of object that it is, and suggests an emotional reaction that it might spark in an observer from the present. Players must then each write a short description of an object that fits the constraints of the prompt. These descriptions are then read aloud (without attribution), and players vote on which description they find the most interesting, provocative, or funny. The winner of each round keeps the cards put into play for that round, and whoever has the most cards when the game ends is declared the overall winner.[69]

In revising the game, Pollock and Brooks encouraged their students to add cards to the deck that were reflective of their experience and cultures. Noting that student experiences are an underutilized resource not just for technological futures but also for futures of social change, Pollock and Brooks argue that "we work to unleash the imaginations of our students and to elevate the status of their deferred dreams where they have undervalued their own innovative capacities of mind."[70] The CSU-EB Game Jams are just one element of the wider Black Speculative Arts Movement, in which Brooks also plays a prominent role. While the movement goes far beyond pedagogy and gaming, these techniques remain an important way to draw in nonstudent and nonspecialist populations.

For example, Brooks revisited the Minority Report game at two public events, one called Black Imagine Oakland, a festival during the winter of 2018, and the other Technology + Entertainment Convergence, in Los Angeles.

Games are not widely practiced in commercial trend forecasting, much less those that elicit feedback from the public. Most of the means for public engagement happen through instruments such as surveys or through surveillance. Gaming thus has radical potential in both the method of Afrofuturism it proposes and its interventionist gestalt. Additionally, as much as both the trend industry specifically and futurism more generally seek professional legitimacy, it is important to consider what it means that futurist methods aren't necessarily widely accessible. "I think it's a slippery slope when you start saying you can only practice futurism if you have these methodologies," explained Alida Draudt, futurist and author of *What the Foresight.* "There's a huge opportunity for people from every walk of life and every background, not just people who happen to be wealthy enough to be able to think about the future, because that is a privilege at the moment."[71]

Conclusion

In their 2016 book *Inventing the Future: Postcapitalism and a World without Work,* Nick Srnicek and Alex Williams make a provocative point about the relationship between history and the future. "The complex and often disastrous record of the twentieth century demonstrated conclusively that history could not be relied upon to follow any predetermined course," they write. "There was nothing inherent in the nature of history, the development of economic systems, or sequences of political struggle that could guarantee any particular outcome."[72] In other words, we can't count on the future to fix the world for us. It will not be better because some discourse of "progress" would prefer it to be so. And when we hear ideas about developments that promise to improve our lives, we must always ask, "Better for whom?" The future requires the active participation of those who want it to unfold in a certain way.

This is a perspective that is already familiar to trend forecasters, who insist that one of the goals of using their services is to veer action toward desirable futures and away from undesirable ones. Yet for all of this belief in the possibility of taking advantage of the future, trends are not carriers of progressive politics. Instead, trends usually serve the interests of those people, institutions, and forces that make most of us feel as though the future is out of our control. As futurists Luke Goode and Michael Godhe have argued, present-day conditions work to "[persuade] citizens that there is no alternative to the onward march of globalized markets, finance capitalism, deregulation and environmental deg-radation."[73] Tasked with the purposes of making money, circulating newness, and readying businesses rather than societies, trend commodities and the fore-casting companies that sell them have no one to be accountable to. They don't usher in "events," because they don't have to.

Profit may not be the ideal driver for eventful futures. At the same time, we live in a moment in history where we can't ignore the power of business or hope that the current system evaporates overnight. Businesses must be held account-able for their actions and be aware of and thoughtful about their social role. Of all places, the trend industry has the power and the means to generate new senses of imagination and possibility that can permeate not just trend companies but also other industries. Alternative sites for futures likewise need to be encour-aged and grown, and Afrofuturism offers one version of an answer. In addition, we need to engage the public fully in the work of the future and democratize the practices of trends. Trends can be more than just private commodities. They can be public tools for thinking and action.

Public Futures

Trends are extremely powerful tools for anticipating and shaping the future of consumer culture. That power affects everyone, even though a very small number of people regularly participate in the conversation and contrivances around trends. The discrepancy between who manufactures trends and whom they affect is as crucial to think about as the changes that trends themselves might usher in. It's important that we not only understand what trends do and how they do it but also find ways to moderate and redirect their power. Ideally, we can democratize how trends come into being and empower every one of us to actively shape rather than passively receive our collective future.

How will that happen? The goal is lofty, and the way there is complicated. It can be partially attained, though, if we focus on the reckoning with trends' social and cultural influence that has begun already. While I was writing this conclusion, a backlash against the power of trends was brewing. The focus was on the somewhat unlikely target of trending algorithms. Facebook discontinued "Trending Topics" in June 2018 due to the ongoing fallout from the 2016 US election, the scandal surrounding Cambridge Analytica, and other serious breaches of trust in the United States and beyond. News stories that followed overviewed the problems trending features can cause on social media platforms. In a story for *Wired*, for instance, Louise Matsakis recounted the history of blunders surrounding Facebook's management and definition of "trending," from human editors accused in 2016 of suppressing conservative news sources, to an algorithmic system that "repeatedly surfaced conspiracy theories and outright false information."[1] Other social media platforms also raised alarms around how easy it was for trending algorithms to be gamed, manipulated, or abused. After a YouTube video falsely claiming that a school shooting survivor was an actor became the number one trending video on the platform, journalist Issie Lapowsky declared trending "broken," too easily compromised by bots and fake news: "Based largely on conversation volume, trending tools naturally drive the public consciousness toward topics of outrage; an outrageous topic trending only adds to the outrage. How many times have you clicked on a trending topic on Twitter, only to see an endless scroll of Tweets decrying that the topic is trending in the first place? The conversation about the trend becomes the trend itself, an interminable loop of outrage that all started because some line of code decided to tell millions of people that topic was important."[2]

Of the many conclusions one might draw from this debate, a central one is the pervasive attachment that people have to the idea of "trends"—an attachment that, I argue, has been growing since the early twentieth century. We pay attention to trends because they tell us something about ourselves—what the community of "us" is talking about, thinking about, doing, standing up for, or bemoaning. From there, trends point us in a direction. Whether we've fallen into the rabbit hole after clicking through a trending topic, seen hashtags like #BlackLivesMatter and #FamiliesBelongTogether become movements, or simply heard about such trends second- or thirdhand, we increasingly live in a world where trends mold our awareness of cultural change and, through that, our awareness of ourselves. The negative response to trending is commentary on how opaque technologies that govern arenas of public discourse adversely affect our sense of reality and self-determination. "Algorithmic processes also become a part of social action," explains sociologist David Beer, "based . . . not just upon what they do but on how individuals and organizations respond to what they do."[3] Even if most of us do not fully understand how trending works, we react to and exist within the frames it creates. And because trends are more than mere barometers of public sentiment, the people and technologies that create and circulate them are more than passive reflectors. They have real influence.

The trend labor I have focused on in *On Trend* differs from what happens on the internet, but it too is performative and recursive. In the trend industry, computational and human "algorithms" handle colossal amounts of information, utilize them to detect early signals of new behaviors, and, from there, anticipate where the world might be going. The resulting trends impose a sense of order on the otherwise chaotic dynamics of life and in so doing make cultural change easier to spot, evaluate, and simulate. Trends predict, but they also prescribe—they help us to understand changes percolating around us, as well as assist in those changes taking further hold. For this reason, corporations both buy and buy into trends: for both the views they provide and the greater idea that cultural change can and should be harnessed and directed in this manner.

Forecasters, futurists, and the other trend professionals I've studied in *On Trend* are several orders of magnitude less fearsome than corporate leviathans like Facebook and Google. As small, intermediary companies that aren't consumer-facing, trend forecasters don't carry along with them the same concerns about oligopolism, privacy, or political manipulation. Because they work under a range of titles, they are also more difficult to make sense of in a holistic way (at least prior to this book). Many who have heard of this field often struggle to take them seriously—even their most convincing claims can be swaddled in hype—though one aim of *On Trend* has been to caution against knee-jerk dismissal. These disclaimers aside, in crucial ways, the objectives of the trend industry are not only as ambitious as those of Big Tech but also as perfectly harmonious with them. Deciphering the cultural future to make better business decisions is exactly what Facebook and Google promise advertisers. It's exactly what Amazon is attempting to do for itself with its troves of shopper data. What distinguishes the pursuits of the trend industry, for now, are the nature of the forecasts, the time horizon, and the methodologies. And compared to tech behemoths, trend forecasting's work has even less public awareness.

Obscurity does not mean lack of influence or narrow perch. Trend forecasting is deeply invested in all manner of public culture, especially as consumerism intensifies around the world. The field's perspicacity about the pulse of our consumer-driven culture is what makes trend forecasting such a fascinating line of work. There is no cultural happening that falls outside its purview, nothing "off topic," nothing uninteresting. As should be evident from these pages, the breadth of this understanding means that trend forecasting has gotten a lot of things right: correctly spotting fringe or underground movements that grew to be mainstream, promoting intercultural exchange and global understanding, and championing many of the age's most forward-thinking beliefs. Certainly, there have been misses, too—someone interested in writing a book about fallacious cultural predictions would have no shortage of material. But it turns out that people who read and travel, who speak to experts and consult research, and who are well-connected and well-positioned are (unsurprisingly) pretty good at seeing where things might go. They also excel at the all-important skill of convincing other people that they are in the know and should be believed.

For these reasons, the trend industry has also been a significant actor in the long march of "trend" toward commodification, where the term signifies not

so much the general drift of society as it does a proprietary commodity manufactured out of public culture. Trend-oriented thinking on an industrial scale
means that quirky developments exist not on their own terms but as indicators
of possible new consumer groups or marketable social arrangements. Likewise,
when "trended," major social shifts—around family and romance, ethnicity
and identity, health and the environment—become significant primarily for
the kind of corporate response they will engender. Trend commodities transform social observation into consumer research. Cultural change becomes a
marketing plan. In turn, trends shape the pathways of the future not just for
the businesses that purchase them—not just the retailer wanting to capitalize
on digital clothing, not just the beverage company hoping to tap into the buzz
around cannabis—but for any of us who share their world.

For example, as I was writing this book during 2017 and 2018, many trend
firms had turned their attention to aging.[4] Today's over-fifty group is living in
markedly different ways from previous generations, insisting that stereotypes
about age be revisited and abandoned. "A growing population of Boomers are
redefining the very nature of aging," gushed Sparks & Honey in its report on
trends to watch in 2018; that same year, Trendera examined the backlash against
"anti-aging," while PSFK celebrated Agei.st, a new lifestyle publication that re-
conceptualizes what it means to get older. On the one hand, these are positive,
prescient insights; we should want and expect the market to respond to them.
On the other hand, the graying of the population has implications far beyond the
market, and a cheerful, market-based take obscures the reality that many aging
people continue to deal with. In the United States, "new aging" coincides with
growing poverty among senior citizens, an imperiled welfare state and Social
Security, diminishing fertility, battles over immigration, and more dynamics
that continue to shape the representation and realities of older people. Ability,
class, race, region, and more mean that people age differently, with different
access to opportunities, jobs, and goods; "aging well" is culturally determined,
with the possibility of becoming another burden. The trends that surround
aging are in conversation with all that and will have effects far beyond how
marketers position products. These are important conversations, and not just
because aging is suddenly sexier.

That populations in many industrialized countries are getting older on average is a tangible phenomenon with palpable effects. But regardless of whether a
trend is immediately intelligible or a long way from fruition, even trends on the
"right side of history" can encourage social action that is short-sighted, myopic,
or undemocratic. The power and fallacy of trends is that they are one of the few
genres where systematic thinking about the future regularly happens, but as

sellable commodities, they directly influence the decision making of powerful actors absent any oversight, ethics, representation, or accountability. I noted in chapter 4 that trends exemplify what Peter Taylor has called "corporate social science": profit-driven research written for a private audience. "Such practice does not only betray the possibility of a critical contribution," Taylor writes, "it all but eliminates curiosity without which research is sterile."[5] Trends are part of the increasing volume of corporate research that crowds out other lines of inquiry, other means of answering and asking the most pressing questions of our time.

By the same token, trends inspire disruptive decision making and encourage the consumption of change, thereby increasing the mandates of the future and enlisting all of us to serve. Trend forecasters are the captains among a platoon of forces itching to march into the future as quickly as possible. When we hear incessant claims that driverless cars will revolutionize transport or that virtual reality will change the nature of travel, when we see nimble sixtysomethings contorted in impossible yoga poses or read that marriages are taking place via blockchain, the subtext often is to submit to these developments, even if we don't like them, even if they are against our interests. Trends often present persuasive stories rather than hard predictions, yet either way, they add to the force of an inevitable future that most of us feel very little control over—including, ironically enough, corporations and their workers. Serving that future therefore means not just preparing for tomorrow for ourselves and our progeny but resigning ourselves to unyielding change whose pace and parameters are not ours to set.

That trends increase the weight of the future would be one thing if forecasting were neutral and unbiased. But it isn't. Trend forecasting must serve its own needs and agendas, at the top of which is maintaining the demand for trend content. Daily briefings, nightly emails, weekly webinars, quarterly reports, annual conferences: the sheer magnitude of trend products parrots the nonstop flow of change, guaranteeing that even the most certain proclamations rest on precarious foundations, soon to be followed by different, equally urgent occurrences. Beyond this, the preceding chapters have explained how trends may reflect and accentuate bias, harvest and assimilate difference, and defang and nullify major change. Isolated practices, even happening in tandem, do not necessarily portend a major development or one ready for a bigger audience, but the economy of trends encourages treating them in this way. By connecting them and defining them, trend forecasting can amplify a movement but also genericize it. "Anything that addresses a specific community will have any nuance or difference erased by trend forecasting," said Dena Yago, formerly of

K-Hole. Because trends are fundamentally prejudiced toward commercialism, acceleration, globality, and incrementalism, the result can easily be stasis instead of momentum.

These criticisms reveal the costs of trends, but they are not a call to abandon trends, to fear change, or to attempt to pause the future. I hope I have made clear that trend forecasting is interesting work with much to teach about consumer culture, cultural research, and assuming agency over the way the future unfolds. The trend industry may fade in terms of prominence, but the strategies of cultural forecasting and the utility of the social that it promises are significant contributions that won't disappear anytime soon. While I hope this book has provided readers with historical and critical awareness, it should not be a cause for despair or an excuse to further dismiss the work of trends as simply "manufactured." Rather, it is because these trend practices come from somewhere that we should feel empowered to participate in and re-create them. It is time to ask for more public accountability from the futures industries. It is time to promote thinking in trends as a means to arrive at collectively determined futures. And it is time for trends to become part of the critical vocabulary about consumer culture.

Trending Change, Changing Trends

In his provocative 2018 book, *Winners Take All: The Elite Charade of Changing the World*, journalist Anand Giridharadas points out one of the central fallacies of the current age: that despite near-constant talk of positive change and social altruism, the world has become less equal and less democratic, with meaningful change elusive for the neediest. "When elites assume leadership of social change, they are able to reshape what social change is—above all, to present it as something that should never threaten winners," he writes.[6] We end up with a world where the very rich not only shape the world through the goods, services, and technologies they sell but where, through their philanthropy, rhetoric, and preference for market-based solutions, they also set the agenda and horizons for social activism.

I read Giridharadas's book not just as an important contribution to our understanding of contemporary life but as a signal of possibility, an indicator of a cultural shift, and a sign of a trend making its way through the world. Following five years after *Capital in the 21st Century*, by Thomas Piketty, *Winners Take All* presents a parallel argument about the rise of income inequality but during a time when the toll taken by that inequality is even more conspicuous. Populism and fascism have overtaken many of the world's democracies, political and cultural extremism defines debate, imminent environmental calamity threatens to up-root millions of people, and protest of all kinds is the order of the day. In these ways and many others, across the developed world, the status quo no longer suffices. Addressing these interlocking dilemmas requires asking big, systemic questions and recognizing the need for visionary, unorthodox solutions.

Until now, the trend industry has mostly served the interests of wealth and power either directly in the form of advisement or indirectly through compliance with its worldview. This can no longer continue in good faith. Deep sympathy with elite interests not only perpetuates inequality but also blinds forecasters to sites and sources of change. I offer the following ideas so that trend professionals and the public more generally may seize contemporary agitations and use trending tools to imagine meaningful alternatives.

TRANSPARENCY

Over the course of my research, many companies welcomed me into their offices and conferences, provided me access to their materials, and allowed me to speak with their personnel. I hope other academics and journalists who continue to examine this industry find it equally open. Plenty of topics remain that are ripe for inquiry, including the clients' side of the industry, how futuring and trend methods emerge in-house, the role of venture capital, the development of data science and artificial intelligence, and much more. Better comprehension of the commercial use of trends and futures will supplement the reinvigoration of futurist studies already under way. It will also bring a more nuanced concept of the future and trends into fields across the sciences, humanities, and social sciences that already engage with prognosis or forecasting in one way or another.

The need for research and criticism highlights the fact that much important work in trend forecasting is inaccessible to the public writ large. Trend reports are nearly always proprietary, presentations take place behind closed doors, and conferences are costly. These secluded territories rarely endure public scrutiny, but this also means that they rarely benefit from public insight. There are several ways the trend industry could embrace publicness along these lines. One model is Sparks & Honey's open agency concept, in which the company receives outsiders during certain meetings and sessions. Companies interested in experimenting with this idea could host periodic public forums or events, partner with educational institutions or community groups, or provide reduced conference registration fees and/or virtual conference access to students, educators, nonprofits, and community members. Another path toward transparency is to make research public. Some firms have set a precedent in doing this with some of their reports, and there are several ways in which this practice could become more widespread. For instance, companies could earmark topics that are urgent to the public and share those reports publicly immediately. Reports on other topics could be hosted in a public repository—either within each company, by a centralized body, or through a university—after an embargo period. Firms could also collaborate to develop public reports on our most crucial sociocultural issues.

Transparency around methods also matters. Unlike those surrounding social science conducted in universities, the ethical guidelines around market research are murkier and more poorly regulated. Moreover, when dealing with something as amorphous as the future, the impact of a company's practices can be hard to determine; "harm" and "risk" are thorny concepts that are difficult to calculate. For this reason, ethics within the trends industry must be multipronged and creatively conceived. First and foremost, the industry needs to develop internal ethical guidelines of the sort that typically emerge alongside an industry's professionalization. The dimensions of these ethical questions are too vast to enumerate here but could include the use of social media and artificial intelligence, data sharing, the recruitment of human subjects, and client guarantees and truth in materials. LaFutura, the de facto international organization for trend professionals, might be one place to begin having these conversations and implementing these structures, as might the various futurist societies.

Individually, trend firms might create mission statements or codes of conduct that specify the kinds of projects they take on and/or the clients they will work with, communicating these missions on their websites and other public-facing media. Articulating values reflects what clients and consumers have come to expect in an era when more and more of a company's decisions come into the public eye. One need only look at the controversies that incriminated McKinsey & Company, the American management consulting firm, in 2018 to get a sense of the great risks consultants can potentially run when they neglect to think through the unintended consequences of their actions or appear to be hiding something.[7] Unlike McKinsey, most trend firms are small enough that they can more easily be accountable to a sense of ideals.

The above will all be important steps, but they will not be enough to counter what I hope is increased public interest in the futuring professions. This interest may manifest itself representatively, insofar as governmental or intergovernmental agencies take on exploring the ethical and legal questions that trend work raises. Or technological developments such as so-called smart contracts conducted via blockchain may force the issue of transparency in ways that I can only speculate about now. Such possibilities aside, the more people realize that many outcomes of the future are not magical but planned and imagined years in advance and brought into being, the more I hope people demand to be included. Beyond transparency, there is a potential for action—for the public to become active in the construction and execution of their futures.

ACTION

Action consists of the concrete steps the industry, its stakeholders, and the public more generally can take to bring about meaningfully alternative futures.

Within the trend industry itself, top of mind is diversity and inclusion— not just a display of difference in staffing and output but the full embrace of distinct modes of being and the support for counterinstitutions that arise to fill gaps the trend industry cannot. Hiring more people of color, younger and older people, people of all abilities, people of all genders and sexualities, and people from different class and national backgrounds needs to happen, but it will not happen without conscious effort. Taking a cue from other industries, trend companies can sponsor internship programs, fellowships, volunteer positions, and enriched recruitment efforts that are mindful not only of what people represent but of the perspectives these people bring to the table. In turn, firms must continue to diversify in terms of methodologies, approaches to the future, and questions that defy the narrow, cosmopolitan viewpoints that often dominate in trend shops. As trend forecasting extends around a globe that contains myriad notions of futures, forecasters must be careful not to crowd out local ways of thinking and doing, not all of which are amenable to Western ideation. Forecasting businesses also must broaden whom they turn toward for guidance, outside advisement, and opinion—for instance, making sure their advisory board and expert lists reflect a wide range of people and perspectives.

One strategy for building a multicultural corps of people who are well-suited to do trend work is to pay spotter network participants. Turning these occasional contributors into something akin to freelancers or part-time employees raises quandaries about hiring, management, and cost that certainly don't have easy answers. My focus here, though, is on the positive effects it could have for those workers and for the greater industry. Beyond the inherent virtue in paying people for labor, it might create more dedicated spotters, more potential to cultivate leadership, and a bigger pool of potential job candidates, all of which enhance the stated purpose of these networks to monitor culture across the globe. Paid spotters may eventually start their own companies, which would create more competition, but it would also unearth deeper understanding and spur innovation in the sector.

Beyond the industry, any activism that is geared toward change and movement is already concerned with the future. Likewise, citizens frequently think about what the future holds for them in ways both profound and mundane. None of these things need disappear or be replaced; they do important work. That said, the methods, frames, and systems developed within the trends industry harbor great potential to enhance, accentuate, and push for a broad-based, activist-oriented futurism. Furthermore, the future can become more demonstrably a site of discussion and debate in ways that parallel how societies tend to think about history.

Good models of such action already exist. As I discussed in chapter 6, Afrofuturism has given rise to initiatives, community events, campaigns, and artistic endeavors that combine futurist thinking with social change. Another model worth emulating is the Real Future Fair that took place in Oakland in 2015 and 2016. The gathering, sponsored by Fusion.net, brought everyday citizens in conversation with people working to enact intersectional futures. Strategic foresight increasingly is used across the NGO, nonprofit, and philanthropic sectors in many parts of the world to complement but also contest the corporate use of futures—Trista Harris's *FutureGood: How to Use Futurism to Save the World* is a useful primer on how these practices are taking shape. And both the Institute for the Future and the Association for Professional Futurists have helped to foster conversation and community among people who work on the humanitarian application of future techniques. It is an exciting time for those interested in finding ways to use trends and futures for social good.

Yet there is still a lot more that could be done. Imagine an immigrant rights organization that is not just working on a series of campaigns but also engaging in environmental scanning or scenarios in order to assist its efforts two to three years out. Imagine an antiprison organization that keeps in mind trends in automation, artificial intelligence, and gender identity in order to frame its policy asks or public campaigns. Surely some of this is already happening, both formally and informally, in ways I can't possibly account for here. My point is simply that there is power in democratization of these ways of thinking and that we should think of the application for trends as going well beyond the consumer sphere. As Quinsy Gario and Zwarte Pieteis Racisme have emphatically shown in the Netherlands, these are strategic methods that can be used to question power as much as they can be used to fortify it.

EDUCATION

Education underlies both transparency and action. General awareness of trends and futures can increase through all levels of schooling, as well as through journalism, public programs, and public service campaigns. There are again numerous opportunities both within and beyond the trend industry, as well as useful collaborations between them. I've highlighted just a few ideas below.

I've already mentioned the rebirth of future studies, which is enjoying a moment amid renewed popular attention to the future. Some of this attention is due simply to the proliferating use of language about the future to ask and answer questions or frame research (cue "The Future of X" conferences/papers/etc.). More often than not, some of this interest considers the future as little more than a period of time. Beyond this rhetorical vogue, though, we are also witnessing the emergence of a critical future studies, a field that Luke Goode and Michael Godhe suggest "investigates the scope and constraints within public culture for imagining and debating different potential futures."[8] The idea behind critical future studies is that the frames we use to discuss the future are powerfully constitutive of the futures that then come to pass; critically engaging with and revising these frames can promote substantively different futures. Critical future studies also challenges the perspectives on the future that dominate in many developed consumer economies, where the powerful decree what the future will be, and alternatives seldom gain traction.[9]

The university is an obvious site for the increase in education around trends and futures. Practitioner-based classes in trends already take place at some institutions for higher learning around the world, but these could expand. In addition, critical futurist studies could both be integrated into applied education and proliferate throughout the disciplines. University administrative units could also learn a lot by embracing trends and futurist thinking at all levels—especially since some futurists eagerly predict the demise of universities. The regrowth of futurology and trend research academically can also extend into primary and secondary education, as Erica Bol's Teach the Future well demonstrates.

More critical insights around the future can also take root outside the university. Public programming about the future through community groups and churches, municipalities and small businesses is a great way to carry out this process. If a pub hosts a discussion about the future of the city, it can be an opportunity to generate ideas and raise grievances couched within some of the techniques of trend forecasting and futurism. Churches could hold workshops on how to observe the changing dynamics of religion; schools can host seminars about education in 2050. The Long Now Foundation, based in the Bay Area, provides an inspirational blueprint for how long-term thinking techniques might be shared with a wider audience.

Conclusion

The ideas I have shared here add up to what I call "public futures." This isn't a new idea. The futurism that emerged in the United States and elsewhere in the 1960s and 1970s, a time when many truly believed the future to be infinite, sparked tremendous interest in the utopian and liberatory possibilities of the future.[10] Likewise, that era's futurism had a strong public sensibility and focused on infusing government agencies, building educational programs, and working within communities. Some countries have maintained these futurist entities, to great effect. However, in the United States, many of these structures fell away in the ensuing decades, and the ones that did remain often lost their futurist identity, turned their interest toward private entrepreneurialism, or both. If we make it so, the public spirit for the future can rise again.

I've spoken repeatedly in this book about how trends allow us to witness the future as it unfolds, and that holds true for public futures as well. Despite the lock on certain kinds of future imagining in the private sector and by powerful interests, there is also the whole world of dreams, imaginations, behaviors, and practices unfolding in public view. Being observant of that world and using its signals to address human needs is one way that anyone can become more futurist in their thinking and acting. No matter our walk of life, we can begin to think of trends not as things that happen to us but as things we accept or reject, things we manifest and enact—which gets us that much closer to investing and shaping our future.

To that end, as an educator at a public university, I have started bringing these concepts into my classroom. In the fall of 2018, I taught a class on trends in which my students learned trend forecasting methods, critically assessed futures practice, and created locally based trend content. When I started the class, I had high hopes that the students would do research that could help anyone who can't afford traditional trend content. But I have been humbled to discover that that is only a small part of what they have achieved. My amazing, bright, and engaged students have become bona fide trend watchers who get excited thinking and strategizing about the future but who also will not settle for the assumptions about it that have been handed down to them. It has been my great honor to teach and learn from them, and I hope others emulate what we've done. If this is interesting to you, I encourage you to reach out, share ideas, or follow my work on the website, public-futures.com.

Interview Subjects

First name	Last name	Country	Company	Interview date
Don	Abraham	USA	The Futures Company	January 2016
Hayley	Ard	UK	Stylus	June 2016
Zeynep	Arhorn	Turkey/USA	TRENDDESK	October 2016
Clem	Bezold	USA	Institute for Alternative Futures	July 2016
Erica	Bol	Netherlands	Teach the Future	July 2018
Maja	Bosch	Netherlands	Futureconsult	June 2017
Claire	Brooks	UK	ModelPeople	May 2017
Lonny J. Avi	Brooks	USA	California State University, East Bay	July 2018
Jane	Buckingham	USA	Trendera	April 2017
Lourenço	Bustani	Brazil	Mandalah	September 2017
Max	Celko	Germany	Consulting	April 2016
Nia	Christy	Singapore	TrendWatching	June 2018
Kendra	Clarke	USA	Sparks & Honey	March 2018
Sarah	Davanzo	USA	Sparks & Honey	February 2016
Sem	Devillart	USA	Freelance	July 2016
Els	Dragt	Netherlands	Fontys University of Applied Sciences	June 2017
Alida	Draudt	USA	Strategic Foresight Partners	October 2016
Reinier	Evers	Netherlands	TrendWatching	June 2017
Piers	Fawkes	USA	PSFK	February 2016
Quinsy	Gario	Netherlands	Artist	June 2017
Ted (Theodore)	Gordon	USA	Millennium Project	March 2016
Dan	Gould	USA	Google	June 2016

First name	Last name	Country	Company	Interview date
Will	Higham	UK	Next Big Thing	June 2016
Andy	Hines	USA	University of Houston	February 2016
Kiwa	Iyobe	USA	Freelance	June 2016
Robin	Keeris	Netherlands	Mindcraft	June 2017
Scott	Lachut	USA	PSFK	July 2016
Lieke	Lamb	Netherlands	Trendsverwachting	June 2017
Richard	Lamb	Netherlands	Trendsverwachting	July 2017
Margriet	Larmit	Netherlands	Mindcraft	June 2017
Shepherd	Laughlin	USA	JWT Intelligence	June 2016
Sharon	Lee	USA	CultureBrain	August 2017
Patrick	Lodge	UK	Breaking Trends	June 2016
Max	Luthy	USA	TrendWatching	February 2016
Alexis	Madrigal	USA	Fusion	November 2015
Justien	Marseilles	Netherlands	The Future Institute	July 2017
Avery	McCaffrey	USA	PSFK	June 2018
Ari	Melenciano	USA	NYU Interactive Telecommunications Program	April 2018
Katharina	Michalski	Germany/UK	Consulting	June 2016
Nils	Müller	Germany	TrendOne	December 2017
Katindi Sivi	Njonjo	Kenya	LongView Consult	July 2018
Mphathi	Nyewe	South Africa	Foresight Strategies	July 2018
Florence	Okoye	UK	Afro Futures UK	March 2018
Ayodamola	Okunseinde	USA	Artist	April 2018
Stephan	Paschalides	USA	Now Plus One	June 2016
Katharine	Pegg	UK	Stylus	June 2016
MJ	Petroni	USA	Causeit	August 2016
Faith	Popcorn	USA	BrainReserve	January and March 2016
Hannah	Robinson	UK	The Future Laboratory	June 2016
Carl	Rohde	Netherlands	Science of the Time	June 2017
Hilde	Roothart	Netherlands	Trendslator	June 2017
Eurydice	Sanchez	USA	LIM College	March 2016
Mark	Schipper	Netherlands	freshmark	December 2017
Janet	Siroto	USA	BrainReserve	January 2016
Gregory	Skinner	Canada/USA	MORPACE International	April 2017
J. Walker	Smith	USA	The Futures Company	February 2016
Nanon	Soeters	Netherlands	ROZENBROOD	June 2017
Cecily	Sommers	USA	Consulting	August 2016
Marie	Stafford	UK	JWT London	June 2017
Farid	Tabarki	Netherlands	Studio Zeitgeist	July 2017
Jason	Tester	USA	Institute for the Future	November 2016
Jody	Turner	USA	Culture of Future	January 2016
Caroline	van Beekhoff	Netherlands	C-MarketingStrategie	June 2017
Peter	van Der Wel	Netherlands	FutureVision	June 2017
Freija	van Duijne	Netherlands	Future Motions	June 2017
Jacomine	Van Veen	Netherlands	Likely	June 2017
Henrik	Vejlgaard	Denmark	Consulting	February 2017
Edie	Weiner	USA	The Future Hunters	April 2016
Baysie	Wightman	USA	Hill Holiday	April 2016
David	Wolfe	USA	The Doneger Group	January 2016
Dena	Yago	USA	Consulting	July 2018
Terry	Young	USA	Sparks & Honey	February 2016

Notes

Introduction

1. This depiction is a collage based on three visits I made to the Sparks & Honey offices during 2016 and 2018. The quotations are taken from the Sparks & Honey website from March 2016. The website has since been updated (https://www.sparks andhoney.com/).

2. This depiction is a composite from Daily Cultural Briefings I attended on three separate occasions: March 4, 2016; May 4, 2016; and June 26, 2018.

3. These quotations are taken from the March 4, 2016, briefing.

4. Terry Young, interview with the author, February 2016.

5. Gillespie, "#trendingistrending," 67.

6. Kornbluth, "Now You See It."

7. Peters, *Digital Keywords*, xv.

8. *Oxford English Dictionary*, "trend"; Raymond, *Handbook*, 14.

9. President's Research Committee on Social Trends, *Recent Social Trends*, v.

10. "Business World," *New York Times*, August 26, 1924.

11. Altehenger, Abu-Er-Rub, and Gehrig, "The Transcultural Travels."

12. Levy, "The Drug of Choice."

13. Future Laboratory, "Backlash Culture," unpublished report, London, 2016, 1.

14. Scott Lachut, interview with the author, July 2016.

15. Goode and Godhe, "Beyond Capitalist Realism," 110.

16. Govindarajan, "Planned Opportunism," 56.

17. Koselleck, *Futures Past*, 3.

18. Cornish, *Study*, 83.

19. Featherstone, "Lifestyle," 56, 65–66.

20. Future Hunters website, https://thefuturehunters.com/.

21. Future Hunters, "Work Here, Work Gone: A New Framework," report, New York, 2018, 3; "The New Earthly Epoch," report, New York, 2018.

22. Piers Fawkes, interview with the author, February 2016.

23. Stephan Paschalides, interview with the author, June 2016.

24. Mackay, *Extraordinary*, xx.

25. Le Bon, *Crowd*, 2, 11.

26. Tarde, *Laws*, 11, 17.

27. Riesman, *Lonely*, 21, 78.

28. Katz and Lazarsfeld, *Personal*, 7, 10.

29. Gladwell, *Tipping*, 7.

30. Chun, *Updating*, 25, 26.

31. Ibid., 39.

Chapter 1. Trending

1. Arrington, "Google"; Hansell, "Google Shows."

2. "Twitter Trends."

3. McCarthy, "Twitter CEO."

4. Gillespie, "#trendingistrending," 69.

5. Feldman, "It's Time."

6. Gillespie, "#trendingistrending," 70.

7. Scott-Jones and Watt, "Ethnography," 14–15.

8. Bulmer, "Chicago School."

9. Fletcher, "Significance," 445.

10. For example, see MacLean, "Factory"; Ward, "Utilitarian"; Veblen, "Instinct."

11. Stigler, *History*, 194.

12. Hacking, *Taming*, 1.

13. Ross, *Origins*, 54.

14. Giddings, "Measurement," 1.

15. Ogburn, "Fluctuations," 74.

16. Cobb and Rixford, "Lessons," 5; Porter, *Trust*, 37.

17. Porter, *Trust*, 45.

18. President's Research Committee on Social Trends, *Recent Social Trends*, xiii.

19. Dewey, "Social," 340.

20. Not everyone shared Dewey's optimism about the utility of information. Lillian Symes in "Fact Finding Farce," a February 1932 article in *Harper's*, complained that "since we became sold on what we believe to be the scientific method, the accumulation of facts as a substitute, rather than as a basis for collective action, has become a national gospel" (354).

21. Ross, *Origins*, 7, 8.

22. Quoted in Bulmer, "Methodology," 127.

23. Levenson, *Modernism*, 9.

24. Berman, *All*, 16.

25. Jameson, *Postmodernism*, 310.

26. "Editorial Study," *Trend*, October 2011, 94.

27. Friedman, *Fortune Tellers*, x.

28. Pietruska, *Looking Forward*, 2.

29. Pietruska, "US Weather Bureau," 80.

30. Ibid., 91.

31. Monmonier, *Air Apparent*, 15.

32. C. E. P. Brooks, "Secular Variation."

33. Quoted in Pietruska, *Looking Forward*, 192.

34. Moore, "Economic."

35. Pietruska, *Looking Forward*, 192–98.

36. Friedman, *Fortune Tellers*, 6–7, 181–85.

37. Roy Epstein notes that econometrics allowed "mathematically oriented economists" to explore "the possibilities of using linear differential and difference equations to simulate trend and cyclical movement of times series" (*History*, 47).

38. Porter, *Trust*, 43.

39. Altehenger, "Transcultural."

40. Williams, *Keywords*, 90; see also Hegeman, *Patterns for America*.

41. Benedict, *Patterns*, 49; Mead, preface, vii.

42. Benedict, *Patterns*, 10.

43. Susman, *Culture as History*, 154.

44. Benedict, *Patterns*, 46.

45. Ibid.

46. Igo, *Averaged American*.

47. Barnett, *Innovation*, 14–15.

48. Jewell, "National Academy," 15.

49. "Individuation," *New York Times*, January 5, 1935.

50. See "Short Waves from Afar," *New York Times*, February 21, 1937; White, "Chinatown Turns West"; Horwill, "News and Views"; and Crowther, "Length vs. Strength."

51. "Office Building Outlook," *New York Times*, June 23, 1940.

52. Kozinets and Handelman, "Adversaries of Consumption," 692.

53. Kammen, *American Culture*, 53.

54. McGovern, *Sold American*, 126.

55. Lears, *Fables*, 160.

56. Arendt, *Crisis in Culture*.

57. Douglas, *Listening In*, 5.

58. Kammen, *American Culture*, 75.

59. Gates, "Radio," 13.

60. Rubin, *Making of Middlebrow*, 1, 17–18; Hegeman, *Patterns for America*, 129.

61. Kammen, *American Culture*, 74; Levine, *Highbrow/Lowbrow*, 221–22.

62. Rubin, *Making of Middlebrow*; Hegeman, *Patterns for America*.

63. Arvidsson "On the Pre-history," 461; Schwarzkopf, "In Search," 71.

64. Cherington, "Statistics," 130, 133.

65. Ibid., 133.

66. See Cohen, *Consumers' Republic*.

67. Patsiaouras and Fitchett, "Evolution," 155–56.

68. Veblen, *Theory*, 19, 20.

69. Patsiaouras and Fitchett, "Evolution," 160.

70. Webb and Shawver, "Critical Examination," 23; Patsiaouras and Fitchett, "Evolution," 159.

71. Patsiaouras and Fitchett, "Evolution," 160.

72. Lazarsfeld, "The Art," 27–28.

73. Matt, *Keeping Up*, 5.

74. President's Research Committee on Social Trends, *Recent Social Trends*, 878.

75. Blaszczyk, *Color Revolution*, 8.

76. Blaszczyk, "Rise of Color Forecasting," 39.

77. Blaszczyk, *Color Revolution*, 70.

78. Blaszczyk, "Rise of Color Forecasting," 42.

79. Blaszczyk and Wubs, *The Fashion Forecasters*, 14–15.

Chapter 2. Thinking in Trends

1. Geist, "One Step," B4.

2. Popcorn, *Popcorn Report*, 12.

3. Dougherty, "BrainReserve Taps."

4. Faith Popcorn, interview with the author, March 2016.

5. Popcorn used the term "applied futurism" during our interview.

6. Toffler, "The Future," 109.

7. Toffler, *Future Shock*, 9, 35, 486–87.

8. Van de Kamp, "How We Can Cope."

9. Spielvogel, "Former Advertising Columnist."

10. This is a sample of the many letters Toffler received about the impact of *Future Shock* after its publication. See Arch Patton to Alvin Toffler, August 11, 1971, box 10, folder August; R. Phillip Hanes Jr. to Alvin Toffler, January 13, 1971, box 9, folder January; and Lloyd W. Singer to Alvin Toffler, January 20, 1971, box 45, folder EVR—Motorola; all in Alvin and Heidi Toffler Papers, Rare Books and Manuscripts Library, Columbia University.

11. Green, "Blue Funk," 69, emphasis original.

12. Friedman, *Fortune Tellers*, 1.

13. Williams, "World Futures," 1.

14. Beer quoted in ibid., 25.

15. Toffler, "The Future," 115.

16. On the increasing power of management consultants, see Kiechel, *Lords of Strategy*, 1–9, 21; McKenna, *World's Newest Profession*, 5, 147, 210–11.

17. Bradfield et al., "Origins and Evolution," 797, 800; Turner, *From Counterculture*, 186.

18. Jonker et al., *History*, 16; Bradfield et al., "Origins and Evolution," 799–800.

19. Kleiner, *Age of Heretics*, 123–24.

20. Ibid., 142–47; Turner, *From Counterculture*, 187.

21. Kleiner, *Age of Heretics*, 153.

22. Gordon and Helmer-Hirschberg, *Report*, v.

23. Ted Gordon, interview with the author, March 2016.

24. Gordon, "Forecasters"; "Industry Study Foresees Educational Institutions Dominant in United States," *Futurist*, February 1969, 17; North and Pyke, "'Probes.'"

25. Jouvenel, *Art of Conjecture*, 5.

26. Scott, *Long-Range Planning*, 105.

27. Daniel Bell, one of the most prominent figures in the application of futures thinking to social science, was also a strong proponent of trends. He argued that trends in the economy, society, and culture were often interlocking and causal and proposed that the tools of prediction could be used to steer society toward desirable results. See Andersson, *The Future*, 98–104.

28. Opinion Research Corporation, *America's Tastemakers*, 1.

29. Opinion Research Corporation, *America's Tastemakers No. 2*, 2.

30. Opinion Research Corporation, *America's Tastemakers*; Opinion Research Corporation, *America's Tastemakers No. 2*, 53.

31. Shaw and Jones, "A History," 256.

32. McNair, "How to Sell," 81.

33. Sheth, "A Review"; Yankelovich, "New Criteria."

34. McNair, "Plan Your Department Store."

35. Wells, *Life Style*, v, 15.

36. Cohen, *A Consumers' Republic*, 315–31; Binkley, *Getting Loose*, 89.

37. Cohen, *A Consumers' Republic*, 294–96.

38. Weiss, "Today's Consumer," 39.

39. Katz, Levin, and Hamilton, "Traditions of Research," 238–39.

40. Krugman and Hartley, "The Learning," 622.

41. Katz and Lazarsfeld, *Personal Influence*, 27.

42. Rogers, *Diffusion*, 19.

43. In 1969 Frank M. Bass's article "A New Product Growth for Model Consumer Durables" in the journal *Management Science* helped to build an interest in diffusion within the field of marketing science, the more quantitative manifestation of marketing study. Bass's work drew from Rogers and from Katz and Lazarsfeld to quantitatively model the diffusion process. See Muller, "Innovation Diffusion," 77.

44. Wasson, "How Predictable," 43.

45. Blumer, "Fashion," 276.

46. Blaszczyk, *Color Revolution*; Brannon, *Fashion Forecasting*; see also chapter 1.

47. David Wolfe, interview with the author, January 2016.

48. Cohen, *A Consumers' Republic*, 299–309.

49. Faith Popcorn and Janet Siroto, interview with the author, January 2016.

50. Dougherty, "Advertising"; Fox, "Leo Greenland."

51. Popcorn interview, March 2016.

52. Popcorn and Siroto interview.

53. Tyler, "The New Creativity," 41.

54. Frank, *The Conquest of Cool*, 49, 53–61, 96–97.

55. Ibid., 97.

56. Faith Popcorn and Stuart Pittman to American Tobacco Company, May 8, 1975, Industry Documents Library, University of California, San Francisco.

57. Popcorn interview.

58. Brouilette, "Creative Labor."

59. Popcorn and Pittman to American Tobacco Company.

60. Dougherty, "BrainReserve Taps."

61. Ibid.

62. Popcorn and Siroto interview.

63. Hudson Institute, *The Hudson Institute Report* (1969), 1, 41–46; Hudson Institute, *The Hudson Institute Report* (1970), 41–44.

64. Bradfield et al. "Origins and Evolution," 799; "Institute for the Future Will Begin Operations in Connecticut This Fall," *Futurist*, August 1968, 65–67.

65. Bradfield et al., "Origins and Evolution," 799; Turner, *From Counterculture*, 184–85.

66. Gordon, "Future of Futurists," 322.

67. Edith Weiner, Harold Edrich, and Arnold Brown, Trend Analysis (TAP) reports, undated, p. 3, Weiner, Edrich, and Brown Papers, Hagley Museum and Library, Wilmington, DE.

68. Brown and Weiner, *Supermanaging*, 7.

69. Edie Weiner, interview with the author, April 2016.

70. Traub, "Futurology," 28. In one passage, journalist James Traub explained how the Institute of the Future created a "10-year forecast" that determined that "an increasing proportion of males may not wear underpants because trousers can be washed easily and often" (ibid., 25).

71. Daniells, *Business Forecasting*, 20.

72. Ibid., 20–21; Bradfield et al., "Origins and Evolution," 801.

73. Future Options Room, undated, box 46, folder Projects—Companies/Orgs: Future Options Room, 1975–78, Toffler Papers.

74. Weiner interview; Daniells, *Business Forecasting*, 20–21.

75. "The New York Times Information Bank," advertisement, *New York Times*, September 10, 1974.

76. Futuremics, Inc., press release, April 11, 1975, box 45, folder Projects—Companies/Orgs: Futuremics, Toffler Papers.

77. Bourdieu, "The Production," 76.

78. Urban, *Metaculture*, 4.

79. Abrams, "John Naisbitt."

80. Willard and Lawler, "Megachoices."

81. Naisbitt, *Megatrends*, 2–5.

82. Barmash, "Inside Consumers' Minds."

83. Faith Popcorn, interview with the author, March 2016.

84. McKibben, "Eager," 22.

85. Miller, "Putting Faith in Trends."

86. Popcorn interview, March 2016.

87. BrainReserve, "Quaker, Ken-L-Ration, Love Me Tender Chunks," unpublished report, 1985, New York; and BrainReserve, "The Future of Fast Food," unpublished report, 1987, New York.

88. Popcorn, *Popcorn Report*, 25, 34, 37.

89. Ibid., 100, 13, 22, 190–93, 197.

90. "Trend Spotting on Madison Avenue," *Futurist*, April 1992, 45.

91. Shalit, "The Business of Faith," 23.

92. Tanaka, "Futurism."

Chapter 3. Cool Hunting

1. Dinerstein, *Origins of Cool*, 4.

2. Pountain and Robins, *Cool Rules*, 19; Schor, *Born to Buy*, 47–48.

3. Winick, "Anthropology's Contributions."

4. Field, "Status Float," 46.

5. Scott and Marshall, *Dictionary of Sociology*.

6. Hebdige, *Subculture*, 17, 95, 94.

7. Graeber, "Consumption," 490.

8. Arnould and Thompson, "Consumer Culture Theory," 868.

9. Schouten and McAlexander, "Subcultures of Consumption," 52, 49.

10. Spiegler, "Marketing Street Culture," 29–30.

11. Hollander and Germain, *Was There a Pepsi Generation*, 11; Bogart, *Over the Edge*, x.

12. Ross, introduction, 9.

13. Frank, *Conquest of Cool*, ix–x.

14. "Mr. Cool: An Interview with Tom Frank," *Advertising Age*, November 6, 2000.

15. Jane Buckingham, interview with the author, April 2017.

16. Quote is taken from Rinzler's book's subtitle. See also Rifkin, "Generation X's Mind"; Buckingham interview.

17. Gianastasio, "Houston, Agency Founder"; Rifkin, "Generation X's Mind."

18. Gianastasio, "Houston, Agency Founder"; Buckingham interview.

19. Buckingham interview; Gladwell, "Coolhunt," 85; Grossman, "Quest for Cool."

20. Buckingham interview.

21. Gregory Skinner, interview with the author, April 2017.

22. Ibid.

23. Ibid.

24. Azam, "Cool Huntings."

25. Baba, "Anthropology and Business," 55; Ferraro and Briody, *Cultural Dimension*, 6.

26. Lewin, "Casting"; Graeber, "Consumption," 490.

27. Alsop, "People Watchers"; Foltz, "New Species."

28. Foltz, "New Species."

29. Baba, "Anthropology," 56.

30. De Waal Malefyt, "Understanding," 204.

31. Sherry, "Business," 27.

32. Sharon Lee, interview with the author, August 2017.

33. Lopiano-Misdom and De Luca, *Street Trends*, xi.

34. Luvaas, *Street Style*, 44.

35. Pedroni, "Coolhunting."

36. Ethnographers and anthropologists often contest what does or doesn't count as ethnography. My objective in using this term is not to wade into or enflame these debates. Rather, I am using ethnography rhetorically to explain the motivations behind forecasters' use of in-person and multisite research. Ethnography connotes the objective to observe consumers "where they are" and takes for granted the meaningfulness of place. In chapter 5 I go into more detail about the importance of place to trend work. In addition, distributed ethnography shares certain commonalities with George Marcus's concept of multisited ethnography, but distributed ethnography is carried out by multiple people in multiple sites rather than one or a team of researchers seeking out patterns in multiple sites. See Marcus, "Ethnography," 106–13.

37. Preston, "Malcolm Gladwell Interview."

38. Gladwell, "Coolhunt," 78.

39. Ibid., 78, 87, 87–88.

40. Ibid., 84.

41. Builk, "Cool Hunting Goes Corporate."

42. Southgate, "Coolhunting with Aristotle," 167.

43. Reese, "Quality"; *New York Observer*, February 28, 2005.

44. La Ferla, "Once Hot, Now Not."

45. Gibson, *Pattern Recognition*, 86.

46. *New York Observer*, February 28, 2005.

47. Fleming, "In Search of Cool."

48. Furchgott, "For Coolhunters."

49. La Ferla, "Once Hot, Now Not."

50. Pearce, "As the Centre."

51. Drezner, *Ideas Industry*, 11, 13.

52. Klein, *No Logo*, 72.

53. Here I am referencing the debates that unfolded over the middle of the twentieth century regarding the cultural role of intellectuals. For a characteristic example, see Jacoby, *The Last Intellectuals,* or the special issue "Our Country and Our Culture," *Partisan Review* 19, no. 3 (1952).

54. Lee interview.

55. Ibid.

Chapter 4. Trends, Inc.

1. "Extreme provenance," or the tendency toward hyperlocalism, has been identified by Sparks & Honey as a contemporary trend. See Sparks & Honey, "Extreme Provenance," https://reports.sparksandhoney.com/campaign/extreme-povenance

2. Mapp, "Day in the Life."

3. Davis, "They See the Future"; Raymond, *The Trend Forecaster's Handbook*, 128.

4. From the Future Laboratory website as of July 2018.

5. Hannah Robinson, interview with the author, June 2016.

6. Raymond, *The Trend Forecaster's Handbook*, 44.

7. Robinson interview.

8. Mason, Kjellberg, and Hagberg, "Exploring," 10.

9. Raymond, *The Trend Forecaster's Handbook*, 50.

10. Vejlgaard, *Anatomy of a Trend*, 7, emphasis in the original.

11. Cecily Sommers, interview with the author, August 2016.

12. Marie Stafford, interview with the author, June 2016.

13. Stephan Paschalides, interview with the author, June 2016.

14. Kiwa Iyobe, interview with the author, June 2016.

15. Hayley Ard, interview with the author, June 2016.

16. Scott Lachut, interview with the author, July 2016.

17. Max Luthy, interview with the author, February 2016.

18. Andrejevic, *Infoglut*, 2, emphasis in the original.

19. Ibid.; Striphas, "Algorithmic Culture," 397.

20. Dan Gould, interview with the author, June 2016.

21. Andrejevic, *Infoglut*, 4.

22. Williams, "Analysis of Culture," 47.

23. Brown, *Change by Design,* 49, 37, 70.

24. Bishop, "Pattern Recognition," 1.

25. The innate humanity of pattern recognition contradicts the rise of artificial intelligence within trend forecasting, which I discuss later in this chapter and in chapter 6. Some forecasters have emphasized that machines are capable of finding cultural patterns but cannot explain or interpret them.

26. Piers Fawkes, interview with the author, February 2016.

27. Stafford interview.

28. Gould interview.

29. Sarah Davanzo, interview with the author, February 2016.

30. Future Laboratory, *American Middle*, 11, 18.

31. JWT Intelligence, *Food + Drink 2017*, 2, 12, 16, 18, 38.

32. Beer, *Metric Power*, 9.

33. Callon, Méadel, and Rabeharisoa, "The Economy of Qualities," 199.

34. Lachut interview.

35. Fawkes interview.

36. Dragt, *How to Research Trends*, 108.

37. Ibid., 116, 117.

38. Raymond, *The Trend Forecaster's Handbook*, 47.

39. Van Leeuwen and Jewitt, *Handbook of Visual Analysis*, 1.

40. Patrick Lodge, interview with the author, June 2016.

41. "Five Consumer Trends for 2017," retrieved at https://trendwatching.com/trends/5-trends-for-2017/?utm_campaign=Content+Team+-+Publications&utm_source=hs_email&utm_medium=email&utm_content=37871984&_hsenc=p2ANqtz-826fWjCVeRw9be1ky7dFfqF8xpgvxM6T_0yR1MnsCkup3V4xEBg0xTxhcvm4n0OA76A0yLR1kcKdWPGOMnwc0KMfXN9w&_hsmi=37871985.

42. Stafford interview.

43. Davanzo interview.

44. See http://twin.trendwatching.com/.

45. Luthy interview.

46. Sem Devillart, interview with the author, July 2016.

47. Justien Marseilles, interview with the author, June 2017.

48. Taken from Sparks & Honey's SlideShare, "UnMoney," retrieved at https://www.slideshare.net/sparksandhoney/unmoney-the-value-of-everything.

49. These names are trends from the following companies: Sparks & Honey, the Future Hunters, Futures Group, JWT Intelligence, and BrainReserve. For more on "roboromance," see Popcorn, "Four Survival Trends."

50. "The Status Seekers," *Economist*, December 2, 2010, retrieved July 9, 2018, https://www.economist.com/business/2010/12/02/the-status-seekers.

51. Katharina Michalski, interview with the author, June 2016.

52. Edie Weiner, interview with the author, April 2016.

53. Davanzo interview.

54. Shepherd Laughlin, interview with the author, June 2016.

55. Dragt, *How to Research Trends*, 124.

56. Dale, "Confessions."

57. Dena Yago, email interview with the author, July 2018.

58. Sacks, "That's a Total K-Hole."

59. K-Hole, *Youth Mode*, 28.

60. Sacks, "That's a Total K-Hole."

61. Dena Yago, interview with the author.

62. Luthy interview.

63. Dumitrescu et al., *Trend-Driven Innovation,* 8.

64. Luthy interview.

65. Clark and Salaman, "Telling Tales," 181.

66. IAB Italia, "IAB Forum 2016."

67. Marantz, "Crystal Ball."

68. Slater, "Marketing as a Monstrosity," 35.

69. Ibid.; McFall, *Advertising*, 9–13.

70. McCracken, *Chief Culture Officer*, 1, 13.

71. Earley and Mosakowski, "Cultural Intelligence."

72. Terry Young, interview with the author, February 2016.

73. McKenna, "The Origins," 52–56.

74. McKenna, *The World's Newest Profession*; McKenna, "Strategy."

75. McKenna, "Strategy," 161; McKenna, *The World's Newest Profession,* 11. See also Fincham, "The Consultant-Client Relationship."

76. Fincham, "The Consultant-Client Relationship," 336.

77. Ard interview.

78. PSFK, *Consumer 2020*, 4, 9, 10.

79. Taylor, "Corporate Social Science."

80. Fawkes interview.

81. Janet Siroto, interview with the author, January 2016.

82. Drezner, *Ideas Industry*, 162.

83. Holt and Cameron, *Cultural Strategy*, 22.

84. Jacomine Van Veen, interview with the author, June 2017.

85. Siroto interview.

86. Don Abraham, interview with the author, January 2016.

Chapter 5. Global Futurity

1. Reinier Evers, interview with the author, June 2017.

2. Ibid.

3. Ibid.

4. Altehenger, Abu-Er-Rub, and Gehrig, "The Transcultural Travels."

5. Kotz, "Globalization."

6. Barbrook and Cameron, "The Californian Ideology." The Californian ideology is named after the unique mix of technological utopianism, bohemianism, and libertarianism that is common within Silicon Valley.

7. Friedman, "Did Dubai Do It?"

8. Andersson, "The Great Future Debate."

9. Andersson and Duhautois, "Futures of Mankind," 105, 107.

10. Andersson, *The Future*, 17, 152–53.

11. Saval, "Globalisation."

12. Tsing, "The Global Situation," 330.

13. Nils Müller, interview with the author, December 2017.

14. For more information, see Dubai Future Accelerators at https://dubaifuture accelerators.com/en. All quotes taken from the website.

15. "Bizarre Attractions," *Economist*, September 11, 1999.

16. Nordland, "Welcome to Dubai"; Davis, "Fear and Money."

17. Davis, "Fear and Money," 53.

18. Kanna, *Dubai*, xiii, 7.

19. Ibid., 6.

20. Marantz, "Dubai."

21. Blum, "Oil Won't Last Forever."

22. Schouwenberg, "It's About Time."

23. Fairs, "Good Design."

24. Benoist, "A Brief History," 7–9.

25. Eagleton, *Hope without Optimism,* 4–5.

26. Krier and Gilette, "Un-easy Case," 406.

27. Morozov, *To Save Everything*, 5.

28. Barbrook and Cameron, "The Californian Ideology"; John, "Sharing and Web 2.0"; Van Dijck, *The Culture of Connectivity*.

29. Nanon Soeters, interview with the author, June 2017.

30. *TrendRede 2016*, 8, retrieved May 12, 2018, http://trendrede.nl/wp-content/uploads/2016/01/def.-Trendrede2016-NL.pdf.

31. Lieke Lamb, interview with the author, June 2017.

32. Els Dragt, interview with the author, June 2017.

33. Mark Schipper, interview with the author, December 2017.

34. Ribeiro, "Cosmopolitanism," 2842.

35. Calhoun, "The Class Consciousness," 890.

36. Coates, *Why the Dutch*, 119.

37. Ibid., 3–5.

38. Jonker et al., *A History*, 222.

39. *Trendrede 2016*, 1.

40. Caroline van Beekhof, interview with the author, June 2017.

41. Richard Lamb, interview with the author, July 2017.

42. Teach the Future, "Futures Education Pilot NL."

43. Erica Bol, interview with the author, July 2018.

44. Hilde Roothart, interview with the author, June 2017.

45. Farid Tabarki, interview with the author, July 2017.

46. Webb, *Signals Are Talking*, 2.

47. Marie Stafford, interview with the author, June 2016.

48. Currid and Williams, "The Geography of Buzz," 428.

49. Kiwa Iyobe, interview with the author, June 2016.

50. Nia Christy, interview with the author, June 2018.

51. See, for example, TrendWatching's "Five Key Trends from the Design Indaba" from May 2018, https://trendwatching.com/trends/5-key-trends-design-indaba/; Stylus's "Food Influencer Roundup: Africa" from May 2017, http://www.stylus.com/kdgwjc; or JWT's "The Future 100 MENA: 2018 (Middle Ease—North Africa)," https://www.jwtintelligence.com/trend-reports/the-future-100-mena-2018/.

52. Mphathi Nyewe, email interview with the author, July 2018.

53. Katindi Sivi Njonjo, email interview with the author, July 2018.

54. Lourenço Bustani, email interview with the author, September 2017.

55. Müller interview.

56. Henrik Vejlgaard, interview with the author, February 2017.

57. Max Celko, interview with the author, April 2016.

58. Chan, *Networking Peripheries*, x.

59. Quinsy Gario, interview with the author, June 2017.

Chapter 6. Eventful Futures

1. Ayodamola Okunseinde, interview with the author, April 2018.

2. Brooks, "Playing," 149.

3. Vanderbilt, "Why Futurism."

4. Eveleth, "Why Aren't There More?"

5. Yaszek, "Afrofuturism," 42.

6. Eshun, "Further Considerations," 289, 301.

7. See the Innovation Group, "Genderless Retail, Vinotherapy and More," March 30, 2018, J. Walter Thompson Intelligence, retrieved July 14, 2018, https://www.jwtintelligence.com/2018/03/genderless-retail-vinotherapy/.

8. J. Walter Thompson Innovation Group, "The Future 100," 7, 2018, retrieved July 26, 2018, https://www.jwtintelligence.com/trend-reports/the-future-100-2018/.

9. Banet-Weiser and Mukherjee, "Commodity Activism," 10.

10. Thornton, *Club Cultures*; Frank, *The Conquest of Cool*; Klein, Meier, and Powers, "Selling Out."

11. Gray, "Subject(ed)," 771.

12. Sewell, "Historical Events," 843.

13. Wagner-Pacifici, *What Is an Event?*, 26.

14. Brooks, "Working," 122.

15. Dean, "Communicative Capitalism," 53, 56.

16. "Yes Means Yes," *Cassandra Daily*, email newsletter, April 18, 2018.

17. "The Sexual Mehvolution," *Cassandra Daily,* retrieved July 26, 2018, https://cassandra.co/2015/love/the-sexual-mehvolution.

18. Some trend companies do give away certain trend content for free. For example, some companies archive old reports and share them for free after a certain amount of time. Others prepare free reports on select topics or in partnership with other groups. I will discuss the idea of free reports more extensively in the conclusion.

19. The Futures Company later became Kantar Futures; Abraham left and as of 2018 works for Ipsos Strategy 3.

20. Don Abraham, interview with the author, January 2016.

21. Piers Fawkes, interview with the author, February 2016.

22. Cecily Sommers, interview with the author, August 2016.

23. Popcorn and Siroto, interview, January 2016.

24. Dean, "Communicative Capitalism," 59.

25. Future Laboratory, Workplace Summit Report, 8.

26. Future Laboratory, "The American Middle," 8; Future Laboratory, "The Age of Re-engagement," 9.

27. The Future Hunters, "The New Earthly Epoch," 1.

28. Future Laboratory, Workplace Summit Report, 8.

29. Sharma, *In the Meantime*, 18.

30. Brooks, "Playing," 155.

31. Florence Okoye, interview with the author, March 2018.

32. Gilroy, *Small Acts*, 178; Nelson, *The Social Life*, 3.

33. Lott, *Love and Theft*.

34. Okoye interview.

35. Nelson, "Future Texts."

36. Okoye interview.

37. Womack, *Afrofuturism*.

38. Nelson, "Future Texts," 2; Weyhelie, "Posthuman Voices," 23–24.

39. Eshun, "Further Considerations," 289.

40. Goddess, "Forethought," 7–8.

41. Nelson, *The Social Life*, 7.

42. Ibid., 162.

43. "Time Experiments," Black Quantum Press, Time Camp 001, September 30– October 1, 2017.

44. Newall, "In Sharswood."

45. Quoted in Burton, "Making Space."

46. Quoted in Womack, *Afrofuturism*, 154–55.

47. Dinerstein, "Technology," 570, emphasis original.

48. Eveleth, "Why Aren't There?"

49. See the Innovation Group, "Luxury Space Travel, AI Beauty Blends and More," *JWT Intelligence*, retrieved July 14, 2018, https://www.jwtintelligence.com/2018/06/luxury-space-travel-blend-it-yourself-beauty-and-more/.

50. In May 2018 TrendWatching issued a report about African design called "Five Key Trends from the Design Indaba." The report notes the inspirational power of Afrofuturism, making brief mention of how the concept concerns Africans "rewriting the socio-cultural and economic rulebook." Despite this gesture, the report is primarily focused on consumer brands and design and does not delve into the political affordances of Afrofuturism. See https://trendwatching.com/trends/5-key-trends-design -indaba/.

51. Noble, *Algorithms of Oppression*, 1–2.
52. Webb, *The Signals are Talking*, 256.
53. Weyhelie, "Posthuman Voices," 25.
54. Brock, *Distributed Blackness*, 177, 196.
55. Ari Melenciano, interview with the author, April 2018.
56. Kendra Clarke, interview with the author, March 2018.
57. Jason Tester, interview with the author, November 2016.
58. MJ Petroni, interview with the author, August 2016.
59. Ibid.
60. Dinerstein, "Technology," 572.
61. Kember, "Notes."
62. Brooks and Bowker, "Playing at Work," 117; Bradfield et al., "The Origins," 797.
63. Brooks and Bowker, "Playing at Work," 117–18.
64. Squire and Jenkins, "Games in Education."
65. Brooks, "Cruelty and Afrofuturism," 103–4.
66. Brooks and Pollock, "Minority Reports," 113.
67. Squire and Jenkins, "Harnessing," 10.
68. Lonny J. Avi Brooks, interview with the author, July 2018.
69. http://situationlab.org/project/the-thing-from-the-future/.
70. Brooks and Pollock, "Minority Reports," 121.
71. Alida Draudt, interview with the author, October 2016.
72. Srnicek and Williams, *Inventing the Future*, 73.
73. Goode and Godhe, "Beyond," 110.

Conclusion

1. Matsakis, "Facebook Is Killing."
2. Lapowsky, "Parkland Conspiracies."
3. Beer, *Popular Culture,* 83.
4. JWT, Sparks & Honey, PSFK, and the Future Hunters all touched on aging in 2017 and 2018.
5. Taylor, "Corporate Social Science."
6. Giridharadas, *Winners Take All*, 8.
7. Since 2017, McKinsey has been involved in a series of highly public controversies, all of which revolved around work the firm engaged in for questionable clientele. In 2015 the company signed an illegal contract worth $700 million in South Africa that also linked McKinsey to scandals involving then president Jacob Zuma and the Guptas, a megarich family accused of extensive corruption. As the South Africa story broke between late 2017 and the middle of 2018, another problematic McKinsey contract came to light, this time with US Immigration and Customs Enforcement, or ICE. ICE at the time was experiencing extreme criticism for its involvement in separating immigrant parents from their children; McKinsey suspended its ICE contract in July. Finally, in early 2019, news emerged that McKinsey had advised one of the companies

responsible for the opioid crisis in the United States. While none of these cases was the first time the company had been accused of wrongdoing, they highlighted a new capacity for scrutiny among an industry used to working confidentially. See Walter Bogdanich and Michael Forsythe, "How McKinsey Lost Its Way in South Africa," *New York Times*, June 26, 2018; "Why McKinsey Is under Attack in South Africa," *Economist*, October 12, 2017; David Meyer, "McKinsey Is No Longer Working with ICE, the Agency at the Heart of the Family Separations Scandal," Fortune.com, July 10, 2018; and Michael Forsythe and Walt Bogdanich, "McKinsey Advised Purdue Pharma How to 'Turbocharge' Opioid Sales, Lawsuit Says," *New York Times*, February 1, 2019.

8. Goode and Godhe, "Beyond," 109.

9. Ibid., 109.

10. Andersson, *The Future.*

Bibliography

Abrams, Bill. "John Naisbitt Makes a Handsome Living Reading Newspapers for Big Corporations." *Wall Street Journal*, September 30, 1982.

Alsop, Ronald. "People Watchers Seek Clues to Consumers' True Behavior." *Wall Street Journal*, September 4, 1986.

Altehenger, Jennifer E., Laila Abu-Er-Rub, and Sebastian Gehrig. "The Transcultural Travels of Trends: An Introductory Essay." *Transcultural Studies* 2 (2011). Retrieved January 9, 2017, https://heiup.uni-heidelberg.de/journals/index.php/transcultural/article/view/9073.

Andersson, Jenny. *The Future of the World: Futurology, Futurists, and the Struggle for the Post–Cold War Imagination*. New York: Oxford University Press, 2018.

——. "The Great Future Debate and the Struggle for the World." *American Historical Review* 117, no. 5 (2012): 1411–30.

Andersson, Jenny, and Sibylle Duhautois. "Futures of Mankind: The Emergence of the Global Future." In *The Politics of Globality since 1945: Assembling the Planet*, edited by Rens van Munster and Casper Sylvest, 106–25. New York: Routledge. E-Book.

Andrejevic, Mark. *Infoglut: How Too Much Information Is Changing the Way We Think and Know*. New York: Routledge, 2013.

Arendt, Hannah. "The Crisis in Culture: Its Social and Political Significance." In *Between Past and Future: Six Exercises in Political Thought*, 197–226. New York: Viking, 1961.

Arnould, Eric J., and Craig J. Thompson. "Consumer Culture Theory (CCT): Twenty Years of Research." *Journal of Consumer Research* 31 (2005): 868–82.

Arrington, Michael. "Google Trends Launches." *TechCrunch*, May 10, 2006. Retrieved November 27, 2018, http://techcrunch.com/2006/05/10/google-trends-launches/.

Arvidsson, Adam. "On the "Pre-history of the Panoptic Sort: Mobility in Market Research." *Surveillance and Society* 1, no. 4 (2004): 458–74.

Azam, Sharlene. "Cool Huntings." *Toronto Star*, October 4, 1999.

Baba, Marietta L. "Anthropology and Business: Influence and Interests." *Journal of Business Anthropology* 1, no. 1 (2012): 20–71.

Banet-Weiser, Sarah, and Roopali Mukherjee. "Commodity Activism in Neoliberal Times." In *Commodity Activism: Cultural Resistance in Neoliberal Times*, edited by Sarah Banet-Weisher and Roopali Mukherjee. New York: New York University Press, 2012.

Barbrook, Richard, and Andy Cameron. "The Californian Ideology." *Science as Culture* 6, no. 1 (1996): 44–72.

Barmash, Isadore. "Inside Consumers' Minds." *New York Times*, August 14, 1980.

Barnett, Homer G. *Innovation: The Basis of Cultural Change*. New York: McGraw-Hill, 1953.

Bass, Frank M. "A New Product Growth for Model Consumer Durables." *Management Science* 15, no. 5 (1969): 215–27.

Beer, David. *Metric Power*. New York: Palgrave Macmillan, 2016.

———. *Popular Culture and New Media: The Politics of Circulation*. New York: Palgrave Macmillan, 2013.

Belk, Russell. "ACR Presidential Address: Happy Thought." In *NA—Advances in Consumer Research 14*, edited by Melanie Wallendorf and Paul Anderson, 1–4. Provo, UT: Association for Consumer Research, 1987.

Belk, Russell, Kelly Tian, and Heli Paavola. "Consuming Cool: Behind the Unemotional Mask." In *Research in Consumer Behavior*, edited by Russell Belk, Søren Askegaard, and Linda Scott, 183–208. Bingley, UK: Emerald Group Publishing Limited, 2010.

Benedict, Ruth. *Patterns of Culture*. Boston: Houghton Mifflin, 1959.

Benoist, Alain de. "A Brief History of the Idea of Progress." *Occidental Quarterly* 8, no. 1 (2008): 7–16.

Berger, Jonah. *Contagious: Why Things Catch On*. New York: Simon and Schuster, 2013.

———. *Invisible Influence: The Hidden Forces That Shape Behavior*. New York: Simon and Schuster, 2016.

Berman, Marshall. *All That Is Solid Melts into Air: The Experience of Modernity*. London: Penguin, 1988.

Binkley, Sam. *Getting Loose: Lifestyle Consumption in the 1970s*. Durham, NC: Duke University Press, 2007.

Bishop, Christopher. *Pattern Recognition and Machine Learning*. New York: Springer, 2006.

Blaszczyk, Regina. *The Color Revolution*. Cambridge, MA: MIT Press in association with Lemelson Center, Smithsonian Institution, 2012.

———. "The Rise of Color Forecasting in the United States and Great Britain." In *The Fashion Forecasters: A Hidden History of Color and Trend Prediction*, edited by Regina Blaszczyk and Benjamin Wubs, 35–62. New York: Bloomsbury Visual Arts, 2018.

Blaszczyk, Regina, and Benjamin Wubs, eds. *The Fashion Forecasters: A Hidden History of Color and Trend Prediction*. New York: Bloomsbury Visual Arts, 2018.

Blum, Andrew. "Oil Won't Last Forever, So Dubai Is Betting Big on Science and Tech." *Popular Science*, May 15, 2017. Retrieved July 4, 2018, https://www.popsci.com/dubai -science-tech-innovation.

Blumer, Herbert. "Fashion: From Class Differentiation to Collective Selection." *Sociological Quarterly* 10, no. 3 (1969): 275–91.

Bogart, Leo. *Over the Edge: How the Pursuit of Youth by Marketers and the Media Has Changed American Culture*. Chicago: Ivan R. Dee, 2005.Bourdieu, Pierre. *Distinction: A Social Critique of the Judgement of Taste*. Cambridge, MA: Harvard University Press, 1984.

———. "The Production of Belief." In *The Field of Cultural Production: Essays on Art and Literature*, edited by Randal Johnson, 74–111. New York: Columbia University Press, 1993.

Bradfield, Ron, George Wright, George Burt, George Cairns, and Kees Van Der Heijden. "The Origins and Evolution of Scenario Techniques in Long Range Business Planning." *Futures* 37, no. 8 (2005): 795–812.

Brannon, Evelyn. *Fashion Forecasting*. New York: Fairchild Publications, 2010.

Brock, André. *Distributed Blackness: African American Online Technoculture*. New York: New York University Press, 2019.

Brooks, C. E. P. "The Secular Variation of Climate." *Geographical Review* 11, no. 1 (1921): 120–35.

Brooks, Lonny Avi. "Cruelty and Afrofuturism." *Communication and Critical/Cultural Studies* 15, no. 1 (2018): 101–7.

———. "Playing a Minority Forecaster in Search of Afrofuturism: Where Am I in This Future, Stewart Brand?" In *Afrofuturism 2.0: The Rise of Astro-Blackness*, edited by Reynaldo Anderson and Charles E. Jones, 149–66. Lanham, MD: Lexington Books, 2016.

———. "Working in the Future Tense: Materializing Stories of Emerging Technologies and Cyberculture at the Institute for the Future." PhD dissertation, University of California, San Diego, 2004.

Brooks, Lonny J. Avi, and Geoffrey Bowker. "Playing at Work: Understanding the Future of Work Practices at the Institute for the Future." *Information, Communication and Society* 5, no. 1 (2002): 109–36.

Brooks, Lonny J. Avi, and Ian Pollock. "Minority Reports from 2054: Building Collective and Critical Forecasting Imaginaries via Afrofuturetypes and Game Jamming." *Topia* 39 (2018): 110–35. http://search.ebscohost.com.libproxy.temple.edu/login .aspx?direct=true&db=a9h&AN=133039769&site=ehost-live&scope=site&auth type=uid&user=ebony&password=lewis.

Brouillette, Sarah. "Creative Labor." *Mediations: Journal of the Marxist Literary Group* 24, no. 2 (2009). http://www.mediationsjournal.org/articles/creative-labor.

Brown, Arnold, and Edith Weiner. *Supermanaging: How to Harness Change for Personal and Organizational Success*. New York: McGraw-Hill, 1984.

Brown, Tim. *Change by Design: How Design Thinking Transforms Organizations and Inspires Innovation*. New York: Harper Business, 2009.

Builk, Beth Snyder. "Cool Hunting Goes Corporate." *Advertising Age*, August 1, 2005.

Bulmer, Martin. *The Chicago School of Sociology: Institutionalization, Diversity, and the Rise of Sociological Research.* Chicago: University of Chicago Press, 1984.

———. "The Methodology of Early Social Indicator Research: William Fielding Ogburn and 'Recent Social Trends,' 1933." *Social Indicators Research* 13, no. 2 (1983): 109–30.

Burton, Jazmyn. "Making Space for the Future." *Temple News*, February 27, 2017. Retrieved July 6, 2018, https://news.temple.edu/news/2017-02-27/alumna-afrofuturism -north-philadelphia.

Calhoun, Craig J. "The Class Consciousness of Frequent Travelers: Toward a Critique of Actually Existing Cosmopolitanism." *South Atlantic Quarterly* 101, no. 4 (2002): 869–97.

Callon, Michel, Cécile Méadel, and Vololona Rabeharisoa. "The Economy of Qualities." *Economy and Society* 31, no. 2 (2002): 194–217.

Carson, Rachel. *Silent Spring*. Boston, MA: Houghton Mifflin, 1962.

Chan, Anita Say. *Networking Peripheries: Technological Futures and the Myth of Digital Universalism*. Cambridge, MA: MIT Press, 2014.

Cherington, Paul T. "Statistics in Market Studies." *Annals of the American Academy of Political and Social Science* 115 (1924): 130–35.

Chun, Wendy. *Updating to Remain the Same: Habitual New Media*. Cambridge, MA: MIT Press, 2016.

Clark, Timothy, and Graeme Salaman. "Telling Tales: Management Consultancy as the Art of Story Telling." In *Metaphor and Organizations*, edited by David Grand and Cliff Oswick, 166–84. London: Sage, 1996.

Coates, Ben. *Why the Dutch Are Different*. Boston: Nicholas Brealey Publishing, 2017.

Cobb, Clifford W., and Craig Rixford. *Lessons Learned from the History of Social Indicators*. San Francisco: Redefining Progress, 1998.

Cohen, Lizabeth. *A Consumers' Republic: The Politics of Mass Consumption in Postwar America*. New York: Vintage Books, 2003.

Cornish, Edward. *The Study of the Future: An Introduction to the Art and Science of Understanding and Shaping Tomorrow's World.* Washington, DC: World Future Society, 1977.

Coupland, Douglas. *Generation X: Tales for an Accelerated Culture*. New York: St. Martin's Press, 1991.

Crainer, Stuart. "It's More Than a Matter of Chinos." *Times* (UK), March 9, 2000.

Crowther, Bosley. "Length vs. Strength: An Anxious Reflection upon the Evident Trend toward Longer Pictures." *New York Times*, July 14, 1940.

Currid, Elizabeth, and Sarah Williams. "The Geography of Buzz: Art, Culture and the Social Milieu in Los Angeles and New York." *Journal of Economic Geography* 10, no. 3 (2010): 423–51.

Dale, David. "Confessions of a New York Couch Potato." *Sydney Morning Herald*, July 24, 1987.

Daniells, Lorna M. *Business Forecasting for the 1980s—and Beyond: A Selected, Partially Annotated Bibliography*. Cambridge, MA: Baker Library, Harvard Business School, 1980.

Davis, Johnny. "They See the Future." *Independent* (UK), February 9, 2003.

Davis, Mike. "Fear and Money in Dubai." *New Left Review*, September/October 2006, 47–68.

Dean, Jodi. "Communicative Capitalism: Circulation and the Foreclosure of Politics." *Cultural Politics* 1, no. 1 (2005): 51–74.

De Waal Malefyt, Timothy. "Understanding the Rise of Consumer Ethnography: Branding Technomethodologies in the New Economy." *American Anthropologist* 111 (2009): 201–10.

Dewey, John. "Social Stresses and Strains." *International Journal of Ethics* 43, no. 3 (1933): 339–45.

Diebold, John. *Automation: The Advent of the Automatic Factory*. New York: Van Nostrand, 1952.

Dinerstein, Joel. *The Origins of Cool in Postwar America*. Chicago: University of Chicago Press, 2017.

———. "Technology and Its Discontents: On the Verge of the Posthuman." *American Quarterly* 58, no. 3 (2006): 569–95.

Dougherty, Philip H. "Advertising: Club Serves Up a Potpourri." *New York Times*, November 9, 1970.

———. "A BrainReserve for Hard Times." *New York Times*, February 28, 1975.

———. "BrainReserve Taps Society's Flux." *New York Times*, October 12, 1976.

Douglas, Susan. *Listening In: Radio and the American Imagination*. Minneapolis: University of Minnesota Press, 2004.

Dragt, Els. *How to Research Trends: Move beyond Trendwatching to Kickstart Innovation*. Amsterdam: BIS Publishers, 2017.

Draudt, Alida, and Julia Rose West. *What the Foresight: Your Personal Futures Explored; Defy the Expected and Define the Preferred*. Scotts Valley, CA: CreateSpace Independent Publishing Platform.

Drezner, Daniel. *The Ideas Industry: How Pessimists, Partisans, and Plutocrats Are Transforming the Marketplace of Ideas*. New York: Oxford University Press, 2017.

Drucker, Peter. *Age of Discontinuity: Guidelines to Our Changing Society*. New York: Harper and Row, 1969.

Dumitrescu, Delia, Henry Mason, Maxwell Luthy, and David Mattin. *Trend-Driven Innovation: Beat Accelerating Customer Expectation*. New York: Wiley, 2015.

Eagleton, Terry. *Hope without Optimism*. New Haven, CT: Yale University Press, 2015.

Earley, P. Christopher, and Elaine Mosakowski. "Cultural Intelligence." *Harvard Business Review* 82, no. 10 (2004): 139–46.

Epstein, Roy J. *A History of Econometrics*. Amsterdam: North-Holland, 1987.

Eshun, Kodwo. "Further Considerations on Afrofuturism." *CR: The New Centennial Review* 3, no. 2 (2003): 287–302.

Eveleth, Rose. "Why Aren't There More Women Futurists?" *Atlantic*, July 31, 2015. Retrieved October 20, 2018, https://www.theatlantic.com/technology/archive/2015/07/futurism-sexism-men/400097/.

Fairs, Marcus. "Good Design for a Bad World." *Dezeen*, November 16, 2017. Retrieved July 4, 2018, https://www.dezeen.com/2017/11/16/daan-roosegaarde-good-design-bad -world-louis-vuitton-bag-ferrari-climate-change-pollution/.

Featherstone, Michael. "Lifestyle and Consumer Culture." *Theory, Culture & Society* 4 (1987): 55–70.

Feldman, Brian. "It's Time to End 'Trending.'" *New York Magazine*, February 21, 2018. Retrieved June 30, 2018, http://nymag.com/selectall/2018/02/trending-on-social -media-is-worthless.html.

Ferraro, Gary, and Elizabeth Kathleen Briody. *The Cultural Dimension of Global Business*. New York: Routledge, 2012.

Field, George A. "The Status Float Phenomenon: The Upward Diffusion of Innovation." *Business Horizons* 13 (1970): 45–52.

Fincham, Robin. "The Consultant-Client Relationship: Critical Perspectives on the Management of Organizational Change." *Journal of Management Studies* 36, no. 3 (1999): 335–51.

Fleming, Nic. "In Search of Cool—the Hottest Work in Town." *Guardian*, November 29, 2003.

Fletcher, Alice C. "The Significance of the Scalp-Lock: A Study of an Omaha Ritual." *Journal of the Anthropological Institute of Great Britain and Ireland* 27 (1898): 436–50.

Foltz, Kim. "New Species for Study: Consumers in Action." *New York Times*, December 18, 1989.

Fox, Margalit. "Leo Greenland, an Unconventional Adman, Dies at 91." *New York Times*, June 12, 2011. Retrieved November 26, 2018, http://www.nytimes.com/2011/06/13/ business/13greenland.html.

Frank, Thomas. *The Conquest of Cool: Business Culture, Counterculture, and the Rise of Hip Consumerism*. Chicago: University of Chicago Press, 1998.

Friedman, Thomas L. "Did Dubai Do It?" *New York Times*, December 21, 2017. Retrieved July 4, 2018, https://www.nytimes.com/2014/11/19/opinion/thomas-friedman-did -dubai-do-it.html.

Friedman, William A. *Fortune Tellers: The Story of America's First Economic Forecasters*. Princeton, NJ: Princeton University Press, 2013.

Furchgott, Roy. "For Cool Hunters, Tomorrow's Trend Is the Trophy." *New York Times*, June 28, 1988.

The Future Laboratory. "The Age of Re-engagement." Trend Briefing 2017. Retrieved July 26, 2018, https://www.lsnglobal.com/news/article/20928/trend-briefing-2017 -the-age-of-re-engagement.

———. "The American Middle." US Trend Briefing Report 2017. Retrieved July 26, 2018, https://www.thefuturelaboratory.com/us/reports/trend-briefing-2017.

———. "Workplace Summit Report 2016." Retrieved April 14, 2019, https://www.the futurelaboratory.com/reports/workplace-summit-report-2016.

Gates, Sherwood. "Radio in Relation to Recreation and Culture." *Annals of the American Academy of Political and Social Science* 213 (1941): 9–14.

Geist, William E. "One Step Ahead of Us: Trend Expert's View." *New York Times*, October 15, 1986.

Gianatasio, David. "Houston, Agency Founder, Dies at 52." *Adweek*, August 1, 2003.

Gibson, William. *Pattern Recognition*. New York: Penguin, 2003.

Giddings, Franklin H. "The Measurement of Social Forces." *Journal of Social Forces* 1, no. 1 (1922): 1–6.

Gillespie, Tarleton. "#trendingistrending: When Algorithms Become Culture." In *Algorithmic Cultures: Essays on Meaning, Performance and New Technologies*, edited Robert Seyfert and Jonathan Roberge, 61–81. New York: Routledge. ProQuest Ebook Central, https://ebookcentral.proquest.com.

Gilroy, Paul. *Small Acts: Thoughts on the Politics of Black Cultures*. New York: Serpent's Tail, 1993.

Giridharadas, Anand. *Winners Take All: The Elite Charade of Changing the World*. New York: Knopf, 2018.

Gladwell, Malcolm. "The Coolhunt." *New Yorker*, March 17, 1997, 78–88.

———. "The Science of Shopping." *New Yorker*, November 4, 1996, 66–75.

———. "The Tipping Point." *New Yorker*, June 3, 1996, 32–38.

———. *The Tipping Point: How Little Things Can Make a Big Difference*. Boston: Little, Brown, 2000.

Goddess, Moor Mother. "Forethought." In *Black Quantum Futurism: Theory and Practice*, edited by Rasheedah Phillips, 7–10. Philadelphia: Afrofuturist Affair / House of Future Sciences Books, 2015.

Goode, Luke, and Michael Godhe. "Beyond Capitalist Realism—Why We Need Critical Future Studies." *Culture Unbound* 9 (2017): 108–29.

Goodman, Barak, dir. *Merchants of Cool. Frontline*, February 27, 2001. New York: Films Media Group.

Gordon, Theodore J. "Forecasters Turn to Delphi." *Futurist*, February 1967, 7.

———. "Future of Futurists." *Futures*, December 1971, 322–23.

Gordon, Theodore J., and Olaf Helmer-Hirschberg. *Report on a Long-Range Forecasting Study*. Santa Monica, CA: RAND Corporation, 1964. https://www.rand.org/pubs/papers/P2982.html.

Govindarajan, Vijay. "Planned Opportunism." *Harvard Business Review* 94, no. 5 (2016): 54–61.

Graeber, David. "Consumption." *Current Anthropology* 52, no. 4 (2011): 489–511.

Gray, Herman. "Subject(ed) to Recognition." *American Quarterly* 65, no. 4 (2013): 771–98.

Green, Edward J. "Blue Funk or Blue Skies Ahead?" *Management Review* 59, no. 11 (1970): 66–70.

Grossman, Lev. "Trends: The Quest for Cool." *Time*, September 8, 2003, 48–54.

Hacking, Ian. *The Taming of Chance*. New York: Cambridge University Press, 1990.

Hansell, Saul. "Google Shows New Services in Battle of Search Engines." *New York Times*, May 11, 2006.

Harris, Trista. *FutureGood: How to Use Futurism to Save the World*. Minneapolis, MN: Wise Ink Creative Publishing, 2018.

Hebdige, Dick. *Subculture: The Meaning of Style*. London: Routledge, 1979.

Hegeman, Susan. *Patterns for America: Modernism and the Concept Of Culture*. Princeton, NJ: Princeton University Press, 1999.

Hollander, Stanley C., and Richard Germain. *Was There a Pepsi Generation before Pepsi Discovered It? Youth-Based Segmentation in Marketing*. Chicago: American Marketing Association, 1993.

Holt, Douglas B., and Douglas Cameron. *Cultural Strategy: Using Innovative Ideologies to Build Breakthrough Brands*. New York: Oxford University Press, 2010. ProQuest E-Book Central, https://ebookcentral.proquest.com.

Horwill, Herbert. "News and Views of Literary London." *New York Times*, April 3, 1938.

Hudson Institute. *The Hudson Institute Report to the Members*. Croton-on-Hudson, NY: Hudson Institute, 1969.

———. *The Hudson Institute Report to the Members*. Croton-on-Hudson, NY: Hudson Institute, 1970.

———. *The Hudson Institute Report to the Members*. Croton-on-Hudson, NY: Hudson Institute, 1971.

IAB Italia. "IAB Forum 2016—David Shing, Digital Prophet AOL." YouTube video, December 6, 2016. Retrieved July 9, 2018, https://www.youtube.com/watch?v=_ck1qI-_oJg.

Igo, Sarah. *The Averaged American: Surveys, Citizens, and the Making of a Mass Public*. Cambridge, MA: Harvard University Press, 2007.

J. Walter Thompson Innovation Group. *Food + Drink*. New York: J. Walter Thompson, 2017. Retrieved July 26, 2018, https://www.jwtintelligence.com/2017/05/new-trend-report-food-drink-2017/.

———. *The Future 100*. New York: J. Walter Thompson, 2017. Retrieved July 26, 2018, https://www.jwtintelligence.com/trend-reports/the-future-100-2018/.

Jacoby, Russell. *The Last Intellectuals: American Culture in the Age of Academe*. New York: Basic Books, 1987.

Jameson, Frederic. *Postmodernism, or, the Cultural Logic of Late Capitalism*. Durham, NC: Duke University Press, 1991.

Jewell, Edward Alden. "National Academy Opens Art Exhibit." *New York Times*, January 5, 1935.

John, Nicholas A. "Sharing and Web 2.0: The Emergence of a Keyword." *New Media & Society* 15, no. 2 (2013): 167–82.

Jonker, Joost, J. L. van Zanden, Stephen Howarth, and Keetie E. Sluyterman. *A History of Royal Dutch Shell, Volume 3—Keeping Competitive in Turbulent Markets, 1973–2007*. Oxford: Oxford University Press, 2007.

Jordan, Ann T. "The Importance of Business Anthropology: Its Unique Contributions." *International Journal of Business Anthropology* 1, no. 1 (2010): 15–25.

Jouvenel, Bertrand de. *The Art of Conjecture*. New York: Basic Books, 1967.

Kammen, Michael G. *American Culture, American Tastes: Social Change and the 20th Century*. New York: Knopf, 1999.

Kanna, Ahmed. *Dubai: The City as Corporation*. Minneapolis: University of Minnesota Press, 2011.

Katz, Elihu, and Paul Lazarsfeld. *Personal Influence: The Part Played by People in the Flow of Mass Communications*. Glencoe, IL: Free Press, 1955.

Katz, Elihu, Martin Levin, and Herbert Hamilton. "Traditions of Research on the Diffusion of Innovation." *American Sociological Review* 28, no. 2 (1963): 237–52.

Kember, Sarah. "Notes toward a Feminist Futurist Manifesto." *Ada* 1 (2012). Retrieved July 6, 2018, http://adanewmedia.org/blog/2012/11/11/issue1-kember/.

Kerner, Noah, Gene Pressman, and Andrew Essex. *Chasing Cool: Standing Out in Today's Cluttered Marketplace*. New York: Atria Books, 2007.

Keynes, John Maynard. *The General Theory of Employment, Interest and Money*. London: Palgrave Macmillan, 1936.

K-Hole. *Youth Mode: A Report on Freedom*. New York, 2013. Retrieved July 26, 2018, http://khole.net/issues/youth-mode/.

Kiechel, Walter. *The Lords of Strategy: The Secret Intellectual History of the New Corporate World*. Boston: Harvard Business Press, 2010.

Klein, Bethany, Leslie Meier, and Devon Powers. "Selling Out: Musicians, Autonomy, and Compromise in the Digital Age." *Popular Music and Society* 40, no. 2 (2017): 222–38.

Klein, Naomi. *No Logo: Taking Aim at the Brand Bullies*. New York: Picador, 1999.

Kleiner, Art. *The Age of Heretics: A History of the Radical Thinkers Who Reinvented Corporate Management*. San Francisco: Jossey-Bass, 2008.

Kornbluth, Jesse. "Now You See It, Soon You Won't." *New York Times*, September 24, 2011. Retrieved January 9, 2017, http://www.nytimes.com/2011/09/25/opinion/sunday/trending-twitter-culture.html.

Koselleck, Reinhart. *Futures Past: on the Semantics of Historical Time*. New York: Columbia University Press, 2004.

Kotz, David M. "Globalization and Neoliberalism." *Rethinking Marxism* 12, no. 2 (2002): 64–79.

Kozinets, Robert V., and Jay M. Handelman. "Adversaries of Consumption: Consumer Movements, Activism, and Ideology." *Journal of Consumer Research* 31, no. 3 (2004): 691–704.

Krier, James, and Clayton Gilette. "The Un-easy Case for Technological Optimism." *Michigan Law Review* 84 (1985): 405–29.

Krugman, Herbert, and Eugene Hartley. "The Learning of Tastes." *Public Opinion Quarterly* 24, no. 4 (1960): 621–31.

La Ferla, Ruth. "Once Hot, Now Not, Cool Hunters Are in a Deep Freeze." *New York Times*, July 7, 2002. Retrieved November 22, 2018, https://www.nytimes.com/2002/07/07/style/once-hot-now-not-cool-hunters-are-in-a-deep-freeze.html.

Lapowsky, Issie. "Parkland Conspiracies Overwhelm the Internet's Broken Trending Tools." *Wired*, February 21, 2018. Retrieved July 16, 2018, https://www.wired.com/story/youtube-facebook-trending-tools-parkland-conspiracy/.

Lazarsfeld, Paul. "The Art of Asking WHY in Marketing Research: Three Principles Underlying the Formulation of Questionnaires." *National Marketing Review* 1, no. 1 (1935): 26–38.

Lears, Jackson. *Fables of Abundance: A Cultural History of Advertising in America*. New York: Basic Books, 1995.

Le Bon, Gustav. *The Crowd: A Study of the Popular Mind*. Wellington, NZ: Floating Press, 2009.

Levenson, Michael. *Modernism*. New Haven, CT: Yale University Press, 2011.

Levine, Lawrence. *Highbrow/Lowbrow: The Emergence of Cultural Hierarchy in America*. Cambridge, MA: Harvard University Press, 1988.

Levy, Ariel. "The Drug of Choice in the Age of Kale." *New Yorker*, September 12, 2016. Retrieved January 9, 2017, http://www.newyorker.com/magazine/2016/09/12/the-ayahuasca-boom-in-the-u-s.

Lewin, Tamar. "Casting an Anthropological Eye on American Consumers." *New York Times*, May 11, 1986.

Lopiano-Misdom, Janine, and Joanne De Luca. *Street Trends: How Today's Alternative Youth Cultures Are Creating Tomorrow's Mainstream Markets*. New York: HarperBusiness, 1997.

Lott, Eric. *Love and Theft: Blackface Minstrelsy and the American Working Class*. New York: Oxford University Press, 1993.

Luvaas, Brent A. *Street Style: An Ethnography of Fashion Blogging*. New York: Bloomsbury Academic, 2016.

Mackay, Charles. *Extraordinary Popular Delusions and the Madness of Crowds*. Philadelphia: Templeton Foundation Press, 1999.

MacLean, Annie M. "Factory Legislation for Women in the United States." *American Journal of Sociology* 3, no. 2 (1897): 183–205.

Mapp, Sue. "A Day in the Life of a . . . Futurologist." *Evening Standard*, July 10, 2002.

Marantz, Andrew. "Crystal Ball." *New Yorker*, November 10, 2014. Retrieved July 6, 2018, https://www.newyorker.com/magazine/2014/11/17/crystal-ball-3.

———. "Dubai, the World's Vegas." *New Yorker*, April 18, 2017. Retrieved July 4, 2018, https://www.newyorker.com/culture/photo-booth/dubai-the-worlds-vegas.

Marcus, George E. "Ethnography in/of the World System: The Emergence of Multi-sited Ethnography." *Annual Review of Anthropology* 24 (1995): 95–117. http://www.jstor.org/stable/2155931.

Mason, Katy, Hans Kjellberg, and Johan Hagberg. "Exploring the Performativity of Marketing: Theories, Practices and Devices." *Journal of Marketing Management* 31, no. 1–2 (2015): 1–15.

Matsakis, Louise. "Facebook Is Killing Trending Topics." *Wired*, June 1, 2018. Retrieved July 16, 2018, https://www.wired.com/story/facebook-killed-trending-topics/.

Matt, Susan. *Keeping Up with the Joneses: Envy in American Consumer Society, 1890–1930*. Philadelphia: University of Pennsylvania Press, 2003.

McCarthy, Caroline. "Twitter CEO Jack Dorsey Steps Down." *CNET*, October 17, 2018. Retrieved November 24, 2018, http://www.cnet.com/news/twitter-ceo-jack-dorsey-steps-down/.

McCracken, Grant. *Chief Culture Officer: How to Create a Living, Breathing Corporation*. New York: Basic Books, 2009.

———. "Culture and Consumption: A Theoretical Account of the Structure and Movement of the Cultural Meaning of Consumer Goods." *Journal of Consumer Research* 13 (1986): 71–84.

———. *Culture and Consumption: New Approaches to The Symbolic Character of Consumer Goods and Activities*. Bloomington: Indiana University Press, 1988.

———. "Homeyness: A Cultural Account of One Constellation of Consumer Goods and Meanings." In *Special Volumes—Interpretive Consumer Research*, edited by Elizabeth C. Hirschman, 168–83. Provo, UT: Association for Consumer Research.

McFall, Liz. *Advertising: A Cultural Economy*. London: Sage, 2004. Retrieved July 11, 2018, https://ebookcentral.proquest.com.

McGovern, Charles. *Sold American: Consumption and Citizenship, 1890–1945*. Chapel Hill: University of North Carolina Press, 2006.

McKenna, Christopher D. "The Origins of Modern Management Consulting." *Business and Economic History* 24, no. 1 (1995): 51–58.

———. "Strategy Followed Structure: Management Consulting and the Creation of a Market for Strategy, 1950–2000." *History and Strategy: Advances in Strategic Management* 29 (2012): 153–86.

———. *The World's Newest Profession: Management Consulting in the Twentieth Century*. New York: Cambridge University Press, 2006.

McKibben, William. "Eager." Talk of the Town. *New Yorker,* July 7, 1986, 22–23.

McNair, Malcolm. "How to Sell More Now." *Nation's Business*, August 1963, 38–39, 81–83. Box 28, folder 5, Malcolm P. McNair Papers, Baker Library, Harvard Business School.

———. "Plan Your Department Store for the 1970's Now." Lecture presented at the NRMA Convention in New York, January 11, 1966. Box 28, folder 19, Malcolm P. McNair Papers, Baker Library, Harvard Business School.

Mead, Margaret. Preface to *Patterns of Culture* by Ruth Benedict, vii–x. Boston: Houghton Mifflin, 1959.

Meadows, Donella, Dennis Meadows, Jorgen Randers, and Williams Behrens. *Limits to Growth: A Report for the Club of Rome's Project on the Predicament of Mankind*. New York: Universe Books, 1972.

Miller, Annetta. "Putting Faith in Trends." *Newsweek*, June 1987, 46–47.

Monmonier, Mark. *Air Apparent: How Meteorologists Learned to Map, Predict, and Dramatize Weather*. Chicago: University of Chicago Press, 1999.

Moore, Henry. *Economic Cycles: Their Law and Cause*. New York: Macmillan, 1914.

Morozov, Evgeny. *To Save Everything, Click Here: The Folly of Technological Solutionism*. New York: Public Affairs, 2013.

Muller, Eitan. "Innovation Diffusion." In *The History of Marketing Science*, edited by Russell Winer and Scott A. Neslin, 77–97. Hanover, MA: NOW Publishing, 2014.

Naisbitt, John. *Megatrends: Ten New Directions Transforming Our Lives*. New York: Warner Books, 1982.

Nancarrow, Clive, Pamela Nancarrow, and Julie Page. "An Analysis of the Concept of Cool and Its Marketing Implications." *Journal of Consumer Behaviour* 1, no. 4 (2002): 311–22.

Nelson, Alondra. "Future Texts." *Social Text* 20, no. 2 (2002): 1–15.

———. *The Social Life of DNA: Race, Reparations, and Reconciliation after the Genome*. Boston: Beacon Press, 2016.

Newall, Mike. "In Sharswood, Collecting Personal Histories Both Beautiful and Cruel." Philly.com, December 13, 2016. Retrieved November 18, 2018, http://www.philly.com/philly/news/Sharswood-Rasheedah-Phillips-oral-history.html.

Noble, Safiya U. *Algorithms of Oppression: How Search Engines Reinforce Racism*. New York: NYU Press, 2018.

Nordland, Rod. "Welcome to Dubai. Now, Please, Stop Holding Hands." *New York Times*, November 12, 2017.

North, Harper Q., and Donald Pyke. "'Probes' of the Technological Future." *Harvard Business Review*, May/June 1969, 68–82.

Ogburn, William F. "The Fluctuations of Business as Social Forces." *Journal of Social Forces* 1, no. 2 (1923): 73–78.

Opinion Research Corporation. *America's Tastemakers: A New Strategy for Predicting Change in Consumer Behavior*. Princeton, NJ: Opinion Research Corporation, April 1959.

———. *America's Tastemakers No. 2 : Consumer Values ; How They Help Predict Market Change in a Mobile Society*. Princeton, NJ: Opinion Research Corporation, July 1959.

Osborn, Alex F. *Applied Imagination: Principles and Procedures of Creative Thinking*. New York: Scribner, 1953.

Packard, Vance. *The Hidden Persuaders*. New York: David McKay Company, 1957.

Patsiaouras, Georgios, and James A. Fitchett. "The Evolution of Conspicuous Consumption." *Journal of Historical Research in Marketing* 4, no. 1 (2012): 154–76.

Pearce, Tralee. "As the Centre Becomes the New Edge, KD and Dalton McGuinty Are About to Get Their 15 Minutes." *Globe and Mail*, November 22, 2003.

Pedroni, M.. "Coolhunting, Trending and Fashion Forecasting: The Many Faces of Provisional Research." In *Third Floor Issue 5*, edited by Lisa Mann and Suzie Norris. Retrieved November 27, 2018, https://www.academia.edu/2233203/Coolhunting_Trending_and_Fashion_Forecasting.

Peters, Benjamin. *Digital Keywords: A Vocabulary of Information Society and Culture*. Princeton, NJ: Princeton University Press, 2016.

Pietruska, Jamie L. *Looking Forward: Prediction and Uncertainty in Modern America*. Chicago: University of Chicago Press, 2017.

———. "US Weather Bureau Chief Willis Moore and the Reimagination of Uncertainty in Long-Range Forecasting." *Environment and History* 17, no. 1 (2011): 79–105.

Piketty, Thomas. *Capital in the Twenty-First Century*. Cambridge, MA: Belknap Press, 2014.

Popcorn, Faith. "Four Survival Trends People Will Turn To in 2017 That Marketers Need to Understand." January 5, 2017. Retrieved July 9, 2018, http://www.adweek.com/brand-marketing/4-survival-trends-people-will-turn-2017-marketers-need-understand-175377/.

———. *The Popcorn Report: Faith Popcorn on the Future of Your Company, Your World, Your Life*. New York: Doubleday, 1991.

Porter, Theodore M. *Trust in Numbers: The Pursuit of Objectivity in Science and Public Life*. Princeton, NJ: Princeton University Press, 1995.

Pountain, Dick, and David Robins. *Cool Rules: Anatomy of an Attitude*. London: Reaktion, 2000.

President's Research Committee on Social Trends. *Recent Social Trends in the United States: Report of the President's Research Committee on Social Trends*. New York: McGraw-Hill, 1933.

Preston, John. "Malcolm Gladwell Interview." *Telegraph*, October 26, 2009.

PSFK and Cisco. *Consumer 2020*. New York: PSFK, June 2017. Retrieved July 9, 2017, https://www.psfk.com/report/cisco-2020.

Raymond, Martin. *The Trend Forecaster's Handbook*. London: Laurence King Publishing, 2010.

Reese, Shelly. "The Quality of Cool." *Marketing Tools*, July 1997, 34.

Ribeiro, Gustavo Lins. "Cosmopolitanism." In *International Encyclopedia of the Social and Behavioral Sciences*, edited by Neil J. Smelser and Paul B. Baltes, 2842–45. Amsterdam: Elsevier, 2001.

Riesman, David. *The Lonely Crowd: A Study of the Changing American Character*. New Haven, CT: Yale University Press, 2001.

Rifkin, Glenn. "To Find Out What's on Generation X's Mind, Hire an X'er as Youth Marketing Director." *New York Times*, October 24, 1994.

Rinzler, Jane. *Teens Speak Out: A Report from Today's Teens on Their Most Intimate Thoughts, Feelings and Hopes for the Future*. New York: Donald Fine, 1985.

Rogers, Everett. *Diffusion of Innovations*. New York: Free Press, 1962.

Ross, Andrew. Introduction to *Microphone Fiends: Youth Music and Youth Culture*, edited by Andrew Ross and Tricia Rose, 1–16. New York: Routledge, 2014.

Ross, Dorothy. *The Origins of American Social Science*. New York: Cambridge University Press, 1991.

Rubin, Joan. *The Making of Middlebrow Culture*. Chapel Hill: University of North Carolina Press, 1992.

Sacks, Danielle. "That's a Total K-Hole Thing to Do." *Fast Company*, May 11, 2015. Retrieved July 16, 2018, https://www.fastcompany.com/3045744/thats-a-total-k-hole-thing-to-do.

Sandys-Winsch, Lucy, dir. *The Coolhunters*. BBC 2, 2001.

Saval, Nikil. "Globalisation: The Rise and Fall of an Idea That Swept the World." *Guardian*, July 14, 2017. Retrieved July 4, 2018, http://www.theguardian.com/world/2017/jul/14/globalisation-the-rise-and-fall-of-an-idea-that-swept-the-world.

Schor, Juliet. *Born to Buy: The Commercialized Child and the New Consumer Culture*. New York: Scribner, 2004.

Schouten, John W., and James H. McAlexander. "Subcultures of Consumption: An Ethnography of the New Bikers." *Journal of Consumer Research* 22, no. 1 (1995): 43–61.

Schouwenberg, Louise. "It's About Time We Rethink the Notion of Authorship." *Dezeen*, February 26, 2016. Retrieved July 4, 2018, https://www.dezeen.com/2016/02/26/louise-schouwenberg-opinion-dan-roosegaarde-rethinking-authorship-ownership-collaboration-design-architecture/.

Schwarzkopf, Stefan. "In Search of the Consumer: The History of Market Research from 1890 to 1960." In *The Routledge Companion to Marketing History*, edited by D. G. Brian Jones and Mark Tadajewski, 85–108. New York: Routledge, 2016.

Scott, Brian W. *Long-Range Planning in American Industry*. New York: American Management Association, 1965.

Scott, John, and Gordon Marshall. *A Dictionary of Sociology*. New York: Oxford University Press, 2009.

Scott-Jones, Julie, and Sal Watt. *Ethnography in Social Science Practice*. New York: Routledge, 2010.

Sewell, William H. "Historical Events as Transformations of Structures: Inventing Revolution at the Bastille." *Theory and Society* 25, no. 6 (1996): 841–81.

Shalit, Ruth. "The Business of Faith." *New Republic*, April 18, 1994, 23–29.

Sharma, Sarah. *In the Meantime: Temporality and Cultural Politics*. Durham, NC: Duke University Press, 2014.

Shaw, Eric H., and D. G. Brian Jones. "A History of Schools of Marketing Thought." *Marketing Theory* 5, no. 3 (2005): 239–81.

Sherry, John F. "Business in Anthropological Perspective." *Florida Journal of Anthropology* 8 (1983): 15–36.

———. "The Ethnographer's Apprentice: Trying Consumer Culture from the Outside In." *Journal of Business Ethics* 80 (2008): 85–95.

———. "Postmodern Alternatives: The Interpretive Turn in Consumer Research." In *Handbook of Consumer Research*, edited by Thomas S. Robertson and Harold H. Kassarjian, 548–91. Englewood Cliffs, NJ: Prentice-Hall, 1991.

Sheth, Jagdish. "A Review of Buyer Behavior." *Management Science* 13, no. 12 (1967): B718–56.

Slater, Don. "Marketing as a Monstrosity: The Impossible Place between Culture and Economy." In *Inside Marketing: Practices, Ideologies, and Devices,* edited by Detlev Zwick and Julien Cayla, 23–41. Oxford: Oxford University Press, 2011.

Southgate, Nick. "Coolhunting with Aristotle." *International Journal of Market Research* 45, no. 2 (2003): 167–89.

Spiegler, Marc. "Marketing Street Culture: Bringing Hip-Hop Style to the Main-stream." *American Demographics*, November 1996: 29–34.

Spielvogel, Carl. "A Former Advertising Columnist Interviews Himself." *New York Times*, February 21, 1971.

Squire, Kurt, and Henry Jenkins. "Harnessing the Powers of Games in Education." *Insight* 3 (2003): 5–32.

Srnicek, Nick, and Alex Williams. *Inventing the Future: Postcapitalism and a World without Work*. London: Verso, 2016.

Stigler, Stephen M. *The History of Statistics: The Measurement of Uncertainty before 1900*. Cambridge, MA: Harvard University Press, 1986.

Striphas, Ted. "Algorithmic Culture." *European Journal of Cultural Studies* 18, no. 4–5 (2015): 395–412.

Susman, Warren. *Culture as History: The Transformation of American Society in the Twentieth Century*. Washington, DC: Smithsonian Institution Press, 2003.

Symes, Lillian. "Fact Finding Farce." *Harper's,* February 1932.

Tagliabue, John. "Where St. Nicholas Has His Black Pete(s), Charges of Racism Follow." *New York Times*, November 17, 2013. Retrieved May 12, 2018, https://www.nytimes.com/2013/11/18/world/europe/where-st-nicholas-has-his-black-petes-charges-of-racism-follow.html.

Tanaka, Jennifer. "Futurism: The Trendiest Profession." *Newsweek*, March 2, 1998, 14.

Tarde, Gabriel. *The Laws of Imitation*. New York: Henry Holt, 1903.

Taylor, Peter. "Corporate Social Science and the Loss of Curiosity." *Items: Insights from Social Science*. Brooklyn, NY: Social Science Research Council, August 2, 2016. Retrieved July 6, 2018, https://items.ssrc.org/corporate-social-science-and-the-loss-of-curiosity/.

Teach the Future. "Futures Education Pilot NL." Presentation at Sixth International Conference on Future-Oriented Technology Analysis, Brussels, 2018.

Thornton, Sarah. *Club Cultures: Music, Media, and Subcultural Capital*. Middletown, CT: Wesleyan University Press, 1996.

Toffler, Alvin. "The Future as a Way of Life." *Horizon* 7, no. 3 (1965): 108–16.

———. *Future Shock*. New York: Bantam Books, 1990.

Traub, James. "Futurology: The Rise of the Predicting Profession." *Saturday Review*, December 1979, 24–32.

Tsing, Anna. "The Global Situation." *Cultural Anthropology* 15, no. 3 (2000): 327–60.

Turner, Fred. *From Counterculture to Cyberculture: Stewart Brand, the Whole Earth Network, and the Rise of Digital Utopianism*. Chicago: University of Chicago Press, 2006.

"Twitter Trends and a Tip." Twitter Blogs, September 5, 2008. Retrieved September 9, 2018, https://blog.twitter.com/2008/twitter-trends-tip.

Tyler, William D. "The New Creativity Shakes Up the Old Business Guard." *Advertising Age*, August 4, 1969.

Urban, Greg. *Metaculture: How Culture Moves through the World*. Minneapolis: University of Minnesota Press, 2001.

Van de Kamp, Theodore. "How We Can Cope with Future Shock: The Marketing Brokerage Firm." *Advertising Age*, June 3, 1974, 41–42.

Vanderbilt, Tom. "Why Futurism Has a Cultural Blindspot." *Nautilus*, September 10, 2015. Retrieved November 28, 2018, http://nautil.us/issue/28/2050/why-futurism -has-a-cultural-blindspot.

Van Dijck, Jose. *The Culture of Connectivity: A Critical History of Social Media*. New York: Oxford University Press, 2013.

van Leeuwen, Theo, and Carey Jewitt. Introduction to *The Handbook of Visual Analysis*, 1–9. London: SAGE.

Veblen, Thorstein. "The Instinct of Workmanship and the Irksomeness of Labor." *American Journal of Sociology* 4, no. 2 (1898): 187–201.

———. *The Theory of the Leisure Class*. New York: Dover Publications, 1994.

Vejlgaard, Henrik. *Anatomy of a Trend*. New York: McGraw Hill, 2008.

Wagner-Pacifici, Robin. *What Is an Event?* Chicago: University of Chicago Press, 2017.

Ward, Lester F. "Utilitarian Economics." *American Journal of Sociology* 3, no. 4 (1989): 520–36.

Wasson, Chester R. "How Predictable Are Fashion and Other Product Life Cycles?" *Journal of Marketing* 32 (1968): 36–43.

Watts, Duncan J. *Six Degrees: The Science of a Connected Age*. New York: W. W. Norton, 2004.

Webb, Amy. *The Signals Are Talking: Why Today's Fringe Is Tomorrow's Mainstream.* New York: PublicAffairs, 2016.

Webb, Don, and Donald Shawver. "A Critical Examination of the Influence of Institutional Economics on the Development of Early Marketing Thought." In *Marketing History: The Emerging Discipline; Proceedings from the Fourth Conference on Historical Research in Marketing and Marketing Thought*, edited by Terence R. Nevett, Kathleen R. Whitney, and Stanley C. Hollander, 22–39. East Lansing: Michigan State University, 1989.

Weiss, E. B. "Today's Consumer (and Tomorrow's) Gets a New Look in Our New Society." *Advertising Age*, February 8, 1971, 35–40.

Wells, William D. *Life Style and Psychographics*. Chicago: American Marketing Association, 1974.

Weyhelie, Alexander. "Posthuman Voices in Contemporary Black Popular Music." *Social Text* 20, no. 2 (2002): 21–47.

White, Tom. "Chinatown Turns West." *New York Times*, February 21, 1937.

Willard, Timothy, and Andrew Lawler. "Megachoices: Options for Tomorrow's World—an Interview with John Naisbitt." *Futurist*, August 1985, 13, 16.

Williams, R. John. "World Futures." *Critical Inquiry* 42 (2016): 1–74.

Williams, Raymond. "The Analysis of Culture." In *The Long Revolution*, 41–71. New York: Columbia University Press, 1961.

———. *Keywords: A Vocabulary of Culture and Society*. London: Croom Helm, 1976.

Winick, Charles. "Anthropology's Contributions to Marketing." *Journal of Marketing* 25 (1961): 53–60.

Womack, Yvonne. *Afrofuturism: The World of Black Sci-Fi and Fantasy Culture*. Chicago: Lawrence Hill Books, 2013.

Yankelovich, Daniel. "New Criteria for Market Segmentation." *Harvard Business Review* 42, no. 2 (1964): 83–90.

Yaszek, Lisa. "Afrofuturism, Science Fiction, and the History of the Future." *Socialism and Democracy* 20, no. 3 (2006): 41–60.

Index

marketplace, 38, 49, 67, 93, 103, 106;
democratization of, 78; stratified, 39;
teen consumers in, 70–76
market research, 8, 37, 39, 43, 48, 93;
approaches to, 59, 128; in Asia, 129;
and cool hunting, 18, 63, 77, 78; ethical
guidelines in, 166; on teenagers, 62
market segmentation, 44, 49, 51, 66, 73
mass consumption, 5, 15, 30, 36, 40
McCracken, Grant, 103
McKinsey & Company, 45, 104, 166, 187–
188n7
megatrends, 1, 57, 58, 95, 96
Megatrends (Naisbitt), 57
Meliciano, Ari, 152
Merchants of Cool (Frontline), 62, 63, 64,
79, 80
Merriam, Charles, 29
metrics, 26, 92, 93, 94, 95, 131; of consumer
culture, 18; global cultures as, 97; quantitative, 34
metrification, 92, 94
microtrends, 57, 95, 96
military strategy, 10, 47
minorities. *See* racial minorities
Mitchell, Wesley C., 29, 39
Mobility Theory of Market Prediction, 48
modernity, 10, 27, 30, 35, 41, 118; blackness
as instrument of, 152
modernization, 27, 30, 31, 119
monitoring attitudes program (MAP), 55
Moody, John, 32
Mother Goddess, Moor, 147
Müller, Nils, 114, 115, 131
multiculturalism, 122, 131, 167
music, 67, 71, 72, 89, 105, 126; and Afrofuturism, 135, 149; black, 146; hip hop,
68, 69, 145; Indian, 27; jazz, 37, 65; rap,
68; rock, 37; underground, 138
Musk, Elon, 116, 150

Naisbitt, John, 57, 74
Nelson, Alondra, 147
Netherlands, 112, 119–125, 133, 168
networks, 14, 17, 64, 76, 97, 154; of data,
105; distributed, 72; of futurists, 113; professional, 130; radio, 36; science of, 16;
spotter, 128, 129, 167; of young people, 71

Newland, Ted, 47
New York City, 35, 40, 91, 131, 134, 152;
trend production in, 13
New York Times, 56
No Logo (Klein). *See* Klein, Naomi
nonprofits, 10, 55, 165, 168
normcore, 100
Nostradamous of Marketing, 18, 58. *See also*
Popcorn, Faith
novelties, 2, 17, 30, 50, 65, 95; bottom-up
search for, 74; consumerist, 90; predisposition to, 31; spread of, 15

Okoye, Florence, 146
Okunseinde, Ayodamola, 134, 135
opinion research, 11, 34, 43, 50
Opinion Research Corporation, 48
Osborn, Alex, 53

Paccione, Ornofrio "Patch," 53
packaging, 43, 85, 92, 99, 128, 137; shifts,
84
parent trends, 57, 95, 96f
Paschalides, Stephan, 13, 87
pattern recognition, 55, 77, 89, 90, 181n25
Pattern Recognition (Gibson). *See* Gibson,
William
patterns, 34–36, 108, 127, 128, 180n36;
behavioral, 48; of consumption, 33;
cultural, 26, 35, 89, 181n25; describing, 33, 57; discovery of, 89; in fashion,
40; finding, 17, 28, 90; occupational, 29;
social, 18, 27, 43; trend forecasters seek,
86–87
Patterns of Culture (Benedict), 33–34, 89
pedagogy. *See* education
Persons, Warren, 32
Philadelphia, 148, 149, 151
Phillips, Rasheedah, 149, 150–151
Pittman, Stuart, 42, 52, 53, 58
political change, 19, 55, 95, 111, 136, 137;
and black futurism, 147; drivers of, 48;
invokes fear, 9; potential of, 47; predicting, 57
Polykoff, Shirley, 53
Popcorn, Faith, 18, 51–60, 74, 77, 100; on
creating trends, 142; predictive acumen
of, 42–43

DEVON POWERS is an associate professor of advertising at Temple University. She is the author of *Writing the Record: The Village Voice and the Birth of Rock Criticism* and coeditor of *Blowing Up the Brand: Critical Perspectives on Promotional Culture*.

The University of Illinois Press
is a founding member of the
Association of University Presses.

———————————————————

University of Illinois Press
1325 South Oak Street
Champaign, IL 61820-6903
www.press.uillinois.edu